Jewish
FLAVOURS OF
Italy

A FAMILY COOKBOOK

Silvia Nacamulli

Green
Bean
Books

Green
Bean
Books

This edition first published in the UK in 2022 by Green Bean Books
c/o Pen & Sword Books Ltd, 47 Church Street, Barnsley, South Yorkshire, S70 2AS
www.greenbeanbooks.com

Copyright © Silvia Nacamulli, 2022
ISBN: 978-1-78438-778-5

Printed in China by Leo Paper Products Ltd

Ai miei genitori, Miriam e Bruno, per avermi
insegnato il gusto della vita
e
a Bianca e Thea, con tutto il mio amore e con l'augurio
che continuiate ad essere delle buone forchette!

To my parents, Miriam and Bruno,
for teaching me the zest for life
and
to Bianca and Thea with all my love – may you
continue to be such enthusiastic foodies!

Contents

Contents

"So fare roba buona, pe' vita vostra e mia,
 – disse – cucino bene e con economia;
so fare buoni pranzi, so fare buone cene,
cucino all'israelitica, molto pulito e bene,
son cuoca sperimentata, e sempre ho conservato
il vero cascerudde e non ho mai tarfato.
Grazie al cielo il hazzirre non so che cosa sia,
ve lo posso giurare pe' vita vostra e mia..."

**Da *La Sparsciandata*, autore anonimo, fine XIX secolo
(Poesia completa a pagina 330)**

'I know how to make good things, for your life and mine,
 – she said – I cook well and sparingly;
I know how to make good lunches, I know how to make good dinners,
I cook in the Jewish way, very clean and well,
I am an experienced cook, and I've always kept
the true *kashrut* (kosher rules), and I never ate *taref* (non-kosher).
Thank goodness I don't know what *chazir* (pork) is,
I swear on your life and mine...'

**From *La Sparsciandata*, anonymous author, end of 19th century
(Full poem, in Italian, on page 330)**

Introduction

The best conversations often happen around a table. For as long as I can remember, in my parents' apartment in Rome, or at the family house at the seaside, absolutely everything – frivolous or serious – has been discussed over food, while sitting together or cooking in the kitchen. Food is hugely important to my Italian Jewish family. It's real, and it matters. We see, we smell, we hold, and we transform seasonal produce, bringing to it traditions we have learned from our parents and grandparents and offering it to our nearest and dearest. We talk about artichokes, aubergines, anchovies, pasta, frittatas, baby lamb, courgette flowers, tomatoes, matzah fritters and *pizza ebraica*, just to mention a few favourites. We discuss what we saw that morning in the market, who makes what recipe, how they make it, what's on the plates in front of us and, of course, what we are going to cook or eat for our next meal! I suppose, as a family, we have the double whammy of being both Italian and Jewish – enjoying the best of two cultures that are not shy about their love of food, preferably in abundance, or talking about it with equal abandon.

Jews have been living in Italy for over 2,000 years and Rome, in particular, is home to the oldest continuous Jewish community in the Western world. Italian Jewish cuisine is, therefore, inextricably linked to Italian cuisine as the two developed alongside and influenced each other. What differentiates the two is the adherence to Kosher rules– the Jewish dietary laws – as these have shaped the cuisine of the Jews. In addition, Jews continued to arrive in Italy through the centuries – from Spain and Portugal, Central Europe, the Levant and more recently, Libya – enriching the Jewish presence in Italy culturally and influencing the local cuisine. Cooking and eating 'alla Giudia' or 'all'ebraica' – Jewish-style – made Jews inadvertent culinary forerunners, sometimes infamously, as they were the first to use new ingredients such as aubergines and fennel, which, until the late 19th century, were looked down upon by non-Jews in the centre north of Italy.

This book doesn't pretend to be a complete anthology of Italian Jewish food, rather it is a glimpse into an Italian Jewish kitchen. It features the recipes that I have loved most from an early age, food that has grown and developed with me and my family, plus a few other recipes which I have adopted and created over time. Each one has a story and a reason to be in this book. There are, of course, many more recipes in the Italian Jewish repertoire than I have included here. My focus while writing this book has mostly been to celebrate the dishes that are cooked today and reflect a cuisine which is alive and thriving. This inevitably means I have included some timeless Italian dishes, which Jews, like many other Italians, cook day in and day out. The Italian Jews of today are integrated into Italian society and share much of the local culture and passion for food, yet at the same time they follow kosher rules and celebrate different Jewish festivals. As I am Roman born and bred, Roman Jewish dishes prevail in this book, as that's the food closest to my heart and most familiar to my palate.

Cooking and passing on memories, to me, is one of the most important and effective ways to preserve a culture. I guess that recreating my home cooking helps me live abroad with a firm sense of attachment to my Roman Jewish roots. Going back to Italy regularly refreshes and recharges me, and teaching, cooking and catering for others certainly gives me great pleasure. This is the story of my own Italian Jewish food journey.

MY ITALIAN JEWISH FAMILY

My Italian family are quite liberal and progressive, yet at the same time traditional. My parents' place in Rome has always been an open house, where people come by to say hi, stop for a meal, a drink or a chat. Now in their eighties, my parents remain energetic and hospitable. They both worked hard all their life, growing a successful business of tableware shops and their own lines of Italian handmade ceramics, Modigliani. They instilled in my siblings and me the value of never taking anything for granted.

As a family we loved travelling, and I feel lucky to have been brought up exploring the world and experiencing many different cultures from a young age. Learning about diversity in people, places, customs and food has always been an enriching and stimulating experience for me. My parents continue their passion for travelling, trekking and off-the-beaten-track exploring to this day, and they are a true inspiration. They also gave their children and grandchildren a strong sense of our Jewish heritage and identity: both collectively, by being constantly involved with social and political matters concerning the Jewish community in Rome, and religiously, especially from my

mother's side of the family (my great-grandfather Marco Vivanti was a rabbi in Rome), so we have a solid backbone of traditional values.

My family – the Nacamullis and Dell'Ariccias – have lived in Italy for hundreds of years; we can trace back at least 16 generations on my mother's side and about half that on my father's. The Dell'Ariccias originally came from the small town of Ariccia near Rome; as is often the case with many Italian Jewish last names, the family adopted the name of the town in which they lived. However, we are not sure when they first arrived; they may have come from the south of Italy after the Jewish expulsion there in 1492–1541. Our branch of Nacamullis (previously spelt with one 'L' – Nacamuli) came from Venice, and before that most likely from the Mediterranean island of Corfu.

Both sides of my family have long had a passion for good food. My parents are excellent cooks and are very hands-on in the kitchen and, until recently, they both rode their bikes over to Rome's Trionfale market for their weekly shop. There is always plenty to eat, but meals are never too elaborate. It's an approach to cooking that I still appreciate and share as much as I can. My dad cooks great fish dishes, makes yogurt every other day and creates fantastic jams and marmalades from fruit they have grown or picked themselves, such as lemons, pears, kumquats, green tomatoes, chestnuts and cherries.

Mum's cooking usually wins out at home, however. My dad likes to joke that she cooks so well only because his constructive criticism helps her keep up standards, but she really is in a league of her own. She is my ultimate culinary guru, a presence behind many of the recipes in this book even if seldom mentioned. Despite having a busy life, she always makes sure there is plenty of food on the table; she is the one who keeps the Italian Jewish traditions alive, plying us with dishes that Roman Jews have been making forever, putting pine nuts, raisins, cinnamon and nutmeg in savoury dishes, and mixing sweet and sour flavours. And when it comes to trimming and deep-frying artichokes for *carciofi alla giudia*, she is the master. She cooks for five or 100 people with the same flair – she just gets on with it – alongside a lot of talking, sometimes shouting and a great deal of gesticulating! I learned from her by just being there, helping when needed (a lot!), absorbing tastes and aromas and watching her movements.

My father's mother, Bianca Di Segni in Nacamulli, aka Nonna Bianca, gave me one of my earliest lessons in cooking; on reaching 80, she announced it was high time my sister Simona and I (then teenagers) learned how to make her gnocchi (see page 84). The little potato dumplings that Romans traditionally eat on Thursdays were a high point of her weekly family lunches. I still have my notes from that afternoon; she had no recipe and no quantities, but she taught me to judge 'using your hands and your eyes', something I still do.

For as far back as I can remember, a big crowd of us would gather for lunch on Thursdays at Nonna Bianca and Nonno Bino's home, near the Spanish Steps, the adults having shut their shops for lunch and the children joining after school. There would be between 12 and 15 of us

every week, with extra guests and passers-by always welcome. Everybody loved going there and some of my best memories come from these large meals we ate together. My father's younger brother would be there with my aunt and our three cousins who were a similar age to us, and we shared so many fun times. Nonna Bianca cooked magnificent feasts, heaping our plates generously. She continued this tradition her whole life, even after our grandfather died, only giving up not long before her death at the ripe old age of 96.

Being more religiously observant, it was my mother's side of the family, the Dell'Ariccias-Vivantis, with whom we spent all the celebrations for the Jewish holidays, and we would eat with them every Friday night to honour the entrance of Shabbat, the day of rest. When I was young, we would meet up with our other aunt, uncles and younger cousins at Nonna Emma and Nonno Sandro's. At Nonna Emma's, *frittata di spaghetti* (see page 94) made a constant appearance at the table. She was a good cook, but her food was simple, particularly as my grandfather didn't like garlic, onion or any spices (I know!) and preferred just a few plain dishes to be repeated rather than exploring new flavours. We all ate the same dishes out of respect for him.

By the time I was in my teens, however, the tradition of hosting Friday night dinner moved to my parents' home. Even today they continue to bring in the Shabbat for the family at their apartment. My parents have their own style, with plenty of food and never a fixed menu – seasonality rules. New generations are now at the table, with my older brother Stefano, his wife Loredana Spagnoletto and their children, Ariel and Gad, now in their twenties. Then there is my sister Simona, her husband Morris Di Veroli and their teenage boys, Afranio and Mateo. Finally, my family – my husband Marc Iarchy and our twin daughters Bianca and Thea – joins the Italian family whenever we have a chance to go to Rome, usually for Passover and over the summer holidays.

Both my sister and sister-in-law are great cooks, and we particularly enjoy cooking together at our family seaside house near Rome in the summer, where we have access to my parents' vegetable garden. There, the specialities are wonderful *casalino* tomatoes and courgette flowers, as well as lemons, pears, pomegranates and other fruit trees that my parents grow so lovingly. Every year, 15 members of the immediate family gather there, spending the days cooking, eating, studying, working, playing and relaxing, each of us doing their own thing, yet being together: Nacamulli time at its best. It is a blessing spending time with each other, and our daughters adore going there. They will probably grow up remembering these meals and times together with the same warmth of heart that I remember the lunches and dinners at my grandparents' home.

So, with all this wonderful heritage, I'm proud to say I'm a cook rather than a chef. Although I have been involved with food forever, taken a few culinary courses and worked professionally in the food industry for over 20 years now, what I do is largely self-taught and mostly by choice, as it allows me to maintain a sense of authenticity and a home-cooking style which is what my clients seem to appreciate. Quality of ingredients, tradition and passion are what drive me, along with the pure joy of feeding people. I'm basically an Italian Jewish mamma!

COOKING FOR THE SOUL

I came to cookery in a rather unconventional way, after studies and travels that could easily have taken me in a quite different direction.

I left Rome at the age of 20, living first in Israel, and then in England. I have now lived abroad for longer than I ever lived in Italy – although you may not think so from my strong Italian accent! I went to Israel initially planning to stay for one year and learn some Hebrew, but ended up staying for six years and almost settling there. I got my degree in Political Science from The Hebrew University of Jerusalem. The teaching there was

superb; I learned Hebrew and was exposed to multiculturalism, independence and free thinking. I strengthened my Jewish identity and made friends for life with students from all over the world. We spent Friday night Shabbat dinners together and I cooked a lot over those years, never imagining that this would one day become my profession.

Then, in 1998, I did an internship at the European Union's delegation to Israel, assisting the Counsellor for Economic Affairs, travelled for a few months in Southeast Asia, and finally moved to London to do an MSc in Politics of the World Economy at the London School of Economics. After all those years immersed in politics and economics, however, I came to the conclusion that diplomacy and institutions were not for me; maybe because I'm a hot-blooded Italian who gets straight to the point! I worked for a great start-up in international business development for a couple

of years – it was the dot-com boom, so a very exciting and fast-moving time – before deciding to explore new routes; there was something in me from my family's entrepreneurial background that made me eager to branch out on my own.

Having decided to settle in London, and food having always been a big passion of mine, I was soon giving private Italian cookery lessons, specialising in Italian Jewish cuisine, doing what I knew best. Initially, I did this just as an 'in-between job' while I was figuring out what I wanted to do, but it quickly absorbed most of my days. Clients took me more seriously than I perhaps did myself at the time, appreciating both my food and my informal, laid-back approach. I began to wonder if I could make a business out of this homely niche which I was utterly enthusiastic about. I started giving cookery demonstrations at the Divertimenti cookery school in London, which was a fabulous platform, and ended up teaching there for over 15 years. I call what I do 'Cooking for the Soul'. I love the positivity of bringing people together through cooking, working with the sunny side of life and helping people to celebrate events with plenty of great food.

When I first started cooking as a profession, the UK's interest in food was not nearly as developed as it is today, but I could sense there was real potential. People were open to discovering new flavours, eager to eat well and ready to spend money on it. Creative food trends were emerging, and I was exploring all the new little bakeries and restaurants. I was lucky to be among the first to meet Yotam Ottolenghi back in 2002, when he and Sami Tamimi opened their first Ottolenghi deli in Notting Hill, introducing astonishingly creative, original and fresh flavours to London. I was living around the corner at the time and I used to go regularly for brunch. Being Italian, having lived in Israel, and being a cook myself, I loved his and Sami's food straight away. Even when he was busy bringing out gorgeous-looking platters of food, Yotam would often stop and chat with customers; he was charming, approachable and captivating

and he still is. We've kept in touch ever since, even if sporadically, and a few years ago I was fortunate enough to do a short internship at one of his restaurants, NOPI, which was an inspiring experience. Yotam's family on his father's side is Italian Jewish, and he has kindly contributed one of his recipes to this book, his grandmother's *polpettone* (see page 142), which can also be found in his and Sami's cookbook *Jerusalem*.

Over the years, my business has developed organically, by word of mouth, as I have done countless charity cookery demonstrations (still my favourite activity), food deliveries and catering, lecturing at institutions and universities on the history of Italian Jewish cuisine in the UK, USA, Israel and Italy, and running cookery courses in Tuscany and Umbria. I have contributed recipes to *The Jewish Chronicle* for over 15 years, as well as to a number of cookery books and publications. I love the variety of my work. Parts of this book have been simmering and taking shape in my head and on paper for more than 10 years, while I continued to teach, write, lecture and, most importantly, cook! So, this book is really dedicated to all my students, readers and clients who would have liked to have had this to take home with them many moons ago and have been so patient.

When I stand and teach, I find myself making little gestures which I learned from watching all the cooks in my family – habits and tricks which I try to pass on, like the way to stir a *soffritto*, to tilt a pan lid, or cook vegetables to the perfect golden colour. It is so much easier to demonstrate the right amount of salt or oil in person; on the page, I always find it tricky to give exact measurements. Now that I have finally put pen to paper, however, I've included as many details and tips as possible, so you can either follow the recipes faithfully or use my suggestions to explore your own preferences. If you don't like an ingredient, simply leave it out or replace it with another one you like better. Home cooking is flexible, so enjoy that flexibility. Those of you who know me from demonstrations may even recognise my voice with its Italian accent coming through on the page!

Over the years, my cooking has inevitably evolved. I like to think it has improved, but some may disagree, saying that my having been away from Italy for so long means it has been 'contaminated' with other cuisines and methods. That may be true, but I am proud of that. I believe that being exposed to international cuisines has widened my horizons and challenged my thinking and palate – still within kosher boundaries – allowing me to grow as a cook and as a food expert. Nonetheless, I have tried to stay true to the recipes that I learned at home which are in this book, only proposing variations here and there. In Italian Jewish cuisine, like in many other traditional settings, there are different, even endless, ways of making the same dishes – that's the beauty of cooking. I learned through my journey that there is no right or wrong in the kitchen, just different tastes and traditions. In Italian Jewish cuisine, tastes and traditions rule in equal measure, and we could go on talking about their variations forever. I respect them all and I invite you to open your minds, challenge your taste buds and to experiment a little... and mostly, to enjoy it. *Buon appetito!*

A NOTE ABOUT MY SOURCES AND INSPIRATION

Besides my family and personal stories, which are my core inspiration for putting pen to paper, dozens of books stimulated me throughout my writing journey. However, a few have been my constant companions, and deserve a special mention as they are by authors I particularly respect and admire.

I must start with the grande dame Claudia Roden, who continuously instils her knowledge and passion for food in her books, and who I had the privilege to work with and accompany as co-chair for a cookery demonstration on Italian Jewish cuisine at the Gefiltefest London Jewish Food Festival in 2014. *The Book of Jewish Food* is a jewel and her in-depth analysis of Jewish Italy in it is just superb. Then there is the late Edda Servi Machlin and her wonderful collection of books *The Classic Cuisine of the Italian Jews*, in which she brought to life her charming town of Pitigliano in Tuscany and a community which no longer exists. She inspired me to shape my book as a family cookbook, reminding me that we can share best the things that we know best. I also gained inspiration from Ariel Toaff and his *Mangiare alla Giudia* with its plethora of fascinating stories and in-depth analysis of Italian Jewish cuisine from the late Middle Ages, through the time of the ghettos and up to modern times. *Guida all'Italia Ebraica* by Annie Sacerdoti (with the photography of Alberto Jona Falco) is a beautifully detailed guide through Jewish Italy, showing synagogues, cemeteries and artefacts that are all still accessible for an interested audience – it reminds me of the fact that Italy has two millennia of Jewish cultural and artistic heritage and was a great motivational resource for me while writing this book. I would also like to mention Joyce Goldstein and her *Cucina Ebraica*, in which she describes in detail the fascinating historical background of the Italian Jews and presents important niche historical recipes through a careful American eye. Last, but not least, is the Italian Jewish recipe book *La Cucina nella Tradizione Ebraica*, compiled by Guiliana Ascoli Vitali-Norsa of the Adei WIZO (Association of Italian Jewish Women of Padova), a classic in Italian Jewish households and a manual for the experienced cook, as it gives no temperatures and just approximate timings, but is packed with fantastic recipes and is an absolute gem. I am incredibly grateful to them all.

A CULINARY HISTORY
OF ITALIAN JEWRY

One of the questions I'm often asked is whether Italian Jews are Sephardi or Ashkenazi. To the surprise of many, we are actually neither. We are *Italkim*, in particular the Jews of Rome, who arrived in Italy long before the division into Ashkenazi and Sephardi, and maintained their own distinct *nusach* (prayer format or liturgy) known in English as the Italian rite. The same rite is still in use today, making Rome home to the oldest continuous Jewish community in the Western world. A Jewish presence in Rome was already recorded in the second century BCE; however, the community really started to form around 70AD after the destruction of the Second Temple in Jerusalem, when the Romans brought back thousands of Jews as prisoners of war, or, in essence, slaves. The arch of Titus in Rome, next to the Colosseum, is a testimony of it, depicting the menorah and other objects looted from the Temple of Jerusalem carried in a Roman triumph.

The distinction between Sephardi and Ashkenazi began in the Middle Ages, differentiating the descendants of Jews from France, Germany and Eastern Europe (Ashkenazi) from those from Spain, Portugal, North Africa and the Middle East (Sephardi). Both groups settled in Italy throughout its long history alongside the Italkim, and had an important demographic, cultural and culinary impact, bringing their incredibly varied cuisines and helping to create the huge diversity of dishes that are enjoyed in Italy today.

Italian Jewish cuisine is therefore a story of migration, creativity and necessity; it is a gastronomic osmosis of Italian cuisine and local produce, adapted throughout history according to the underlying kosher rules, the strict dietary laws dictating what a Jew can and cannot eat (see page 38). The keeping of the Shabbat (day of rest), when no cooking is allowed, has also played a central role in the shaping of Italian Jewish cuisine, with dishes created that could be eaten at room temperature or slow-cooked. In addition, the numerous Jewish holidays meant Jews invented special dishes to celebrate specific occasions, such as Passover, Rosh Hashana, Hanukkah or Purim, creating a cuisine with perhaps one of the widest repertoires, especially when it comes to desserts.

Italian Jewish cuisine, just like Italian cuisine, is also regional and, ironically, this has been accentuated by the fact that Jews were confined to ghettos in many cities and towns in Italy for more than 300 years (right up until the abolition of the Papal States in 1870), thus keeping their cultural and religious identity intact. Within this environment, they created unique cuisines, such as Roman Jewish, Venetian Jewish and Livornese Jewish, and I pay particular attention to these three here, but there are many more. Then there is the contemporary 'globalised' cuisine, which includes many classic Italian dishes adapted by Italian Jews to conform to kosher rules, and I have included quite a few in this book, reflecting what Jews mostly eat in Italy today. The cradle of Italian Jewish cuisine, however, sits in the south of Italy, through a rich Jewish history that lasted over 1,500 years before being tragically swept away.

THE LOST SOUTH AND ITS RICH FLAVOURS

On holiday in Sicily a few years ago, I visited the gorgeous town of Taormina, on the east coast of the island. While strolling through the charming narrow streets, I noticed a couple called Vico

Right: Taormina, Sicily
Below right: Relief on the Arch of Titus,
Rome, depicting the menorah looted
from the Temple in Jerusalem in 70AD

Ebrei and Traversa degli Ebrei, which translates as 'alley/alleyway of the Jews'. I became curious, started looking around and also found a Magen David (Star of David) carved in stone on a couple of ancient buildings nearby, including the town hall. It didn't surprise me, yet I'm always fascinated to find Jewish heritage in places where there are no longer Jews living.

Taormina, in fact, is just one of almost 100 locations in the south of Italy where there was once a *Giudecca*, a neighbourhood where Jews lived and formed a community (in contrast to the ghettos in which they were later *forced* to live). Jews had lived across the south of Italy since Roman times – in Apulia, Calabria, Campania, Sardinia, and particularly in Sicily where there was a remarkably large population, reaching 52 Jewish communities by the time the Spanish Inquisition started. Up until then, for over 15 centuries, Jews had mostly lived a peaceful and prosperous existence, contributing to the commercial, cultural and artistic progress of the region.

Tragically, things changed under the Aragonese-Spanish rule, when Jews started to suffer under the restrictions and persecutions which culminated with the Alhambra Decree or 'Edict of Expulsion' of 1492. It ordered the expulsion or conversion to Catholicism of all the Jews from the Crowns of Castile and Aragon and its territories – which included Sicily and Sardinia. The implementation of the Edict was entrusted to the Inquisition, which was a sort of Christian court charged with rooting out 'heretics'. Those convicted of heresy were sentenced to torture or death at the stake. It's believed that about 40,000 Jews fled Sicily. Many more stayed and converted to Catholicism and were called *conversos* or the more infamous derogatory name *marranos* (swine), sometimes keeping, or trying to keep, their secret creed as crypto Jews for centuries. The Kingdom of Naples also eventually fell under Spanish rule and the expulsion of Jews occurred in all its territories, including Calabria, Apulia and Naples, between 1510 and 1541. The historic and thriving Jewish communities of Trani, Bari,

Cosenza, Otranto, Salerno, Lecce and Naples, among many others, ceased to exist. Jews escaped to Rome and to northern Italy, others went to Greece, the Ottoman Empire and the Balkans.

However, the Jews did not leave completely empty-handed. For centuries, Sicily had been an important centre for Mediterranean trade, and Jews living there came into contact with food from North Africa as well as from the Mediterranean. Ingredients such as aubergines, artichokes, rice and many different spices, the combination of sweet and sour flavours, or pine nuts and raisins in savoury food, and cooking methods such as deep-frying were all popular in the Italian south, among the Christians, Jews and Muslims, but they were fairly unknown further north in the country (aubergines, for example, a favourite ingredient in the south, had been mostly rejected in the centre-north for centuries as a food for lowly people and Jews (see page 224). The Jews leaving en masse from the south took with them these ingredients, flavour combinations and cooking methods, alongside their culinary culture, thereby enriching the Italian cuisine of the centre-north of Italy. Many of the ingredients and dishes the Jews brought north went on to become staples of Italian Jewish cooking and the words 'alla giudia' or 'all'ebraica' in dishes which eventually got adopted, gave away either the Jewish origin of a specific dish or the fact that Jews had a long-standing tradition of making it.

THE SETTLEMENT OF JEWS IN THE NORTH OF ITALY

Although there were a few early Jewish settlements in the centre-north of Italy, the influx of Jews increased steadily between the 14th and 16th centuries. The majority of the early migrations came from Central Europe and France, when thousands of Jews were forced to flee as the Black Death spread across Europe between 1348 and 1351; they were mostly fleeing from anti-Semitism, however, rather than from the plague itself, as Jews were falsely accused of having poisoned the wells of the Christians and, as a result, a wave of anti-Semitic massacres annihilated 210 Jewish communities across Europe. Ashkenazi Jews fled and settled in northern Italy, including Venice, Turin, Padua, Ferrara, Verona and Mantua. Further migrations from German states to northern Italy took place in the early 1500s, adding to the already substantial numbers. Throughout the Renaissance, Jews continued to travel to the north of Italy – from Sicily and from Rome thereafter – as well as from Spain, Portugal and the Levant.

The large influx of Jews brought about the creation of the first Italian ghetto, in Venice in 1516, as the Republic found it necessary to pass a decree to organise their presence. The same area today is called Cannaregio.

VENICE, ITS GHETTOS AND ITS COSMOPOLITAN CUISINE

My grandfather, Abramo Nacamulli – aka Nonno Bino – was from Venice. He grew up in Campiello de le Scuole in the Ghetto Vecchio, the little square with two synagogues, Spanish and Levantine, opposite each other. He lived on the top floor of a very tall building – one of those 'skyscrapers' that were created by adding extra floors to existing buildings to accommodate more Jews at the height of the ghetto. I remember visiting Venice with my dad as a child and twice again with my new family later. A few years ago, we stayed in a charming flat in that same campiello, opposite Nonno Bino's apartment. I could just see inside the building high up, imagining myself for a moment as his neighbour and trying to get a sense of his life and all the lives at the time of the ghetto before that.

There were, in fact, three ghettos in Venice with five synagogues (called Scole), reflecting the diverse immigration of Jews. The first, Ghetto Nuovo (New Ghetto), created in 1516, was home to Ashkenazi Jews – German and French – who built the Scola Grande Tedesca and Scola Canton. They lived alongside Italian and Sicilian Jews, who built their Scola Italiana. The Ghetto Vecchio (Old Ghetto) was then created in 1541 to home the Levantine Jews, who mainly came as merchants, and were later joined by the Ponentini Jews – Spaniards and Portuguese escaping the Inquisition (mostly *conversos*) – and two further synagogues were built with the Sephardi rite: the Scola Levantina and Scola Spagnola. In 1633, the third ghetto, Ghetto Novissimo (Very New Ghetto) opened, becoming home to more incoming Ponentini Jews.

Just as the inhabitants of the ghetto represented a cultural melting pot, so too did their food, which was multi-ethnic, sometimes marked by the co-presence or fusion of different techniques and ingredients, but with distinct characteristics between Ashkenazim, Sephardim and Italians. The cuisine was also innovative and, as food writer Claudia Roden puts it, 'exotic and cosmopolitan'. Spices, rice and couscous from the Levant, ingredients such as tomatoes, potatoes, corn, peppers and pumpkins from the New World, together with food from Central Europe, inspired the Jews to create a bold and imaginative cuisine within the Kosher rules.

JEWISH PRESENCE IN ITALY THROUGHOUT HISTORY

12th Century

Legend:
- A few Jews
- Tens of Jewish families
- Larger Jewish communities

Venezia, Bologna, Lucca, Pisa, Roma, Capua, Benevento, Napoli, Melfi, Salerno, Trani, Bari, Taranto, Otranto, Cosenza, Catanzaro, Palermo, Messina, Reggio Calabria, Catania, Agrigento, Siracusa

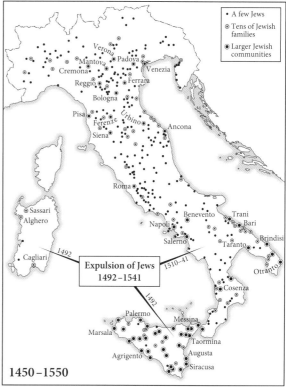

1450–1550

Legend:
- A few Jews
- Tens of Jewish families
- Larger Jewish communities

Verona, Mantova, Padova, Cremona, Venezia, Reggio, Ferrara, Bologna, Pisa, Urbino, Ferenze, Ancona, Siena, Roma, Sassari, Alghero, Benevento, Trani, Bari, Napoli, Brindisi, Salerno, Taranto, Cagliari, Otranto, Cosenza, Palermo, Messina, Marsala, Taormina, Agrigento, Augusta, Siracusa

Expulsion of Jews 1492–1541
1492
1510–41

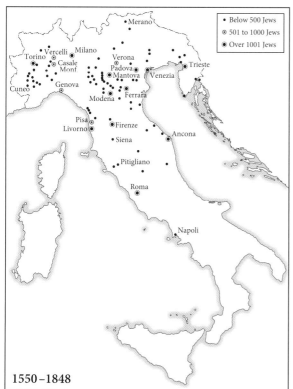

1550–1848

Legend:
- Below 500 Jews
- 501 to 1000 Jews
- Over 1001 Jews

Merano, Milano, Vercelli, Torino, Casale Monf, Verona, Padova, Trieste, Cuneo, Genova, Mantova, Venezia, Modena, Ferrara, Pisa, Livorno, Firenze, Ancona, Siena, Pitigliano, Roma, Napoli

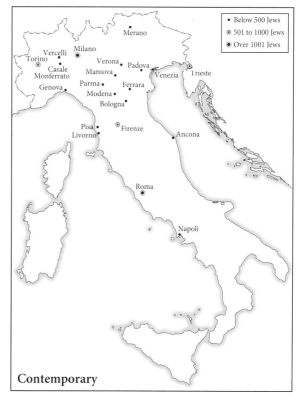

Contemporary

Legend:
- Below 500 Jews
- 501 to 1000 Jews
- Over 1001 Jews

Merano, Vercelli, Milano, Torino, Casale Monferrato, Verona, Padova, Mantova, Venezia, Trieste, Parma, Ferrara, Genova, Modena, Bologna, Pisa, Livorno, Firenze, Ancona, Roma, Napoli

Jews arriving in the ghetto brought hitherto unfamiliar ingredients with them. The Portuguese, Spanish and Sicilian Jews, as well as the Levantine, brought aubergines, and pine nuts and raisins became an almost trademark combination in their food. They were put in many dishes, from *carote sofegae*, a sweet and sour carrot dish, to spinach and also in polenta, the Italian maize meal, just to mention a few.

Rice and risottos were cooked with a variety of spices, vegetables or even dried fruit. In went saffron for *risi e zafran*, or *riso giallo del Sabato* (also known in Ferrara), or artichokes for *risi coi articiochi* as well as the famous *risi e bisi*, a dish of rice cooked in a stock made from boiled and blended fresh pea pods, or raisins for *risi e uette*.

Access to the Adriatic Sea put fish in pride of place on Venetian Jewish tables: for the Ashkenazim, who created *pesse in gelatina* (fish in jelly); for the Levantine and Sephardi Jews, who used sardines to create, for example, the famous *sarde in saor* (fried sardines marinated with onions and vinegar); and for the Italian Jews who created *bigoli in salsa* (buckwheat spaghetti with anchovies and onions) amongst other fish-based dishes. Sephardi Jews also adapted fish soup to kosher practice, using only kosher (in this case, white) fish to create *sopa di pesce spina*, a delicious flavour-rich dish including tomatoes, saffron and wine.

The influence of Ashkenazi cooking can be further seen in the interesting *cugoli in brodo*, which remind us of matzah balls, rolled into oblongs and simmered in chicken broth; their shape, consistency and Italian origin earned them the

name of *gnocchi all'ebraica*. Also popular among the Ashkenazi was the use of goose, which became particularly common in the Jewish communities of northern Italy and was called 'the pork of the Jews', as it was used for a variety of cold cuts of meat in the same way that Christians would use pork to make prosciutti and salami (see page 156). Goose was used across many dishes such as *fugazza cole grigole* (focaccia with fried goose skin mixed into the dough), or *frisinsal* (*ruota di faraone*), a tagliatelle bake with goose, raisins and pine nuts, popular today not only in Venice but also in Trieste and Ferrara, and with quite a story behind it (see page 112).

There is then the food for Jewish festivals, in particular sweets such as bolo, a delicate sweet bread with raisins, also known as *bollo* or *buccellato* in other parts of Italy, and as *bulo* in Libyan Jewish cuisine, traditionally eaten to break the fast of Kippur and enjoyed for Sukkot. For Purim, there are the famous *recie di Haman*, or for Passover, the *scacchi* (a meat and vegetable matzah bake), the *azzime dolci* (sweet matza), or the numerous

sweets of Sephardi origin, which are all quite similar and simple to make: *bisse, impade, apere, mandorle* and *sucherini*. These are all still popular today – many people bake them at home and they are also available from the kosher bakery Volpe in Venice.

Despite the restrictions of keeping kosher, the Jews in Venice had a more varied diet than the Christians. It included many different vegetables and pulses resulting in a cuisine that was both healthy and economical. And economy was certainly a necessity in the overcrowded ghetto where the inhabitants were, at times, particularly poor – *testine di spinasse*, stems of spinach leaves cooked with oil and garlic and a splash of vinegar, are a good testimony to that.

Even though the Jews living in the Venice ghetto were barred from free movement for the 300 years of the ghetto's existence, their cooking was not subject to such restrictions, and after Napoleon opened the gates in 1797, this rich mix of ingredients and original dishes became an integral part of the broader Venetian cooking we know and love today.

THE CREATION OF THE ROMAN GHETTO

A papal bull of 1555, issued by Pope Paul IV, revoked all rights of the Jews of Rome. They were no longer permitted to own any property, and were allowed only unskilled jobs such a ragmen, fishmongers and pawnbrokers (the latter prohibited to Christians). The bull also obliged them to move to a separate walled and gated quarter, not officially called a ghetto, but rather *serraglio degli Ebrei* (enclosure of the Jews). It was the poorest of the ghettos in Italy and the one which lasted the longest, for over 300 years. The chosen area, Sant'Angelo in Pescheria – opposite Trastevere – was where many Jews already lived and was one of the most undesirable quarters of the city, next to the fish market and subject to frequent flooding due to its proximity to the Tiber River. All Jews from nearby towns were moved to the Roman ghetto, and when outside of the ghetto, they were forced to wear a distinctive mocking piece of clothing. As in the Venice ghetto, conditions were cramped, so buildings grew upwards,

Left: Ettore Roesler Franz – Il Portico d'Ottavia Guardando a Destra (1887)
– Watercolour – Roma, Museo di Roma in Trastevere
Below left: Piazza delle Cinque Scole, Rome

making the streets dark and unsanitary. Today, only a couple of the backstreets remain, as the area was knocked down and redeveloped at the turn of the 20th century. A large main piazza (square) in Portico d'Ottavia (called Piazza Giudia or simply Piazza) is the core of the Jewish quarter today: a vibrant and fashionable neighbourhood (quite a contrast with the past!), home to the Jewish school, restaurants, bakeries and (of course) a large synagogue built in 1904, still run with the same Italian rite.

During the time of the ghetto, Jews were allowed to have just one synagogue, so they squeezed five synagogues into one building (three using Italian rites and two using Sicilian rites) and Piazza delle Cinque Scole is a reminder of that. Jews were also forced to attend church sermons on Shabbat designed to convert them. Today, there are a variety of synagogues in Rome, including Sephardi, Ashkenazi and Libyan, each with their own rite, although the Italkim are still the majority.

The local dialect, *Giudaico Romanesco*, a sort of mixture of Italian and Hebrew which was spoken more in the past than it is now (although many words remain popular to this day), is also worth a mention. The dialect was found in plays and poetry, once popular, and my favourite piece is a culinary poem, *La Sparsciandata*, which I found in Ariel Toaff's book *Mangiare alla Giudia*. The poem, written by an anonymous author probably at the end of the 19th century, is about a Roman Jewish cook who, when asked what she knew to make, lists over 200 dishes reflecting what Roman Jews, and Italian Jews more generally, ate at the time (see page 330).

THE 'INVENTIVE THRIFT' OF ROMAN JEWISH CUISINE

Roman Jewish cuisine is the closest to my heart and palate, the one I know inside-out and that I grew up with. As a child, I thought the whole wide world ate the same food as I did, only later realising that it was really a (delicious) niche, as none of my non-Jewish friends added pine nuts and raisins to their spinach, ate matzah fritters in April or had *concia di zucchine* (fried marinated courgettes) as bruschetta toppers. I am not an *Ebrea di Piazza* – a Jew from Piazza Giudia; I grew up in the centre of Rome and I did not go to a Jewish school. Yet I am deeply Roman Jewish, and have a profound feeling of belonging, even after many years of living abroad. My connection with the food is particularly strong and I honestly believe it is one of the best and most interesting cuisines in the world. It is certainly one steeped in history.

Over time, as a large number of Sicilian Jews settled in Rome after their expulsion, many dishes from the south were fully assimilated into Roman Jewish cuisine and adapted using local produce. Aubergines were quickly adopted for *melanzane alla giudia* and combined with sweet and sour flavours to make *caponata di melanzane alla giudia*, for example. *Concia di zucchine* (or *melanzane*), fried courgettes (or aubergines) marinated in vinegar, a sister dish to *zucchine alla scapece* from Naples and originally from Sicily, became a staple of Roman Jewish cuisine. *Cassola*, a popular ricotta bake, reminds us ever so slightly of the Sicilian cassata, even if it's simpler in flavour.

A wonderful variety of artichoke called mammole or cimarolo, grows around Rome, and Jews became experts in trimming them. The dish par excellence from these is *carciofi alla giudia*: deep-fried, crunchy and absolutely delicious, and THE emblem of Roman (if not Italian Jewish) cuisine.

Talking of fried food – and there is a lot of it in Roman Jewish cuisine – *fritto misto* (see page 204), mixed fried morsels of vegetables and fish, was particularly popular in the ghetto, and Christians used to come from outside to eat it. Over time, it became a classic of Roman cuisine and grew to include cod and courgette flowers as well, the latter – stuffed with mozzarella and

anchovies – is one of my favourites. The Sicilian combination of pine nuts and raisins also became a norm in Roman Jewish cuisine, added to spinach, red mullet and salt cod.

The fish market, *La Pescheria*, was on the border of the ghetto and this made its mark on the cuisine within. Small bony fish became popular in Roman Jewish cuisine, especially anchovies, as they were once considered, particularly by the Catholic Church, to be fish bait rather than food and were thus cheap (see page 170–172). These resulted in dishes such as *aliciotti con l'indivia* (anchovy and endive bake), *alici fritte* (fried anchovies) and a fantastic fish soup made with fish heads and bones and Romanesco broccoli.

A good example of both creativity and necessity is the use of *carne allungata* (literally 'stretched meat') – minced meat to which other ingredients are added, such as courgettes, celery, carrots or onions, in order to 'stretch' the meat so it can feed a larger number of people. Classic dishes in this style are *zucchine ripiene* (stuffed courgettes), or *ngozzamoddi* (chicken meatballs) which originally included crushed pieces of bone to add volume and flavour and feed more people. In addition, the use of offal, usually from beef or veal, such as *milza* (spleen), *trippa* (tripe) or *cervello* (brain), became traditional in Roman Jewish cooking as it was cheaper and more accessible than the more refined cuts. Today, offal is still popular throughout the city. Another staple dish is *stracotto*, meaning literally 'overcooked', a Shabbat meat dish which is cooked slowly for hours. This slow cooking was required to soften the tough and gristly cuts of meat it used, but fortunately we use more tender cuts of beef today.

As elsewhere, Roman Jews also adapted many traditional local dishes to conform to kashrut (Jewish dietary laws), and in the process created new and original recipes. For example, inspired by the popular Italian cold cuts, mostly of pork, which is not kosher, the Jews of Rome created delectable cuts of cured beef such as *coppiette*, *carne secca*, *coda di pezza* and *salsicce*. Made for hundreds of years, they are still popular today, and remain relatively unknown outside the Jewish community. My favourite use of them is a sandwich of pizza bianca with *carne secca*!

A more contemporary approach to adapting traditional local dishes to conform to kosher rules can be seen in dishes such as pasta 'carbonara' or 'amatriciana' made with cured beef instead of pork (and omitting the Parmesan cheese), or made vegetarian using courgettes, which I propose here. Similarly, for *pasta e fagioli*, which usually includes pancetta (cured pork belly), Jews remove the pork from the *soffritto* and make the dish their own. Pulses, economical and rich in nutrients, were – and still are – key ingredients in the diet of Roman Jews, and another classic dish reflecting this is *pasta e ceci*, a thick chickpea soup that's still popular today.

Finally, we cannot forget desserts: from *pizzarelle col miele* (matzah fritters dipped in honey) for Passover to *orecchie di Amman* and *tortolicchio* for Purim, and *pizza ebraica* to celebrate all the simchot (happy occasions) such as births, weddings and bar/t mitzvahs. *Pizza ebraica* (a delicious fruitcake) is sold in the tiny (but very famous) bakery Boccione, where they make only traditional Roman Jewish desserts, including *ginetti*, *biscottini* and *torta di ricotta e visciole*.

GHETTOS THROUGHOUT ITALY

Other ghettos were created throughout Italy by successive popes, and unique regional cuisines developed. Until the beginning of its Risorgimento (unification) in 1848, Italy was a conglomerate of independent states: some were Papal States and others were ruled by specific families. It is interesting to note that the different dates on which the various ghettos were established depended on the family that was ruling the city or province at the time, how tolerant they were towards Jews and how

dependent they were on the Papal State.

For instance, one of the most important Jewish communities in Italy in the 13th century was in Ferrara, and it developed rapidly under the Dukes of Este in the 15th century. Jews from Spain and Portugal further expanded the community and by the 16th century the city was considered one of the most secure shelters for Jews of all backgrounds. The last Duke of Este died with no male heir and the pope claimed the duchy, establishing the ghetto in 1627.

From a culinary perspective, the Ashkenazi influence in Ferrara is demonstrated by the use of goose and turkey, and the Sephardi influence can be seen in *buricche* (pastry parcels). But Ferrara also has special dishes to celebrate the Jewish festivals, such as *zuccherini* and *montini* – sweets for Purim – or *scacchi ferraresi* – a savoury matzah bake for Passover. Other dishes include *riso in brodo al limone* – a warming broth for the breaking of the fast of Yom Kippur, and *zucca fritta con lo zucchero* – sweet fried pumpkin, also for Yom Kippur. And for a summer dish there is fried aubergines with melon, which replaces the classic (non-kosher) Parma ham and melon dish, often served as a starter in Italy.

Another important city in the Italian Renaissance was Florence: in the 15th century, Jews were invited by the ruling Medici family to come and live in the city, where they worked in finance, art and culture. The Medici family often protected them, in particular Lorenzo il Magnifico, who was in power for 50 years. However, Jewish fortunes changed with whichever member of the Medici family was at the helm and eventually, in 1571, they were forced to live in a ghetto. I have included in this book a fascinating old recipe from Florence for a spinach and almond cake (*torta di spinaci e mandorle*).

The region of Piedmont had numerous ghettos including in Turin, Vercelli and Casale Monferrato, the latter being well-known for the Jewish tradition of eating goose (see page 156).

In Mantua, as elsewhere, Jewish fortunes

varied depending on who was in power, with periods in history when they were allowed to run businesses and work in the professions, but even there, under pressure from the Papacy, the ruling Gonzaga family enforced the creation of the ghetto in 1612. Pumpkin, which arrived from the newly discovered Americas, became particularly popular there and was cooked in a variety of ways; perhaps the most classic pumpkin recipe is *tortelli di zucca*, now widely found throughout Italy.

As in Ferrara, Mantua and Florence, Jews elsewhere often flourished culturally and economically before eventually being persecuted, and so they kept on moving throughout central and north Italy whenever they could to avoid the discrimination of the Papal State. The same happened in the small Tuscan towns of Pitigliano, Sovana and Sorana. Jews had settled there from the 15th century onwards, and under the rule of the tolerant Orsini family, this community became known as *La Piccola Gerusalemme* (Little Jerusalem). The community grew and flourished, but a change in ruling families to the Medici brought in stricter laws for Jews, and a ghetto was eventually established there. Edda Servi Machlin, who grew up in Pitigliano and moved to New York in the 1950s, writes beautifully about this in *The Classic Cuisine of the Italian Jews*. I have included the recipe for *sfratti* in this book, symbolising the time of the creation of the ghettos and the way Jews were evicted ('sfrattati') from their homes.

LIVORNO, *PORTO FRANCO*, AND ITS SEPHARDIC AND LEVANTINE CUISINE

There were two important exceptions to the ghetto era: Livorno and Pisa. They are the only major Italian cities never to have had a ghetto, and the role of Livorno is particularly interesting. They were both governed by a member of the Medici family (Ferdinando I de'Medici, Grand Duke of Tuscany) who, at the end of the 16th century, declared Livorno to be a *porto franco* or 'free port', and approved the *Leggi Livornine*. These laws gave special privileges to Jews, guaranteeing the religious, personal and commercial freedom of any newcomers from any nation or creed. Numerous Jews arrived to take advantage of these rights and Ferdinando I was especially keen to include Spanish and Portuguese *conversos*. Livorno became an incredibly important trading town as the Jewish merchants had contacts throughout the Mediterranean area. It's interesting to note that, until the Fascist period in the 1930s, the Jews of Livorno never suffered persecution, nor were any restrictions imposed upon them during the entire time of their residence in the city. Their synagogue was one of the finest architectural monuments of the city, but it was sadly destroyed during World War II.

The Livornese Jewish cuisine reflected its fascinating and diverse community, with Spanish dishes such as *roschette* (little ring crackers), or the Portuguese sweet, *uova filate*. Many Jews also arrived from Tunisia and Libya, and their influence can be seen in dishes such as *cuscusssù' alla Livornese*. The humble tomato, which is believed to have been brought from the New World to Italy by Spanish *conversos*, also played an important role. It quickly became a key ingredient and the Jews used it with fish in particular to create the classic *pesce alla mosaica*, or *all'ebraica* (fish – mostly the local red mullet – in tomato sauce), which later became *alla Livornese*, and in soups such as the famous *cacciucco* – a rich fish soup with tomato, which nowadays includes seafood, making it non-kosher, but which some say was originally made just with kosher fish.

THE UNIFICATION OF ITALY AND ITS AFTERMATH

The last ghetto to be abolished was the one in Rome in 1870 after the final collapse of the Papal States and the unification of Italy. Jews were granted equal rights, and big new synagogues were built across the country as a sign of emancipation; outstanding examples can be found in Rome, Florence and Turin. Many Jews were keen to integrate themselves into the wider Italian community and assimilation occurred on a grand scale. Under Mussolini, Jews were so integrated in Italian society that some of them were members of the Fascist party. This, for them, reflected their being Italian, but they were soon proved wrong when, in 1938, Mussolini introduced racial laws and Jews were once again highly discriminated against.

During World War II, approximately 8,000 Italian Jews perished (see pages 30–31) and many small communities tragically ceased to exist.

'An event of historical import', as the Jewish community defined it, was the first meeting in 2,000 years between a pope and a rabbi in 1981, which was followed by another significant public event in Rome in 1986, when the same pope, Jean Paul II, met Chief Rabbi Elio Toaff and visited a synagogue for the first time, marking a turning point in the history of Jewish-Christian relations.

In total today (the last public records being for 2019) there are just over 23,200 Jews registered within 21 communities in Italy, with probably a few thousand more that are not registered. All Jewish communities in Italy have always been, and still are, orthodox in structure – although as Italians our philosophy has perhaps often been more conservative in nature. The UCEI (Union of the Jewish Communities in Italy) plays a crucial role in representing the body of Italian Jewry as one: both nationally when dealing with the Italian state, and internationally as the Italian affiliate of the World Jewish Congress.

The largest Jewish communities today are in Rome and Milan. The latter increased in numbers mostly in the 20th century and has the most international texture of all with, among others, Persian, Lebanese and Italian Jews. Florence and Turin are the next largest, while all other communities have fewer than 500 registered Jews; however, tourism and Jewish foreign university students play a vital role in increasing numbers

and helping maintain regular synagogue services, such as in Venice and Bologna.

In the south, in recent years, there has been a growing movement to revive the Jewish communities among crypto Jews, the *Anusim*. Today, descendants seem to remain in Apulia, Calabria and Sicily and some of their stories are fascinating. Numbers, however, are small and many challenges lie ahead.

New Jewish immigrants arrived in Italy in the last century, many coming from Libya, Egypt, Lebanon and Iran, and settling mainly in Rome and Milan. These immigrants came following the expulsion of Jews from the Arab states after the creation of the state of Israel (1948), the Suez crisis (1956) and the Six-Day War (1967). Their stories are all significant and unique.

I share here a snippet on Libyan Jewish cuisine and include a few recipes, as it is perhaps the most predominant new influence on Italian Jewish cuisine.

THE NEWCOMER – LIBYAN JEWISH CUISINE

Of the more recent contributors to Italian Jewish cuisine, Libyan Jews are extremely important, in particular to the Roman Jewish community. The story of the Libyan Jews in Rome started in 1967, when about 5,000 of them were evacuated to Italy after the Six-Day War, leaving everything behind (Libya was an Italian colony from 1911–43). Of these, the majority settled in Rome while others continued to Milan, Livorno, Israel or the USA. Libyan Jews re-energised the Roman Jewish community, bringing a new vitality through their North African warmth, hard work and rich traditions; traditions that were quite different from the Roman ones, but nonetheless deeply Jewish, adding a vigour to religious rules and strengthening a sense of community.

They also brought with them their precious cooking traditions. From a culinary perspective, Libyan Jewish cuisine (known as *cucina tripolina* because many of the Libyan Jews came from

Tripoli) is an important part of the cuisine of Rome today, introducing a rich combination of flavours dominated by spices and ingredients such as caraway, cumin, cinnamon, paprika, garlic, chilli and tomato paste/purée, just to mention a few – some of which they had adopted in turn from Italian cuisine during their years as a colony. They introduced to us dishes such as the spicy fish *haraimi*, *mafrum* (stuffed vegetables) and various stews, including *lubia b'selk* with beans and spinach and *lubia bel cammun* with beans and cumin. There is then the famous *shakshuka*, poached eggs in spicy tomato sauce, *merduma*, my favourite spicy, garlicky tomato dip, and delicious desserts such as *sefra*, an aromatic semolina bake with a honey glaze. I have included a few of these recipes in the book as I have been lucky enough to eat them all thanks to good Roman and Milanese Tripolitanian friends (and their mums!), who cook divinely and still preserve their unique culinary tradition. These dishes are gradually being incorporated into Jewish Italian cuisine and can now be found in kosher restaurants in Rome. At the same time, the Libyan Jews are also enriching their own culinary traditions with the use of Italian ingredients, continuing this fascinating gastronomic osmosis.

The rich and complex Italian Jewish cuisine is, therefore, continuing to evolve.

A PERSONAL STORY: HOW MY FAMILY SURVIVED THE WAR

Each year, at Rosh Hashana in London and Passover in Rome, when we finally sit down at the dinner table after frenetic preparations to enjoy a delicious and plentiful meal, I look around the table with a sense of wonder, especially at the children, with their beautiful innocence. I feel blessed and privileged to be alive and to see the family growing.

I think of the six million Jews who were persecuted, deported and brutally murdered by Nazi Germany during the Holocaust just because of their religion, and my heart pounds with sorrow. I also think of my great-aunts and uncles who I never met, and of all my 'would-be' cousins who were never born.

To be alive today as a European Jew is, to me, nothing short of a miracle, and I feel it is my duty to honour and remember all those who perished, as it is something we should never forget. Here, I share the story of how my family, and in particular my parents, survived during World War II. This story is a big part of my identity and one of the reasons why I want to keep my own family traditions alive.

If anyone feels I have simplified history by just telling my personal tale, I apologise, but you could take my story as a symbol of the countless other stories which could be told instead. For instance, in one of life's coincidences, my husband's father, Jean Iarchy, was also a Hidden Child in Belgium during the war for over three years. This is my parents' tale.

HISTORICAL CONTEXT IN A (TINY) NUTSHELL

In 1938 in Italy, under the Fascist rule of Mussolini, racial laws were brought into force against Jews. These laws defined who was a Jew and stripped them of basic rights; they could no longer study or teach in any state school or university, hold any public office, work in banks or insurance or employ staff, and marriage to non-Jews was forbidden. This was a body blow to all Italian Jews, who had been contributing so much to the young Kingdom of Italy, and their living conditions became extremely hard and humiliating. The few who were farsighted enough and could afford it sought to emigrate, especially to Switzerland and the US, but the great majority remained, never imagining what horror lay ahead.

Italy entered World War II as an ally of Nazi Germany in 1940, however, curiously enough, Jews were deported from Italy only after it swapped sides, when in September 1943 the Kingdom of Italy signed an armistice with the Allies. German troops then invaded Italy and mass deportations of Italian Jews to Nazi death camps in Germany and Poland began.

By September 1943 there was an atmosphere of paralysing fear and rumour among the Jews of Rome, and they were being increasingly repressed by the state. In one infamous episode, on 26th September, the Nazis demanded 50kg (110lb) of gold from the Jewish community in Rome, to be collected and handed over within 36 hours, or else 200 Jewish men would be deported. Most Jews, who were already impoverished by the war and lack of work due to the racial laws, gave their last precious valuables away and some non-Jews helped by contributing their own gold. In the end, 50.3kg (111lb) were given to the Germans. However, the Germans did not keep their promise as only a few weeks later they deported all of the Roman Jewish community they could find, and not only men, but also women and children.

In the early hours of Saturday 16th October 1943, Nazis raided the area of the former ghetto in Rome, where many Jews still lived, and throughout the day entered every single Jewish household across Rome. In a single day, 1,023 Jews were deported and put onto cattle trains to Auschwitz; of those, more than 200 children were murdered in gas chambers within a day of arrival. Only 16 of these Jews returned to Rome in 1945, when the war ended, and of these there was only one woman.

More than 1,000 more Jews were arrested in Rome and deported in the months that followed, right up until 4th June 1944. Jewish communities elsewhere in Italy were decimated, including in the great historic centres of Florence, Milan, Genoa, Turin, Venice, Ferrara and many other smaller communities of the north. Jews were first arrested – large numbers were put in the concentration camps of Fossoli near Modena, and Bolzano, and others in local jails, such as the Carcere Le Nuove in Turin – then deported, mostly to Auschwitz. It is estimated that around 8,000 Italian Jews became victims of the Holocaust – 22 per cent of the Italian Jewish population at the time.

Though there were, unfortunately, spies among the Fascist population who tipped off the whereabouts of Jews to the SS (often for money), most of the Jews who survived owe their lives to the solidarity and generosity of Christian religious institutions and ordinary Italians, who risked their own lives by sheltering them, supplying food in places of hiding and helping them in whatever way they could. My family stories are a testimony to their benevolence and generosity and I will be forever grateful to them.

'MEMME BEVILATTE' – MY MOTHER'S STORY

Miriam Dell'Ariccia, my mother, was born in 1941, so she was only a toddler during World War II, but she still has memories of her days in hiding and the sound of German soldiers talking and their boots pounding.

Her grandfather, Rav Marco Vivanti, worked in the offices of the *Comunità Ebraica di Roma* (Roman Jewish community) and witnessed, on 29th September 1943, the raid by German officers who impounded a multitude of documents, including all the registers containing the names and addresses of the Jews in Rome. That same day, his daughter Enrica went to pick him up from work and happened to meet a Jewish refugee from Poland. This woman told my great-aunt what was happening to the Jews in the rest of occupied Europe, how the Germans had collected registers and then deported and murdered all the Jews, and she urged her to hide as soon as possible.

Thankfully Enrica listened, as just over two weeks later, when the Nazis raided the homes of Rome's Jews and went to my great-grandparents' apartment, there was nobody there as they had already gone into hiding.

They were saved by their former housekeeper of 16 years (until her summary dismissal in 1938, when Jews were no longer allowed to employ non-Jews). Teresa Giovannucci and her husband Pietro Antonini bravely risked their lives by hiding them in their home in the small town of Riano, outside Rome.

Teresa was pregnant at the time and on 30th September 1943 came to Rome for a doctor's visit. As usual, she went to visit my great-grandparents as she regularly brought them eggs and vegetables from the countryside. When she didn't find them at home, she got worried, but the concierge told her they were hiding in the cellar of the next-door oil and wine shop, so she found them there and convinced them to come back to Riano with her at once.

Back home, she told the people in the town that they were her family from the south, refugees from Apulia, looking for temporary shelter. My family ended up staying for nine months in their small house and Teresa and Pietro gave up their room for them, sleeping on the floor despite Teresa's pregnancy. To begin with, only six members of the family lived there in hiding: my great-grandparents Marco and Silvia, their daughters – my great-aunt Enrica and my grandmother Emma – plus Emma's husband Alessandro Dell'Ariccia and my mother Miriam. A few months later, they were joined by a cousin of my grandmother's, Sandra Bassan, and my grandfather's twin brother, Giacomo (called Mimmo). He ended up marrying Enrica, so the twin brothers married two sisters! But that's a different story...

Sadly, two of my Grandfather Dell'Ariccia's brothers, Ernesto and Manlio (with his wife and two young children) and several other members of our wider family were deported to Auschwitz and tragically never returned. At the time, Teresa was running Riano's communal bread oven, which was in the same building as their house, and German soldiers came daily to buy bread,

hence my mum's memory of the sound of pounding German boots and their voices.

During the family's time there, they had many narrow escapes. Although some of them had fake IDs – my grandfather, Alessandro Dell'Ariccia, for example, was 'Alberto Sandro Mori', and had his fake ID even before going into hiding – it still wasn't safe, as people could easily denounce them. One time, when the Germans entered the house to carry out a search, my great-grandfather hid in the chimney and the others escaped through a back window into a ditch and then into the forest, causing my grandmother (who was also pregnant) to have a miscarriage, and she almost died from a haemorrhage. Another time, they were kept locked in a single room for 20 days as tensions in the town were running high and Teresa told everyone that they had left.

The hardest part was keeping my mum, who was just over two years old, quiet and still for the whole time; she still remembers sitting on a small chair for hours on end. I have children myself now and I often think of this episode and how hard it must have been, both for my mother to keep still and for her parents to keep her so.

When Riano was eventually liberated by the Americans on 6th June 1944, they found German registers stating that just four days later, on 10th June, my mother's family would have been shot in the main square alongside Teresa and Pietro for hiding them; someone from the town had notified the authorities. Once free, everyone else in the village came up to embrace and salute my family and it became clear that everyone suspected or knew they were Jews, despite pretending to be refugees, and they had all (but one) kept the secret throughout the nine months.

The ex-deputy mayor of Riano, Italo Arcuri, wrote a book telling the story of my mother and her family during this time called *Memme Bevilatte salvata da Teresa* (Memme the Milk-drinker saved by Teresa – my mum was known as 'Memme Bevilatte', and my grandfather called her Memme for many years after the war). In

Above: Fake ID of my grandfather during the war

1993, as a result of their brave actions during the war, Teresa Giovannucci and Pietro Antonini were given the title of 'Righteous Among the Nations' by Yad Vashem, the World Holocaust Remembrance Center in Jerusalem, and a commemoration stone was put outside their home in Riano in 2010. In 2015, a room in Riano's City Hall was named after them.

My mum always says that her mother gave her life, but Teresa preserved it and she will be forever grateful to her. We all are. To this day, our families continue to have a close relationship and one of Teresa's daughters, Laura, was my nanny when I was born and still calls me every year for my birthday. She then worked in my parents' store for many years, so the cycle of life and mutual giving continued. Felice, Teresa's eldest daughter, still lives in the same house in Riano and regularly visits my parents in Rome. Every year she bakes a wonderful Christmas dessert that her mother used to make called *pangiallo*, made of nuts marinated in liquor, chocolate and dried fruits, and she always gives one to our family – I share the recipe on page 324. My mum then gives some to her children. I share it with my own daughters, telling them my mother's story, adding a bit of extra information every year as they grow up, until they are ready to hear the full story.

Today, my mother is a regular speaker at schools and institutions across Italy as a Holocaust survivor. She tells her story to thousands of children every year so that future generations will hopefully never forget, and she spreads the message from the Talmud which says that saving one life is like saving all of humanity (the exact quote is 'whosoever saves a single soul is regarded as though he saved a complete world'). Just think – more than 30 people have been born as a result of the saving of my grandparents' lives.

Above: Plaque outside Teresa and Pietro's house
– Zia Enrica, Teresa and Nonna Emma (right)

My father hiding at Collegio Nazareno during the war. He's the first one right on the the third row.

MY FATHER'S STORY

Bruno Nacamulli, my father, was born in 1935 and is the eldest of two brothers; his brother Franco was born in 1939. My grandfather, Abramo Nacamulli – we called him Nonno Bino – was from Venice and came to Rome in 1933, followed by his much younger brother Giorgio, and each ended up marrying a Roman Jewish girl. The Nacamullis who stayed in Venice (Abramo's mother, sisters and nephews) were sadly all deported and perished in Auschwitz; I've always been told that I look like one of my grandfather's sisters, Rori, and I wish I had met her. Some other cousins managed to escape to the US and there are still Nacamullis living there today, so it was a lovely surprise to find and meet a couple of them a few years back.

My grandmother, Bianca Di Segni, was from Rome – her family had been there for numerous generations. They lived in the city centre, where they also ran a small household shop. Fortunately, they didn't live in the area of the former ghetto, which was the first place to be raided on the 16th October 1943. By the time the Germans arrived at their home to deport them, they had already been alerted by a neighbour, who kindly hid them for a few hours.

Within a few days, after moving between several different hiding places, the family decided to split up as they couldn't find anywhere that could take the four of them. Thanks to Catholic institutions and kind human beings they all managed to hide and survive the war. My grandmother and her younger son were taken in by a convent in Via della Lungaretta in Trastevere. My father and three of his cousins, Sergio, Fausto and Umberto Tagliacozzo, went to the Collegio Nazareno, a Catholic boarding school near the Spanish Steps. My grandfather and his brother went to Palazzo Ruspoli, a gorgeous 16th-century palazzo in the centre of Rome. There they were hidden by the Austrian wife of the driver to Prince Ruspoli; she was a regular customer in our family shop and had become a friend. Interestingly, they often hosted card parties for German soldiers and both my grandfather and great-uncle played cards with the SS without them ever guessing their true identity.

My father was in third grade by this time and his mother told him never to tell anyone he was Jewish, so he and his cousins went to mass every day (but sat at the back) and did everything

together with the other children. His memories of the Collegio are of a relatively normal time; he was able to continue studying, and in the afternoons, he often went to play football in the Villa Borghese gardens nearby. He remembers that the food was poor but sufficient, so they weren't hungry. His favourite meal each week, however, was when his mother came to visit, bringing him egg sandwiches. He has a clear memory of her making four sandwiches out of one hard-boiled egg crushed with water, drops of olive oil and a little salt – thrifty cooking at

its best. He would share those with his cousins, whose mother Tosca had sadly been deported in the meantime. My dad stayed in the Collegio until the end of the war, when he remembers watching the American trucks driving through and liberating Rome on 4th June 1944. He was almost nine years old then and, still today, he describes it as one of the happiest days of his life.

Sadly, Nonna Bianca lost Riccardo, one of her brothers, who had been deported to Auschwitz with his wife Rita and young daughter Gianna. Nonna's sister, Tosca, who had been deported,

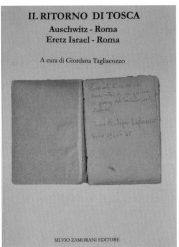

Left: Rita Caviglia, Gianna Di Segni and Riccardo Di Segni, deported and assassinated in Auschwitz

was one of the very few Roman Jews who returned from concentration camps (although there she lost her husband, Gino Tagliacozzo). Their four sons, thinking that their mother was probably dead, all emigrated to then Mandatory Palestine, with their aunts and uncles, to start a new life there as soon as the war in Italy was over. It took Tosca almost seven months to come back to Rome from Auschwitz – and not find her children!

One of Tosca's granddaughters, historian Giordana Tagliacozzo, compiled a wonderful and important book, *Il ritorno di Tosca* (The return of Tosca), telling the vicissitudes, through Tosca's personal diary and family letters, of her return from Auschwitz-Birkenau and Theresienstadt to Rome, as well as her subsequent journey to Eretz Israel (Land of Israel) to see her children and then their return to Rome all together.

My grandparents re-opened their shop just days after liberation, with only 30 lire in the till and a small stock of iron pans which Nonna Bianca had managed to hide. They sold out quickly as people needed everything, but they bought more stock and before long the shop was as busy as ever. Over the years, they developed a successful business, opening a few stores in the centre of Rome, and eventually my father and his brother took over the business with their respective wives. My parents' passion has always been to create and sell colourful Italian glass and ceramic tableware, and they were among the forerunners in the industry. I spent many happy days in the shops as a child and teenager, and helping to sell items during the busy Christmas period. The nature of the business changed over the years, but the passion is still going strong almost 80 years later, led now by my brother Stefano, who runs the family business and creates gorgeous hand-crafted Italian ceramics under the brand Modigliani.

Top: My dad Bruno (left), Nonno Bino (centre), Nonno Bino's brother Giorgio (right) and a client in their Via del Leoncino's shop in the 1950s; Left: My parents' wedding in 1961; Above: Their 60th wedding anniversary in 2021

KOSHER RULES

Kosher rules, or Kashrut, is the set of dietary laws at the core of Judaism. It dictates what food is permitted (*kasher* in Hebrew means 'fit to eat') and what is forbidden, 'non-kosher' or *terefah*.

The set of laws stem from the Torah, the first five books of the Bible, and they have subsequently been interpreted and elaborated in the Talmud (the primary source of Jewish oral law and theology). These rules are universal and apply to all Jews worldwide. They are a common denominator to Judaism and have been fundamental in shaping, strengthening and preserving Jewish life throughout the millennia.

The reasons behind kosher rules stem from the belief in sacred writing: as a divine commandment, one should follow the rules as a given tenet, and this is combined with philosophical, social, moral, mystical and health-related reasoning.

Kashrut not only regulates what we eat and the way we nourish our body and soul every day, it also gives us roots, awareness of our daily actions and choices and a sense of identity, history and community and, not least, it keeps traditions alive. More orthodox Jews follow kashrut completely, while less religious Jews (and the variations between orthodox and non-orthodox are very wide) adapt any of the rules in a more relaxed way. The degree of choice comes down to each individual and, if you are ever in doubt, you should consult your rabbi.

As a general guideline, these are the rules of kashrut.

It is prohibited to mix meat and milk or any other dairy products

In the Torah, it is repeated three times that one must not cook a lamb in its mother's milk. This has been taken by rabbis and sages who worked on the Talmud in the Middle Ages as a clear

separation between meat and any dairy products. This means that meat and dairy cannot be prepared, cooked or eaten within the same meal and a kosher kitchen must have separate sets of crockery, cutlery and utensils (plus two extra sets for Passover only!) and some people even have separate dishwashers and fridges.

Consequently, a meal can either be 'meaty' or 'milky' but not both. For example, no Parmesan cheese is allowed on a Bolognese sauce, a risotto or soup cannot include both butter and chicken stock, lasagne cannot contain meat and béchamel sauce, and no buttery or cheese dessert can be served after a meat meal... and

no caffè macchiato either!

Today, you can easily find dairy alternative products, such as soya, oat or almond milk and non-dairy cream, all of which are allowed to be used with meaty meals. However, this is a relatively new phenomenon and traditional Italian Jewish cooking calls more for ingenuity and creativity rather than like-for-like substitutions, such as making a lasagne with spinach instead of meat, or the many dairy-free desserts that have been created to accompany meat meals, usually served on Shabbat or High Holidays.

In addition, a specific length of time must pass between the consumption of meat and dairy, usually

a few hours, but longer after meat as it takes longer to digest, and timing rules change within the different communities and rabbinical authorities.

Today, kosher cheeses are made with vegetarian rennet, when rennet is required, making sure there is no animal trace. *Parve* (or *parev*) products are 'neutral' and include fish, vegetables, fruit, pulses, cereals and any other products which have no traces of dairy or meat. These products can be eaten with either a meaty or milky meal. Fruit and vegetables must be washed thoroughly and checked for the presence of worms and insects, which need removing as they are not kosher.

No meat and fish can be served in the same dish

Although fish is *parve* and can be eaten both in a meaty or milky meal, it cannot be served in the same dish as meat. This is a relatively late arrival in the kosher rules; it is not written in the Torah but in the Talmud, where rabbis regarded it as an unhealthy practice. So, you can have fish soup followed by a meat main course (or the other way round), but you must use a different plate.

Pure and impure animals

According to Jewish beliefs, before the Great Flood, humans were vegetarian and only after Noah's story did they start eating meat. Some rabbinic scholars, most famously Rav Kook, have said that at the end of time mankind will return to being vegetarian and that God's permission to eat meat is only a temporary privilege and man should not abuse or break any natural equilibrium. Not all animals, however, are permitted. The Torah lists the different categories of animal based on their habitat and has precise lists of those that are and are not permitted.

Four-legged land animals must both chew the cud and have cloven hooves to be permissible, so cows, sheep, goats and some wild animals such as deer are allowed. All other animals are considered impure and therefore forbidden, including pork, rabbit, horse, camel, boar, etc.

From the sea, only fish that have both fins and

scales are kosher. All other seafood, shellfish and crustaceans are forbidden, so no lobster, prawns/shrimps, eel, octopus, squid or sea urchins, just to mention a few. Also, larger animals such as sharks, or mammals like dolphins and whales, are not permitted.

Of the birds, the Torah lists only the ones which are forbidden, which includes all birds of prey and scavengers, as well as ostriches, owls and many others. In theory, all those not listed are permitted, but in reality only a handful of species are eaten. Today, the most commonly eaten birds are chicken, goose, duck and turkey. Other less common (yet still permitted) birds are pigeons, partridges and pheasants – they cannot be hunted and killed but must be slaughtered by *shechita* (see below) like all other birds and land animals, which means it is rare to find them in kosher butchers.

All insects are non-kosher, except locusts. However, as in most Jewish communities, there is no tradition of eating locusts, they became non-kosher by default, except where there has been a continuous tradition of eating them, for example for the Yemenite Jews.

No blood is permitted, and *shechita*
Blood is a symbol of life in the Torah and it must not be eaten. All land animals and birds which are permitted are not automatically kosher unless they are slaughtered in a specific manner under rabbinical supervision. This method is called *shechita*, where a very sharp knife is used to make a swift and precise cut in the large blood vessels of the neck, causing the animal to lose the maximum amount of blood and ensure a sudden and as painless a death as possible. The person who performs the *shechita*, which must always be accompanied by a blessing, is known as a *shochet*. The first thing the meat needs is a thorough inspection to check it is blemish-free. It is then soaked in cold water, covered with salt, then rinsed again three times under cold water; the timing

of each phase varies in different communities. Nowadays, meat from kosher butchers has already undergone all these processes; however, until a few decades ago, it was the task of housewives to soak and salt the meat. I clearly remember my mother doing it at home.

Only animals killed by *shechita* are regarded as kosher, and that's a cardinal tenet. Animals which died from natural causes, or have been stunned, shot or hunted, are not kosher. Fish do not need a *shechita* or any specific way of slaughtering and all the fish that are permitted are automatically kosher.

Interestingly, during World War II and my family's nine months of hiding (see page 31), my great-grandfather Marco, who was a rabbi and *shochet*, used to perform the *shechita* on chickens on the rare times that they were lucky enough to have one for Shabbat or a High Holiday, so the whole family could eat it.

The sciatic nerve must be removed, and no fat is allowed
One of the stories in the Bible tells of when Jacob was attacked in the middle of the night by an unusual angel. Jacob won the fight, however, during the struggle he was struck by the angel on the sciatic nerve in his hip socket, leaving him with a limp.

The Torah says that, as a result, Jews must not eat the sciatic nerve and that it must be removed from the hindquarters in order for an animal's leg to be kosher. This is a delicate and difficult operation performed by a *menaker* (a porger – someone who specialises in removing the sciatic nerve, residual blood and forbidden fat) and in most communities worldwide nowadays the hindquarter is simply not eaten and regarded as not permitted. So, cuts such as filet mignon, rump or sirloin are not easily found in kosher butchers, as they are cuts from the rear side near the sciatic nerve. The same applies for leg of lamb, which is not available in communities that don't have a *menaker*. Lamb roasts, therefore, are usually done using shoulder, shank or cutlets.

Wine – only Jewish handling is allowed

In order for wine to be kosher, it must be handled throughout (from the initial pressing of the grapes, through bottling, to opening and pouring) by orthodox Jews who keep Shabbat. The reason for this is both religious and social. Historically, wine was used in the worshipping of idols, and Jews wanted to make sure that they were not consuming wine which was meant to sanctify other gods, so they made their own. The main use of wine was, and still is, for the *kiddush* (blessing on wine) before each meal on Shabbat and High Holidays. Socially, wine is the oldest of 'drugs' and needed to be regulated so that Jews would not drink – and get drunk – with non-Jews, as this might lead to promiscuous relationships and assimilation.

Today, you can get *mevushal* wine (or 'cooked' wine) which can be opened and served by non-Jews or non-religious Jews. However, the production process and bottling must still be handled under rabbinical supervision. Most Italian Jews have drunk non-kosher wine for centuries as rules were relatively lax, however, this has changed in the last few decades, and today Italy produces fully-supervised kosher wine which is easily available, appreciated and exported worldwide.

RULES VS. CUSTOMS AND PRACTICES

Besides the paramount universal rules of kashrut written in the Torah and Talmud, there are customs and practices, or *minhagim*, which have developed in each Jewish community. These are important as they eventually dictate what is allowed, or forbidden, within each specific community whenever a question arises which does not have a straightforward answer in a sacred text. What is traditional and has been applied for centuries is usually what dictates the practice, whether this relates to food, prayer or lifestyle. What is regarded as kosher by one group of Jews may not be considered kosher by another group, and this is due to their different *minhagim* in following specific rules.

A good example with food is during Passover,

when Italian, Sephardi, Mizrachi and Yemenite Jews all eat rice, seeds and pulses and consider them 'kosher-for-Passover', as these are not *chametz* (leavened food, prohibited on Passover), while Ashkenazi Jews prohibit them and call them *kitniyot*. This follows a custom that Ashkenazi Jews developed in the Middle Ages which eventually became practice, saying that as *kitniyot* might in some way become confused with true *chametz*, they were forbidden altogether. The different practices are both valid within their own communities.

Broadly speaking, Ashkenazi Jews have been stricter over the centuries in following rules and practices, including kashrut, while Sephardim (including Italian and Mizrachi Jews) have been somewhat more relaxed. This is perhaps because the latter have always been more engaged and interested in the world and country they lived in, while Ashkenazi Jews lived a more insular life, not wanting to be influenced by the outside world for fear of losing their identity.

This does not make one group more or less religious or virtuous than another, as great scholars and rabbis came and still come from all backgrounds and communities. It is simply a different approach and interpretation of sacred texts and reflects the way of life in different regions over the centuries, when globalisation was not yet part of the equation.

Today, the Chief Rabbinate of Israel – chaired by two rabbis, one Ashkenazi and one Sephardi – tends to centralise the orthodox rules with a strong religious rigour, often called Ultra-orthodox. Diaspora orthodox Jews don't have to accept their ruling, as this in theory applies only to Israel and there is not a Pope-like governing figure in Judaism. However, many communities are often inclined to accept it, altering or removing some customs and practices which have existed for centuries in communities in Italy and around the world. The upside of having a universal approach in today's world is the guarantee that you can find and recognise kosher food worldwide by clear labelling on product packaging, so any Jew can shop with confidence, and by using restaurants with a kosher licence.

SHABBAT AND THE JEWISH HOLIDAYS

Jewish Holy Days are central to Jewish life, each having its own religious significance, symbolism and customs and, of course, there is no shortage of special foods. To me, they reinforce my Jewish identity and keep family traditions alive. Growing up in Rome, I remember seeing our home getting busy, refreshed and ready for each of the Jewish holidays: from the house being turned upside down with deep cleaning in preparation for Pesach (Passover), to long tables being filled with corn, wheat, pomegranate and honey for Rosh Hashanah, and our regular Shabbat dinners on Friday nights. Each celebration is unique, the only common denominator in our house, as in many others, is a very busy kitchen!

According to tradition, the Hebrew calendar started at the time of the Creation of Adam, placed at 3761 BCE. At the time of writing, the Hebrew year is 5782. It is interesting to note that the Jewish calendar is solar-lunar rather than only solar like the Gregorian calendar most of us live by. This means that the years are based on the cycle of the sun, and the months on the cycle of the moon, so each day, or 'date', starts and ends at sunset rather than at midnight, which changes slightly every day! Shabbat and the Jewish holidays are therefore celebrated when they 'enter', which is just before sunset, usually by going to synagogue, followed by a special family meal, and they end after sunset, once three stars appear in the sky, either the following day or a few days later, depending on the festival.

Jewish holidays can be split into three main groups. The first are solemn days or Yamin Noraim ('Days of Awe'), which include Rosh Hashanah, Yom Kippur and the 10 repentance days in between the two. Then there are the Three Pilgrimages, or Shalosh Regalim, which include Pesach (Passover), Shavuot and Sukkot. All three holidays are connected as they all have both religious and agricultural components, and refer to the time when the Temple in Jerusalem existed and the Israelites were commanded to perform a pilgrimage to the Temple and bring offerings to God. Finally, there are the rabbinic holidays, which include Hannukah, Tu BiShvat and Purim.

I should also mention the days of *moed*, commonly called Yom Tov – literally 'a good day' but meant as 'festive day' – which are in all the biblically-mandated holidays. These are essentially festive days within the different festivals! Work and all activities which are prohibited on Shabbat are also prohibited on *moed* days, except for some related to food preparation. So, for instance, on Yom Tov you are allowed to cook food that will be eaten that same day, as long as the stove used for cooking is lit with a pre-lit candle or fire (no electricity) – one that was lit before the festival in question started, and which can stay lit throughout the duration of Yom Tov.

This chapter includes an overview of the festivals in the Italian Jewish tradition, including a few family anecdotes, in the order they occur in the Jewish calendar. I will start, however, with Shabbat, often described as 'the Queen' or 'the Bride', marking every week. Throughout millennia, the keeping of Shabbat is one of the main reasons that Judaism survived and thrived, giving it continuity, strength and an identity like no other.

SHABBAT

Shabbat is the most important celebration of all and the only one which is mentioned in the Ten Commandments; it is the Fourth Commandment, and it says: 'Remember the Sabbath day, to keep it holy'. According to the Torah (the first five books of the Hebrew Bible), God created the world in six days and blessed and rested on the seventh day – the Sabbath (in Hebrew Shabbat). It is, therefore, a holy day of respite, where no work of any type is permitted, and time is dedicated to prayer, family and rest. In today's world, it also means no use of electronics is allowed, so no phones, TV or computing. It means no writing, driving, working, sawing, fire-lighting and no cooking either. So, through the centuries, Jews had to come up with some very clever ways of avoiding cooking on Shabbat and creating dishes which would keep well overnight.

Shabbat takes place every week; it begins on a Friday shortly before sunset with the lighting of two candles, usually lit by the women of the house, and it ends once three stars appear in the sky on the Saturday evening. There are three meals during Shabbat: the first one on Friday night, then lunch on the Saturday, and a lighter meal just before the end of Shabbat, *seuda shlishit* ('the third meal'). The Friday night dinner and Saturday lunch both start with the blessing of the wine, *kiddush*, thanking God for creating the world and for giving us a day of rest, followed by the blessing of two loaves of special bread, *challah*, referring to the double portion of manna that God provided to the Jews in the desert.

Planning the food is crucial, as everything needs to be cooked before Shabbat starts. In ancient Judea, Israelites prepared a dish that was cooked and kept hot in a pit overnight so it could still be eaten hot for Shabbat lunch. Because of this tradition, pre-cooked food may be kept hot for the Shabbat meal by a provision in the rabbinic oral law, which explains why Jews may use a fire that was lit before Shabbat to keep food warm. This tradition of 'one-pot slow-cooking' or, technically, continuous heating (called *hamin* in the Sephardi tradition and *cholent* in the Ashkenazi one), is still maintained today in Jewish communities around the world, with a multitude of dishes in both traditions. The Roman Jewish *stracotto*, one of my favourite dishes, literally means 'cooked over and over', stewing the originally tough cuts of beef until tender, making the tomato and red wine flavours intense.

Shabbat Shalom

Today, of course, there are hot plates and timers on electrical appliances, making it much easier to warm up food without needing to keep a fire lit or doing any 'work' by switching on an oven or stove. However, until not so long ago, and *hamin* and *cholent* aside, we had to rely on a menu which did not require warming up, and if we go even further back in time, before the advent of fridges, we mostly had to prepare food that would keep well at room temperature for one or two days. Out of this necessity comes the tradition of sweet and sour flavours and the use of vinegar to preserve food, as in *caponata di melanzane alla Giudia*, *cipolline in agrodolce*, *concia di zucchine* and *sarde in saor*.

For my family in Rome, the Friday-night Shabbat dinner has always been the main meal of the week and a very special time for us. When I was a child, we used to go to my maternal grandparents – Nonna Emma and Nonno Sandro – with my cousin, aunt and uncles. Nowadays, my siblings with their families go to my parents' house in Rome. The menu at my Nonni's house always started with the *frittata di spaghetti*, which we all loved, and as they were keeping the Shabbat, all the food was prepared ahead and ready to serve. To celebrate birthdays which fell on Shabbat, instead of putting candles on top of the cake (which could, of course, not be lit), we would each put up fingers which the birthday person would 'blow out'. This is a tradition that we still enjoy doing today.

The menu at my parents' home in Rome for a Friday night dinner, and our house now in London, is seasonal and varies from week to week. There are many recipes suitable for Shabbat in this book. I make more than half of them regularly for any Shabbat meal (especially from the Meat, Poultry and Fish and the Vegetable Dishes chapters). Here are a few you can try – traditional ones my family prepares, as well as some more generally Italian Jewish ones, and some from the delicious newcomer of Libyan Jewish cuisine.

Here are some menu ideas for Shabbat:

ROSH HASHANAH

Rosh Hashanah is the Jewish New Year and occurs in September or early October, on the first of the month of Tishri, and it lasts two days, both of which are Yom Tov. It is a time of joyous celebration as well as reflection, thinking about how we live our lives and about our relationship with God, our family and the community we live in. In fact, it marks the start of a 10-day period, the solemn days (Yamim Noraim), which culminate with Yom Kippur. A *shofar* (a ram's horn) is blown during prayers to 'raise a noise', to shake and gather our souls to prayer and God.

The notes of the *shofar* are the same everywhere, although the actual sound, tone and intensity of the blow differs within the various communities and, of course, with the actual blower. I am lucky enough to come from the Jewish community in Rome where the sound of the *shofar* is one of the most powerful, harmonious sounds I have ever heard. We belong to the Oratorio Di Castro Synagogue in Via Balbo (Rome's second largest synagogue), where Rav Pino Arbib has been blowing the *shofar* for decades. To me, his *shofar* blow encapsulates Rosh Hashanah: it is a real 'call', especially the last long, powerful sound of Rosh Hashanah morning's service.

The food served at Rosh Hashanah celebrates growth and prosperity, as the holiday looks forward to the year ahead. Sweet food, such as apples dipped in honey, is customary, and no bitter or sour food (in particular lemons and vinegar) is usually served. There are four celebratory meals – two evening meals and two lunches.

Italian Jews, like Sephardi Jews, have a tradition of doing a Seder (pre-meal ritual) for the first night of Rosh Hashanah, although thankfully not as long as the one for Passover! The food, individually blessed, may differ slightly within the various communities, but the common message is one of a sweet and prosperous new year.

At my parents' home, Rosh Hashanah has

always been a very joyous time, with lots of family and food around. We all get involved in preparing the nine different foods (see foods on pages 46 and 47) to put on everyone's plate for blessing. As there are so many of us, long tables are put up and my mother takes out her crockery for special occasions and her embroidered tablecloth, and the table is then decorated with pomegranates (usually home-grown), honey, corn and wheat. It is, in fact, an Italian Jewish custom to grow *grano e granturco* (corn and wheat) for Rosh Hashanah and to keep them until the end of Sukkot, three weeks later. They are considered a good omen and symbolise prosperity, and they look so gorgeous. The kernels are scattered on a plate and watered every day. By the end of the three weeks, they are a beautiful grass-like intense green.

The evening meal starts with the blessing of the wine, the washing of hands and the blessing of the *challah* bread and apples, which are both dipped in honey. The *challah* for Rosh Hashanah is usually made in a round shape to symbolise the cycle of the year and the continuity of life.

The Roman Jewish Seder then starts with a blessing, both in Hebrew and Italian, of each of the nine foods on the plate: fig, fennel, leek, pumpkin, date, chard (*bieta* in Italian), pomegranate, fish and lamb's brain. We all say the blessings, one person reading the Hebrew and another the Italian. There are joyous blessings on the fig, fennel and pomegranate for a sweet new year and to multiply our merits; there are wishes to proliferate like fish (if anyone in the family is trying to have children, they are invited to say the blessing!); and there are more serious ones on the date, leek, chard and pumpkin, which represent the eradication of our sins and destruction of one's enemies. There is then the lamb's-brain blessing (some Sephardi Jews cook a whole sheep's head) that we 'may be the head and not the tail'.

There are no rules on how to cook or prepare any of these foods, as long as they are all on everyone's plate ready to bless and eat. In my family home in Rome, we serve pomegranate seeds, dates, fresh figs (we are lucky to have the most delicious sweet figs in September in Italy) and raw fennel slices or seeds. For the fish, we serve red mullet cooked with pine nuts and raisins. There is then the pumpkin, which we either fry, coated in flour, or roast. We then make two frittatas with the leek and chard.

Although lamb's brain is available in kosher butchers in Italy, I have not yet found it in London, so in the UK, I usually serve a small piece of grilled lamb – when my mother came to us from Rome, she used to often bring frozen brain! To cook it, it should first be blanched and then sautéed with a drizzle of extra virgin olive oil, salt, pepper and a little splash of white wine. To some, the idea of eating brain doesn't appeal; however, if you are adventurous with your food and can get hold of it, then do give it a go – I find it quite delicious.

For the actual meal in my family, we usually create dishes using one or more of the ingredients that are part of the Seder plate, such as pumpkin risotto or soup, or escalopes of veal or chicken with pomegranate and honey, which has now been a tradition in our family for over 30 years.

Our daughters were born just a few days before Rosh Hashanah, and since their birth, we have been celebrating it in London, with my in-laws usually coming from Belgium, and occasionally my parents from Rome. It is one of the busiest times of the year for me and my catering work, and I love that English Jewish families choose my Italian Jewish cooking to celebrate their Holiday.

Once my deliveries are all done, I make sure that we have everything ready for our Italian Seder. We have a lovely tradition to celebrate the first night: we set the table with colourful plates, each one different from the other, from Modigliani Ceramics, our family's store in Rome. The second night we have an Ashkenazi meal, following my husband's tradition from growing up in Belgium. Although he is Sephardi (as you get that from your paternal last name), he is actually three-quarters Ashkenazi and Rosh Hashanah is the one time in the year he brings that out! For this meal, we use a beautiful white tablecloth from his late grandmother Thea, as well as her stunning porcelain and silverware. There is no Seder, we just do the blessing of the wine, and the challah, and dip apples in honey. Marc's parents usually bring gefilte fish from Belgium, and we then have pickled beef tongue with a tomato, Madeira and mushroom sauce. I really like this marriage of traditions and for our girls to learn about their different roots.

Here are some menu ideas for Rosh Hashana:

YOM KIPPUR

Yom Kippur is the Day of Atonement and it marks the end of the *Yamim Noraim* that started with Rosh Hashanah. It's the holiest and most solemn day in the Jewish year, when we repent and ask for forgiveness for our mistakes and sins, both to God and to the people we might have upset or hurt in the last year. It is marked by fasting; in fact, no food or drinks are allowed for 25 hours, starting at sunset on the tenth of the month of *Tishri* and ending after sunset the following day. It is traditional to wear white clothing for purity, and leather clothing, such as shoes and belts, are not allowed.

The pace of the day on Yom Kippur does not resemble any other. This is not only because of fasting and the fact that no work of any kind is allowed, but because reflection, repentance and prayer are at its core. It is perhaps the one day a year that even secular Jews tend to observe and go to synagogue.

As a child, I remember walking back home from the synagogue's evening service with our Nacamulli cousins, aunt, uncle and Nonna Bianca, who insisted on walking all the way well into her nineties. Wonderful chats and open-hearted discussions somehow happened during these walks, as we were perhaps unconsciously embracing the spirit of introspection.

The following day, I used to walk back to synagogue with my siblings from our home near Piazza del Popolo. We went through the historic centre of Rome, near the Spanish Steps, the Pantheon and all the way across the Tiber to Trastevere, where our synagogue for Yom Kippur is. Roman Jews have a long tradition of being shopkeepers. On Yom Kippur, my siblings and I used to enjoy counting the number of shops that were closed for the festivities, ours included, counting easily 50–60 shops along the way. Things have changed in the last couple of decades, with the retail scene changing to large brands, and a greater variety

of professions now practised by Roman Jews; however, the odd closed shop can still be found on Yom Kippur.

Now let's talk about the food... It is customary to serve a generous but simple meal before the fast, usually with little or no salt or spices (to avoid getting thirsty during the fast). A light meal is served at the end of the fast, usually with tea and coffee served with small savoury pastries and sweets such as the *bollo* (or *bulu* to Libyan Jews) from Venice or the *dictinobis* from Ferrara, both leavened sweet breads with raisins (or sultanas).

Well, that's what most people do. My family in Rome is quite unusual, serving more than 15 different dishes before the fast, and breaking the fast with tea and biscuits at the synagogue, and then chicken soup and a delicious BBQ steak at home! The steak tradition changed a few years ago – and I'm aware it is rather unusual – but it was in place until I left home, and continued well beyond that.

The Dell'Ariccia cousins come to my parents' home for the meal before the fast; there are usually about 20 of us, and it lasts around three hours, which is certainly long, but it is such a special meal. The menu is usually the same, just the side vegetables may change depending on what my parents find fresh at the Mercato Trionfale. I have listed the main dishes here, but I have not included all of the recipes, or else a fifth of the book would have been dedicated to food on Yom Kippur!

We start with the most delicious chicken and beef soup, which my mum makes only once a year, especially for Yom Kippur, with small quadrucci pasta and topped with offal and liver – the latter addition is very Roman. We then serve the chicken and beef from the soup with a few boiled and steamed vegetables such as chicory (endive) and broccoletti, as well as potatoes and naturally sweet shallots cooked in tomato sauce. There are also two other meat dishes; a veal stew with peas, and the classic Roman Jewish meatballs with tomato and celery, *ngozzamoddi*, which always goes down well with both adults and children. We then take a short break after the meat course to make space for the fish! A typical side dish to accompany the red mullet would be a raw fennel salad or grated raw carrots. My mum cooks everything savoury and rarely makes the desserts, so for dessert we usually have my aunt Isa's fruit salad, my sister Simona's chocolate mousse, or a cake from my sister-in-law Loredana, and desserts from Boccione bakery in the Jewish quarter. Finally, of course, a good espresso coffee, or else we would all fall asleep on our way to synagogue after so much food!

Here are some menu ideas for Yom Kippur:

Nacamulli-Dell'Ariccia lengthy lunch before the fast of Yom Kippur

SUKKOT

Sukkot is one of the Shalosh Regalim – Three Pilgrimages – together with Shavuot and Pesach. It takes place in mid-September or October, five days after Yom Kippur, on the fifteenth of the month of Tishri. It is a week-long festival, with the first two and last two days being Yom Tov in the Diaspora (and just the first and last day in Israel). It commemorates the 40 years the Israelites spent in the desert after leaving Egypt. Like Shavuot, Sukkot is also a Harvest Festival as it comes at the end of the farming season, so it is also a celebration of the bringing in of the harvest.

The word *sukkot* means huts or booths, and so the festival is a reminder of those precarious times in the desert. Traditionally, a *sukkah* is built (*sukkot* is the plural of *sukkah*) – a small hut covered in palm fronds, bamboo canes or pine branches. Religious Jews eat and sleep in the *sukkah* for eight days and take the Lulav or Four Kinds – an etrog (citron), a palm frond, three myrtle twigs and two willow twigs. On each day of the festival (besides Shabbat), Jews pick up

the Four Kinds, recite a blessing and wave them in all directions. This symbolises and reminds us that Jews are made of different kinds (hence the Four Kinds), all of which are important and complementary to each other, and that we should live together in harmony.

We seldom built a *sukkah* at my parents'; however, we always went to synagogue for the festival and ate in the *sukkah* there. I can still smell the palm leaves used to cover the sukkah and the palm frond of the Lulav, which we shook vigorously, as tradition dictates, on Oshana Rabba, the last day of Sukkot, in order to get rid of any outstanding sins that may just be lingering from Yom Kippur. Of course, as a child, I was much more interested in shaking the Lulav as we were allowed to make a mess and noise and I was quite oblivious of my sins! We often had lunches, aperitifs, dinners or after-dinner desserts at friends' homes under the *sukkah* and I particularly enjoyed helping decorate the *sukkah* with fresh fruit and children's drawings, something I still enjoy doing today with my daughters in London.

the Torah'), which celebrates the conclusion of the annual cycle of public Torah readings, and the beginning of a new one. I remember going to the children's service every year, where it is traditional to dance with and around the Torah and be merry, and sweets are given and thrown in large quantities at the end of the service. This tradition is still very much alive, both in Italy and across Jewish communities worldwide.

As for food, the focus of the festival is more about eating under the sukkah rather than what we eat; any food which represents the harvest, such as fresh seasonal fruit and vegetables, is popular and, of course, food is never lacking. There is, however, one sweet bread with raisins (or sultanas) – and sometime anise – that is a staple for Sukkot throughout Italy, but interestingly it is known by different names in different places. In Venice it is called *bolo* or *bollo*, showing its Sephardi origin (in Spanish 'bollo' means 'bun'); in the Veneto region it is *bussolà*; and in Tuscany and Central Italy it is *buccellato*. Libyan and, more generally, North African Jews also have their own version, *bulu*. It is made both for Sukkot and even more to break the fast at Yom Kippur.

For us children, the end of Sukkot was a particularly joyous time, as another two days of festivals occur: Shemini Hatzeret (literally 'the eighth day') when prayers for rain and a good harvest are made for the coming year, and Simcha Torah ('rejoicing of

Here are some menu ideas for Sukkot:

HANUKKAH

Hanukkah, or the Festival of Lights, celebrates the re-dedication of the Second Temple in Jerusalem in the second century BCE. It is celebrated for eight days, starting on the twenty-fifth of the month of *Kislev* according to the Hebrew calendar, which is in late November or December. There are no days of Yom Tov during Hanukkah.

In the second century BCE, Judea was ruled by the Seleucids (Syrian-Hellenists). King Antiochus IV Epiphanes outlawed the Jewish religion and ordered the Jews to accept Greek culture and beliefs. Jerusalem's Second Temple was desecrated by erecting an altar to Zeus and sacrificing pigs. The ancient Israelites rebelled, led by Judas Maccabeus, and against all odds, a group of faithful but poorly armed soldiers defeated the mighty Syrian-Greek army, drove them from the land, reclaimed the Temple in Jerusalem and re-dedicated it to the service of God.

According to the story, when the soldiers went to light the menorah in the Temple, they found only a small amount of olive oil – just enough for one day. The oil ended up lasting eight nights, enough time for new, pure oil to be prepared, hence the miracle of Hanukkah.

In celebration of this story, over the eight days of the festival, the candles of the nine-branched menorah, called a Hanukkiah, are lit, one each night. The ninth candle, the *shammash*, is used to light the eight others. The sight of lit candles is so beautiful and mesmerising, and it is a joyous time when songs are sung and presents are exchanged. Today, large public lightings happen all over the world. Over the last decade, this has even begun to happen in the south of Italy, in Puglia, Sicily and Calabria – 500 years after the expulsion of the Jews from those areas.

Since the miracle of Hannukah involved oil, it is traditional to eat fried food. Any fried dish goes, and there is no shortage of these in Italian Jewish cuisine, or in this book! Perhaps the most well-known dish for this holiday is *sufganiot* (fried doughnuts, usually filled with jam). Even if not Italian Jewish in origin, they are now common and can be found in kosher bakeries around the time of Hanukkah – particularly popular in Italy are the ones filled with custard cream or chocolate. Italians make the most delicious *'bomboloni'* which are available throughout the year and are quite similar, so Italian Jews were quick at adopting their versions for Hanukkah. I make my own version with Nutella and chestnut spread.

Other traditional Italian Jewish dishes for Hanukkah include fried chicken on the bone, fried potato fritters (Ashkenazi in origin) and fried apple fritters. I also found a fascinating recipe, which I am sharing in this book, for *precipizi* from Ancona – mini pieces of dough fried and coated with honey, which I have personalised by adding ricotta cheese. Eating dairy at Hanukkah is, in fact, another tradition, as it reminds us of the story of the brave and beautiful heroine, Judith. According to the story, in 164 BCE, she helped save the Jews in Bethulia by seducing the brutal Assyrian general Holofernes and feeding him lots of salty cheese; he then drank wine to assuage his thirst and fell asleep. Judith then cut off his head and the Assyrians, scared and having lost their leader, dispersed, and Israel was saved.

Hanukkah is probably my favourite festival; perhaps because I was born on the third day of Hanukkah, so it is often around my birthday, or perhaps because I always enjoyed the lighting of the candles and love all the blessings and songs, or perhaps because we used to receive a present every evening for the eight days (yes!), or could it just be the delicious fried food? I honestly cannot choose; it is just a perfect package of a festival to me!

Here are some menu ideas for Hanukkah:

Anything else fried...

TU BISHVAT AND SHABBAT BE SHELACH

BiShvat traditionally marks the time when the trees in Israel come out of winter hibernation and start the new cycle of life. It is, in fact, also called the New Year for Trees, or in Hebrew, Rosh Hashanah Leilanot. The name is also its date – 'tu' is how the Hebrew letters for 15 are pronounced, and the festival comes in the Hebrew month of Shevat (end of January to early February). It is not Yom Tov. Jews mark the occasion by planting new trees and eating fruit, particularly fruit that is mentioned in the Torah: grapes, figs, olives, dates and pomegranate, as well as wheat and barley.

An old tradition to do a Seder in Italy, which had been lost, has been revived by Rav Shalom Bahbout in his interesting and delightful publication 'Seder di BiShvat', which he compiled on the occasion of his daughter's bat mitzvah in 1986, and it has been welcomed and widely used since.

Like at Pesach, we drink four glasses of wine: however, instead of representing the gradual path to freedom, at Tu BiShvat the four glasses of wine represent the liberation of nature, from the cold winter to early spring, with the sprouting of plants and fruits. White wine is a symbol of winter and its sleeping nature, while red wine is the symbol of spring and the awakening of nature. We start the Seder, therefore, with the first glass being only white wine, and we drink it after eating wheat (as in biscuits or cake), olives, dates and grapes – each with its relative symbolism and blessing. The second glass of wine is white with a little red wine in it, and we drink it after eating fig, pomegranate, etrog (citron) and apple. The third glass of wine is half white and half red and we drink it after eating walnuts, almonds, carob and pear. The fourth and last glass of wine is all red, representing spring, and we drink it after eating rowanberries, apple, cherries, hazelnuts, medlar and lupin bean.

I grew up with a more simplified version of this wonderful Seder, eating a wide variety of nuts and fresh and dried fruits and reciting the blessing for each. I have now, however, adopted the longer version at home. During the years that I lived in Israel while at university, I truly understood the meaning of this festival, which is very much connected to the land of Israel and its seasons. I remember travelling to the north in late January/February and seeing green fields and flowers starting to bloom: such a rare, precious and short-lived sight in the dry land of Israel.

Quite a different story connected to this holiday is one of a fascinating dish that is usually prepared for Shabbat Beshalach, the Shabbat that falls either on or around Tu BiShvat. On this day, we read the story in the Torah of the Israelites coming out of Egypt and crossing the Red Sea. Italian Jews, particularly in the north-east, celebrate this Shabbat with a special dish, the *ruota di faraone* or *frisinsal*, or Pharaoh's Wheel, a delicious pasta bake which has a rather unusual and captivating story (see page 112).

PURIM

Purim is a joyful festival. It is on the fourteenth of the month of *Adar*, which usually falls in late February/early March, and it is not Yom Tov. There is a colourful story behind the festival, which is read in synagogue from the Book (or 'Scroll') of Esther (*Megillat Esther* in Hebrew).

In the fourth century BCE, the Persian King Ahasuerus was looking for a new wife. He found and married a beautiful girl called Esther, but she didn't tell him she was Jewish. Around the same time, Ahasuerus appointed a new prime minister, Haman. Esther's cousin and guardian Mordechai refused to bow in front of Haman, and in response, Haman got the King to issue an edict to kill all the Jews of Persia. He used a lottery (*purim* in Hebrew means *lots*) to choose a particular day, the thirteenth of *Adar*, for this terrible event. When she heard about this, Esther asked the king and Haman to a special feast. There, she told her husband her true identity as a Jewish woman and also revealed Haman's evil plan and begged him to save all the Jews. The King agreed on a new edict for Jews to defend themselves and also decided to hang Haman instead of Mordechai, who was made prime minister in his place. So the Jewish people were saved and the following day, the fourteenth of *Adar*, the day of deliverance, became a day of feasting and rejoicing.

It is customary to offer and exchange edible gifts with friends and family at Purim – *mishloach manot* – and to dress up, usually as characters from the Book of Esther, but anything goes, especially in non-strictly-religious communities. It is also the only Jewish holiday where alcohol drinking is encouraged. As a quote from a fourth-century rabbi says, a Jew should drink 'until he does not know the difference between "cursed be Haman" and "blessed be Mordechai"'. However, clearly one should also not become so drunk as to violate other commandments, the law or become seriously ill!

There are many interesting literary references and poems on the ways Italian Jews celebrated Purim during the Renaissance in Venice, Livorno, Mantova, Rome and across the smaller communities of the centre-north of Italy. Large banquets consisting of over 20 courses were popular, with a wide variety of fish dishes, followed by cold cuts of meat (beef or goose) and elaborate cooked dishes of beef's tongue, veal, turkey, lamb and pigeon. Lots of spices were used, and savoury and sweet dishes were mixed and served together, as was the custom until not too long ago. Finally, wine, and lots of it, was, and still is, always on the menu.

Today, the food at Purim is mostly about treats and sweets, and the most famous one in Italy is *orecchie di Amman* – Haman's Ears. These are a little different from the popular Haman's Pockets, made by Ashkenazi and Sephardi Jews: delicious triangular baked pastries filled with jam or poppy seeds that have found their way into Italy over the last few decades. The traditional Italian version is a light and scrumptious fried pastry topped with icing sugar,

but with no filling. It looks and tastes more like *frappe* or *chiacchere*, pastries that Italians eat around Carnival, which often falls at a similar time of the year to Purim. In this book, I propose both the simple fried version and a personal variation of filled ones. Interestingly, across Italy for centuries Christians called Purim the 'Carnival of the Jews'.

I always used to dress up as a child, and often still do even now, as Purim is a festival for everyone to enjoy and celebrate. We used to go to synagogue in Rome and make lots of noise, with boos, hisses, and stamping of feet, when the name of Haman is read out during the reading of *Esther's Megillah*. I remember Haman's Ears and how, as my mum was frying them, they would disappear from the plate before she could make the next batch. I'm sharing in this book my family recipe for *orecchie di Amman* (and there are probably as many recipes for this as there are Jewish families in Italy!). Edda Servi Machlin fondly mentions more than a dozen other Purim sweet recipes from the Italian repertoire in her book of recollections and recipes, *The Classic Cuisine of the Italian Jews*, most of which include almonds, such as *mustacchioni* and *montini* from Trieste and Padova, varieties of marzipan from Ancona, Padova and Livorno, as well as *moscardini dolci*. One of my favourite almond-based recipes is for amaretti, which I make both for Purim and Pesach. Finally, I've included the lovely Ferraresi *buricche*, small pastry parcels that are ideal party food and eaten on several Jewish holidays.

PESACH

Pesach, or Passover, is one of the Three Pilgrimages – starting on the fifteenth day of Nissan which falls in March/April. It lasts for eight days (seven in Israel), and it is Yom Tov on the first two and last two days in the Diaspora (just the first and last day in Israel). It is a holiday of freedom, commemorating the exodus of the Israelites from slavery in Egypt over 3,000 years ago. On the evening Passover starts, there is a ceremonial dinner called Seder, which takes place for two nights (except in Israel where it is one), when the story of the exodus is told through the reading of the *Haggadah*. The Seder has everything in it: prayers, ceremony, songs, history, and thoughtful and joyful moments. Everyone, in taking part in the Seder, relives in person the ancient story of the liberation from Egyptian slavery.

Special food is eaten from the 'Seder plate', each having a symbolic meaning. In the Italian Jewish tradition, it is sometimes a plate (mostly in the north) and sometimes, as in the Roman Jewish tradition, a basket, but the elements inside are the same. There is: *maror*, or bitter herbs, usually lettuce, to represent the bitterness of slavery; *zroa*, a lamb shank bone (not to be eaten), in memory of the sacrificial lamb, both on the eve of the exodus from Egypt and the offering to the Temple; *charoset*, a sweet paste, made of fruits and nuts, representing the mortar the Israelite slaves used when building. There is then *karpas*, usually celery, as a symbol of the spring harvest, which gets dipped in vinegar or salted water to remind us of the Jewish tears under slavery. There is also *betzah*, a hard-boiled egg, which has a double meaning: it's a symbol of mourning to remember the destruction of the Temple in Jerusalem, but it is also a symbol of life and our determination to keep our faith. Hard boiled eggs are then served as a starter together with a variety of kosher salami.

Interestingly, it is customary in some Roman Jewish families (including ours), to also add a few raw broad (fava) beans to the basket. No blessing for these, just the enjoyment of eating them. Finally, not on the plate or in the basket, but rather next to it on the table, there are three covered matzot, or unleavened breads; these remind us that the escape from Egypt was sudden, and there was no time for the bread to rise, hence the tradition to eat matzah. In fact, for the duration of Passover, anything *chametz* (food considered leavened) is forbidden.

Therefore, any bread, cakes, biscuits and pasta made with one of the five grains – wheat, spelt, barley, oats, rye – that has been in contact with water and has been fermented or leavened are not allowed. To avoid any confusion, matzah is indeed made of flour; however, it is made with kosher-for-Passover flour, meaning flour that is supervised throughout the production process to make sure it does not get fermented.

Ashkenazi Jews, additionally, don't eat *kitniyot* – rice, corn, pulses and many seeds – during Pesach, following a custom developed in the Middle Ages. In Italy, however, we consider them kosher since the Italkim arrived straight from Judea before the split into Ashkenazi and Sephardi Jews. This was way earlier than the ban on *kitniyot*, so eating rice and pulses has never been an issue, as technically they are not prohibited but rather it is a custom that the Ashkenazi developed.

Every Jewish community across Italy has not only their own traditional dishes, but also special tunes for reading the *Haggadah*, which is still read in Hebrew and sung throughout, making the whole experience of the Seder unique and personal. The Roman Jewish melodies are just wonderful and close to my heart, and I am lucky enough to come from a family where most know the liturgy and sing beautifully in tune – an important element for a pleasurable evening!

At home in Rome, as in many other homes, the weeks and days before Pesach are dominated by frantic and thorough spring cleaning, when every cupboard and drawer is emptied and cleaned of

any *chametz* that might have lingered from the last year. Growing up, I was responsible for cleaning my room and helping in the kitchen with my siblings, where we were given cloths, small tools and cleaning products and tasked with reaching the smallest parts of every cupboard. All the china is packed and replaced the following day with kosher-for-Passover china, all the cutlery, pots and pans boiled for deep cleaning and the hob and fridge dismantled in a way I was not even aware was possible!

As a child and teenager, once everything was clean and reassembled, usually rather late the night before Pesach started, we were ready to start baking. We baked *ginetti* and *ciambellette* using kosher-for-Passover flour, as the Italian Jewish community was allowing, at the time, the private use of kosher-for-Passover flour at home before the festival started. This was a time for late-night chats, for sharing confidences, while grating orange zest and chopping nuts, a time which I particularly enjoyed as my mum is a very matter-of-fact person, so I cherished the times when she opened up and shared some good chats and memories.

As we host the Seder at my parents' home on the first night, the setting up starts just after the burning of *chametz* in the late morning, officially ending any leftover cleaning. The house suddenly becomes busy with a joyous festive buzz. There is the setting up of tables and chairs to seat our 30–35 close family relatives on my mother's side. All the kosher-for-Passover china gets put out, copies of the *Haggadah* come off the shelves and everyone gets involved. The kitchen, of course, comes alive with my mum's amazing cooking. Lastly, when everything is almost ready, my father, siblings and any grandchild who happens to be around prepare the different 'pesach baskets' with overflowing lettuce, the different *charosets* and all the other elements of the Seder plate.

My mum is in charge of the savoury menu, and as no Seder is complete without *carciofi alla Giudia* (Jewish-style fried artichokes) she always prepares those. Hers are the best ever – perfectly trimmed, with crunchy leaves and a soft, sweet heart. I help as much as I can – my mum is the only one who is allowed to boss me around in the kitchen – and I am in charge of making *charoset* and a couple of desserts. My sister or sister-in-law also brings a dessert or two.

Some families also have *pizzarelle col miele* (matzah fritters dipped in honey) on Seder night, as they are a staple of Roman Jewish cuisine for Passover, but in our family, we dedicate a whole evening during the week to them, which just shows how special they are to us.

On the second Seder night, we usually split up as a family, each generation with their peers, and we tend to get together with our cousins and friends for a pot-luck Seder, in a different house each year.

As Pesach falls during spring, the weather in Italy is usually turning, with gorgeous sunny, mild days. It also often coincides with the Easter holidays, all excellent reasons to go on outdoor picnics or day trips. In fact, I am not sure I remember a Pesach without one. Rome has stunning parks, such as Villa Phamphili and Villa Borghese, or there are fields near old Roman aqueducts to visit; outside of Rome we might go for hikes up in the mountains, or go to the house at the seaside. The *azzimino* – literally meaning 'small matzah' but used to mean a matzah sandwich – is a classic to take along, often filled with beef salami, *carne secca* or *concia*. *Pomodori col riso* (stuffed tomatoes with rice), anything with artichokes, and frittatas also seem to be the perfect accompaniments. Desserts are usually *ginetti* or *ciambellette* – so easy to carry around – either 'homemade' from the community centre or bought from Boccione, the kosher bakery. One thing is certain: we are never short of food and by the end of the week we have definitely eaten too much!

Here are quite a few ideas for your Pesach week. Please note that some of the dishes are not considered kosher-for-Passover for orthodox Ashkenazi as they have *kitniyot*, so do bear this in mind as I certainly do not want to offend, or invite anyone to prepare or eat food which is not considered kosher in their tradition.

Here are some menu ideas for an Italian Pesach (including kitniyot):

SHAVUOT

Shavuot is one of the Three Pilgrimages, together with Pesach and Sukkot, and it falls on the sixth of Sivan, around May/June. It lasts two days in the Diaspora, both of which are Yom Tov, and one day in Israel. It celebrates the receiving of the Torah with its Ten Commandments, given by God to Moses at Mount Sinai. It is also a Harvest Festival – celebrating the spring harvest of wheat, as well as when the first fruits (bikkurim) were brought to the Temple as part of the Pilgrimage. Shavuot in Hebrew means 'weeks'; in fact, it takes place seven weeks from the second night of Passover, and these 49 days (called the 'Counting of Omer') are a build-up of excitement and a countdown to the receiving of the Torah.

In Italy, there is a tradition to decorate the synagogue with plenty of beautiful flowers, mostly, but not only, roses. The sacred vestments of the synagogue are changed to floral ones and I remember going to synagogue every year and being struck by its beauty and the scent of fresh flowers.

It is the custom to eat dairy food for Shavuot,

mostly to emphasise the purity of the Torah and the Ten Commandments, as they are considered to be as pure as milk and honey (Song of Songs 4:11). However, there are a number of other explanations for this custom in rabbinic literature, a few connected with the spiritual, numerical and gematria meaning of the festival.

As Shavuot is the festival of harvest and new fruits, my family tends to concentrate on this rather than eating dairy. We would wait until Shavuot to eat any new-harvest fruit, so even if new-season fruit such as cherries, apricots, peaches or strawberries were available earlier at the market, my mum would wait until Shavuot to buy them so that we could bless each of them individually, and also collectively as the new harvest. Cherries were always particularly popular. When the cherry season started, friends with homes in the countryside would invite us to help them pick their cherries, so we had lots of fun climbing trees to get them. We would come home with baskets overflowing with big lumpy cherries (which I adore) and then a few days of jam-making by my dad would

Above: Synagogue Oratorio Di Castro, Rome
Left: Great Synagogue of Rome, decorated with plenty of flowers for Shavuot

follow. When I see how expensive cherries are nowadays, I realise how lucky I was as a child to have almost unlimited access to them. My parents still pick cherries at their friends' houses – lucky them!

Here are some menu ideas for Shavuot:

Any fresh seasonal fruit

SILVIA'S COOKING TIPS AND BASICS

Here are my top tips on getting the best results from your cooking, from choosing the right kit to seasoning your food correctly, and making the most of leftovers. Nothing too complicated, just like my food!

Eat a balanced diet and use fresh ingredients.
I'm a strong believer in a balanced diet and moderation; if you combine both, then no food group or method of cooking should be off-limits – unless, of course, you have a food intolerance, allergy or health reason to do so. The only type of food I eat as little as possible is processed food. I use fresh ingredients and, whenever I can, seasonal ones. Enjoy roasting, sautéing and boiling as well as frying and baking; there is a time for everything in life and food is very much part of it. The key element is to have a healthy relationship with what you eat, without guilt or obsession, and know your limits – these limits are different for every one of us. Appreciate the good range of food we have, enjoy cooking and eating (without overindulging) and please avoid waste.

Make the most out of leftovers.
Don't forget that leftovers are delicious! Most food is perfectly fine to eat two or three days after it has been made (if it's properly stored), and some dishes, such as soups or stews, even improve in flavour. Of course, leaf-based salads and fresh raw dishes should be eaten on the day. I usually cook enough food for a couple of days' worth of meals and when I prepare more elaborate or time-consuming dishes, such as lasagne, *melanzane alla parmigiana* or stuffed courgettes, I often make an extra batch and freeze it, so I have a meal ready for whenever time or energy run short.

In the recipes in this book, I've advised where a dish is suitable for making ahead or freezing. You can also often transform leftovers into a new dish. For example, if you have leftover sautéed broccoli or beef stew in tomato sauce, then use it to make a pasta, or if you have leftover chicken soup, then use the stock to make a risotto, or leftover spinach or courgettes to make a frittata. The options are endless.

Get one (or two!) non-stick frying pans.
More than half of my cooking happens on the hob using a non-stick frying pan – the larger the better, so the food will cook more evenly. Make sure you only use silicone spatulas or wooden spoons for stirring (avoid using metal spoons, spatulas or cutlery as they can scratch and damage the non-stick coating). Don't hoard old, scratched pans, replace them regularly. Ceramic non-stick pans are also great.

Use good knives and keep them sharp!
Good, sharp knives are a kitchen essential. If you can invest in high-quality knives – which can be expensive – then do, as they are worth it and a pleasure to use. Otherwise, buy the best you can afford. Whichever type you have, please keep them sharp, as even expensive knives go blunt if they are not sharpened regularly. A sharp knife is, in my view, (almost) more important than a good-quality knife, as it allows you to cut, slice and chop easily and safely. Most of the time, I use a 'chef's knife' which is a relatively large knife with a blade that's 18–20cm (7–8in) long and 3–4cm (1¼–1½in) wide. In addition, smaller carving knives are handy, as are serrated knives (which don't need sharpening) – these are great to cut through the smooth slippery skins of ingredients like

tomatoes and aubergines, and other fruits. I find that large sharp knives are safer to use for chunky food as you can keep your hands away from the blade and use less pressure when cutting. Having said that, you should always use a knife that you feel comfortable holding: we all have a unique grip and some people can be put off by large blades. Get into the habit of sharpening your knives regularly – anything between once a week to monthly, depending on how much chopping and slicing you do.

Don't rush your soffritto!
Soffritto (literally 'slow shallow-fried') is the first step in building layers of flavour in most Italian dishes, especially soups, stews and sauces. The base is usually oil or butter – I like to use extra virgin olive oil – to which you add either one simple ingredient, such as garlic, which is quite quick to cook, or onion, which can be cooked long and slowly, or a combination of a few ingredients such as onion, celery, carrot, garlic and fresh herbs. I also sometimes like to add an anchovy fillet to give the *soffritto* an extra kick and hidden tang, as well as a good splash of white wine. When using a combination of ingredients, these should be cooked slowly until they soften and become aromatic. To make a good *soffritto*, time is all-important – I see it a little bit like building a relationship: if you take time and build a good solid base, then what follows will bear fruit. In a recipe, if you build a good base, it will enhance the flavour of the main ingredients and result in a tasty dish.

Chop and freeze.
Chop or slice batches of onion, or onion, celery and carrot, for your *soffritto* – either by hand or with a few pulses in a food processor – then freeze them. Use sealable bags and freeze the mixture flat and thin so that whenever you need some, you can easily break off small amounts and put them straight into the cold or lukewarm oil. Never put frozen

food straight into hot oil or it will splatter and you could easily burn yourself.

Extra virgin olive oil.
I genuinely love extra virgin olive oil and am a strong advocate of it. I use it for all of my cooking, although I prefer to use a light olive oil or sunflower oil for deep-frying. There are different schools of thought on oil, and I belong to the Italian-Mediterranean diet 'school' which believes that extra virgin olive oil is the healthiest oil – both for using raw and for cooking – with the lowest amount of saturated fat; it is flavoursome and adds a wonderful depth to your dishes. If you find it too strong, replace it with a regular olive oil instead. The important thing – for any oil – is not to let it reach smoking point or it will burn, become harmful to your health and give your food a bitter flavour, so just make sure to put food in the pan before the oil gets too hot.

I have two types of extra virgin olive oil at home: a standard oil, available from any supermarket, to cook with, and a cold-pressed, good-quality, extra virgin olive oil which I buy at farmers' markets or smaller retailers (or Italy!) and that I use as a condiment and for salad dressings.

Salt.

A few points on 'mighty' salt – a vital component in any dish. Firstly, I use sea salt or other natural salt for cooking and for dressings – coarse or kosher salt, crystals, flakes or fine. Pink Himalayan and Celtic salt are quite fashionable these days, and both are good, however, different salts have different flavours: taste a few to see which one you like best. My favourite salt, which I use regularly, is natural sea salt flakes. I gently crush the flakes when adding them to food and in regular cooking. I also use coarse or kosher salt (kosher salt has a slightly smaller grain than coarse salt) for cooking pasta and soups. I then use fine sea salt for desserts and baking. Avoid using 'table salt', as it has the highest percentage of sodium and contains additives and anti-caking agents.

Secondly, please use salt in your cooking! It is important to add salt to food (in moderation) in order to bring out its flavour, especially when you are cooking with natural fresh ingredients as I do in this book (unless you have a medical condition that requires a low-salt diet). I even add a pinch of salt to all my desserts, as it enhances flavour and helps to balance the sweetness.

I don't give exact quantities of salt in the recipes unless relevant, as every palate is different, and it's up to you and your taste buds to judge, but if a dish (like a soup, for example, where I never use any stock) tastes bland, do add a pinch of salt.

Thirdly, don't forget to generously salt the water when cooking pasta. In theory this is a simple concept, but I've found it is one of the hardest things to get across to my students in all my years of teaching. You need plenty of salt in pasta cooking water or it will taste bland. In the recipes in this book, I give a rough amount of 1 tablespoon per 500g (1lb 2oz) of pasta which goes into a large saucepan filled with 4–5 litres (135–175fl oz/17–21½ cups) of water. The salt is a means to an end and you won't eat all of it, so don't get put off by the quantity. It will flavour the pasta while it's cooking, so it will be tasty in its own right and ready to match any sauce. If you've gone to the trouble of making a wonderful sauce or fresh pasta, and if the cooking water is not salty enough, the final dish will taste bland, or it will feel like something is missing.

Garlic.

I love garlic and use it in most of my savoury recipes, however, the inner shoot (in Italian, the *anima* or 'soul', also known as the 'germ') in the middle of each clove can be difficult to digest. If you have no problem digesting it, leave it in, but if you are using it raw or cooking for guests, I would recommend removing it. Halve each clove lengthways and you will see the *anima*: it has a different texture to the rest of the clove. The *anima* also tells you the age of the garlic: when it's small and firm, the garlic is fresh. It then grows in size and slightly changes colour into green and starts to sprout, showing that the garlic is less fresh and is stronger in flavour. Ideally, store garlic at room temperature in a breathable dark container, but (as with onions and potatoes) never in the fridge.

Onions.

When slicing or chopping an onion, try to keep the root intact as it holds all the layers together to make it easier to cut. You can discard the root at the very end.

When chopping onions in advance, sprinkle some freshly ground black pepper on top after chopping them – this will help appease the smell. This is a great trick that a lovely group of Iraqi Jewish ladies taught me many years ago. It works!

When shallow-frying onion, I advise adding a little water to the pan and cooking it over a low to medium heat. This helps the onion to cook while preventing it from burning. The water will eventually evaporate and the onion softens and cooks.

Mixing garlic and onion.

You rarely combine garlic and onion in the same dish in Italian cooking, unless you are looking for a rich combination of flavours with lots of ingredients (in a *minestrone* or a *puttanesca* sauce, for instance). In fact, they have rather different tastes: garlic is sharp and onion is sweet. If you want to mix onion and garlic, I suggest softening the onion first for a few minutes before adding the garlic, as it needs less cooking time and tends to burn faster.

Risotto rice.

To make a good risotto, you must use risotto rice. Carnaroli, Vialone Nano and Arborio are all wonderful risotto varieties. Please don't attempt to make a risotto with long-grain or basmati rice (which I adore by the way, just in appropriate dishes). Never rinse risotto rice before cooking it (as you may do with other varieties), as you don't want to wash off the starch – the starch is what helps to create the delicious creamy consistency that is unique to risottos.

Lievito per dolci ('vanilla baking powder').

I use this for all of my cakes which call for baking powder. It is a great Italian leavening agent, with a subtle taste of vanilla, that's used to bake cakes and pastries. It is usually available in Italian delicatessens. It comes in 16g (½oz) sachets (*bustine*) and is usually used as one-sachet-per-cake-recipe for regular sponges, or in smaller quantities if less raising agent is required (or for small cakes). It can be substituted by using 1½ tablespoons of baking powder plus 1 teaspoon of vanilla extract or powder, but to be completely honest, I find that the end result does not taste quite the same!

Egg size.

I generally use large free-range eggs, however for the recipes in this book it doesn't really matter if you use another size: my food is home cooking in style, and is forgiving in terms of ingredient variations.

Use disposable gloves when dealing with raw meat, poultry and fish.

Use disposable gloves and discard them straight away after preparing the flesh; it reduces the risk of cross contamination. I also find them useful when handling vegetables that discolour your hands, such as artichokes, aubergines or carrots, or for food that has a strong smell like onions or garlic and especially for fresh chilli! I also recommend wearing disposable gloves when handling a mandoline or sharp knives, as it helps minimise the chances of nasty cuts.

Make your own vegetable stock.

It's easy to make and incredibly versatile; in this book, I use it to make risottos, but a good stock is invaluable for enhancing the flavour of (and adding moisture to) all kinds of dishes. Homemade vegetable stock is so much better than the reconstituted powder and cube shop-bought versions. Here's how I make mine, but feel free to add any other vegetables of your choice (avoiding anything starchy). Bring 2 litres (68fl oz/8½ cups) of water to the boil in a large pan with 1 peeled carrot, 1 peeled onion, 1 celery stick, 1 tomato, 1 courgette, a small bunch of fresh flat-leaf parsley and a teaspoon of coarse or kosher salt. Simmer, partially covered, for 1½–2 hours, then strain and discard the veggies.

As the stock freezes well, it's worth making larger batches to have a supply on hand for next time. If you can't make your own stock, choose a natural vegetable bouillon powder without any added MSG (monosodium glutamate).

Use dairy-free spread instead of margarine.

If you're looking for a butter alternative for your baking, or to finish off a delicious risotto to make your dish *parve* (dairy-free), I recommend using a non-dairy spread rather than margarine, as the latter is extremely unhealthy: it is high in trans fats, which increase blood cholesterol

can sometimes be inaccurate. The first time you try a recipe, you might like to set the timer for 5–10 minutes earlier than the specified time, especially when baking. Some ovens also heat unevenly, meaning one part of the oven is hotter than another. If this is the case with your oven, rotate the dish or tray towards the end of the baking or roasting time to allow the dish to cook evenly.

I always use a fan setting when roasting and baking. All oven settings (conventional, fan, Fahrenheit and gas mark) are provided in recipes where you need to use the oven, however, my recipes have all been tested using the fan setting, so bear this in mind. It might be considered unusual to use a fan oven for baking, which perhaps demonstrates that I'm a cook rather than a chef (in the good sense!) and I do what feels right for what I'm doing, rather than following fixed rules.

Use a food thermometer.
If you don't have one already, then buy one. It is an inexpensive and handy kitchen tool, especially for frying if you don't use a deep fryer, or for roasting meat and chicken.

Above all, enjoy yourself and have fun in the kitchen! Cooking is about nourishing both your body and your soul, and sharing homemade food is a wonderful way to spend time with loved ones and show them how much you care.

A note on measurements: All the recipes have been tested using metric measurements – grams and ml – so for best results and accuracy, please use kitchen scales and a measuring jug.

A note on cheese: All references to cheeses in the book, including Parmesan, are based on the use of kosher cheese, which uses vegetarian rennet (rather than animal) where required.

levels and the risk of heart disease. There are many dairy-free spreads out there, so look for the most natural one. You will notice the benefit in taste, and it will benefit your health, too!

Partially cover your pans when cooking.
In my recipes, you'll see that I often mention that a pan should be 'partially covered'. By this I mean that the lid should almost cover the top, leaving just a small opening on one side. This allows some of the cooking liquid to evaporate, while still maintaining a good temperature in the pan so the dish cooks through. Splatter screens are also great and have the added benefit of preventing sauces or oil from spitting; I often use them instead of a lid, especially when making a tomato sauce.

Check your oven temperature!
Baking and roasting times may differ from oven to oven so beware, as oven thermostats

CHAPTER 1

Soup, Pasta, Matzah and Rice

Without pasta and risotto there would not be Italian cuisine, or even Italian Jewish cuisine. These are national staples, with many regional variations. Soups are equally important in Italian cooking and are characterised by their chunky consistency rather than the smooth, puréed texture more common in northern Europe. Texture is given to Italian soups mostly by the addition of vegetables, pasta, rice, pulses, meat or fish and as far as Italian Jewish cuisine is concerned, also by matzah – cubes or balls – found in recipes such as *zuppa imperiale di Pesach* and *cugoli in brodo*. The idea of being without pizza or pasta for over a week during Passover is hard to imagine, so Italian Jews creatively make all kinds of matzah pizza and lasagne – I have included a couple of family favourites.

A few of the dishes I've featured here are best eaten at room temperature, ideal for Shabbat, when Jews are not allowed to cook or do any work; this includes dishes like *tagliolini freddi per Shabbat*, *pomodori col riso*, *ruota di faraone* and *pappa al pomodoro*. I've also included dishes that recall my childhood, with recipes from my late grandmothers – Nonna Bianca with her fabulous *gnocchi* and Nonna Emma with her delicious *frittata di spaghetti*. Then there are family dishes like *risotto ai funghi porcini*, which arose from my dad's passion for mushroom picking, or my mum's *spaghetti con ricotta, zucchero e cannella*, which I loved as a child and still make today.

Other recipes are a clear testimony of how traditional Italian dishes have inspired the Jewish cook and how these have been adapted to conform to kosher rules, such as *carbonara di zucchine*, which uses courgettes instead of bacon, or *lasagne al sugo* with cheese and tomato but not the meat the traditional Italian recipe calls for, again to meet the kosher rule of not mixing dairy and meat.

The rest of the recipes in this section use ingredients that have a Jewish heritage, such as pumpkin, aubergines, anchovies and fish roe, or are part of my everyday repertoire – Italian and Italian Jewish dishes with a soul.

TIP: *If you are not planning to eat all the soup immediately, cook only as much pasta and broth as you need. Cook new pasta in the remaining broth when you next serve it.*

Brodo di Carne

CHICKEN AND BEEF SOUP

Preparation: 15 minutes
Cooking: 3 hours

SERVES 6–8

Ingredients

1.2–1.4kg (2lb 12oz–3lb 2oz) chicken,
ideally an older bird ('boiler'),
halved or quartered
300–400g (10½–14oz) lean beef
such as top rib, in one piece

**4.5–5 litres (152–175fl oz/19–21½
cups) water**
1 teaspoon coarse or kosher salt
1 onion, peeled
1 celery stick, quartered
2 carrots, peeled and halved
bunch of fresh flat-leaf parsley,
stalks included
1 tablespoon tomato paste or purée
200g (7oz) small pasta shapes,
such as quadrucci

C hicken soup can be found throughout Jewish cooking. My mother makes this wonderful version, mixing chicken with beef, for the special, sizeable meal we have before the Yom Kippur fast, and again afterwards to break the fast. For my family in Rome, it's a special once-a-year soup, whereas many Ashkenazi Jews will have chicken soup every Friday night for their Shabbat meal. At home in London, I cook chicken and beef soup every so often as we all adore it, especially our daughter Thea. Chicken soup also cures any cold (well, we believe so!), so no wonder it is often called Jewish Penicillin!

Being Italian, we like to cook small pasta shapes, like quadrucci, in the broth, and we eat the chicken and beef separately as a main meal with olive oil or mayonnaise, but you can, of course, shred it into the soup instead or even as well. The broth can form the base for many other soups, such as zuppa imperiale di Pesach (see page 73) and cugoli in brodo (see page 74). You'll find that you only need water, not stock, as long as you use good-quality, fresh ingredients and the right amount of salt. It is best prepared a day ahead.

I buy a quartered 'boiler' from a kosher butcher to make this soup, an old hen which has tougher meat but makes a great broth (in Italy there's a saying, 'gallina vecchia fa buon brodo' – 'old hen makes good broth' – which is often used to say that wisdom comes with age, but let's take it literally here, for the soup!), however, you can use a regular chicken if you prefer, halved or quartered by your butcher.

1 Trim any extra fat from the chicken and beef, but leave the skin on the chicken. Fill a large saucepan with the water, then add the chicken and beef together with the coarse or kosher salt. Cover, bring to the boil over a medium heat and skim off any scum.

2 Add the onion, celery, carrots, parsley and tomato paste or purée, reduce the heat to low, partially cover the pan with a lid and leave to simmer, stirring occasionally and skimming regularly, for 2 hours.

TIP: *I use a large stainless-steel spice ball to contain the onion, celery and parsley so they don't float around and are easy to remove at the end, but you can wrap them up in a piece of muslin tied with string if you prefer, or do without.*

3 After this time, remove the chicken and set it aside, covered. As soon as it's cool enough to handle, remove the skin, then remove the meat from the bones and shred it into strips. This is much easier to do while the chicken is still warm, rather than cold.

4 Leave the beef and vegetables to simmer for a further 30–40 minutes, covered, until the beef is tender and breaks up easily with a fork (cook it for longer if the meat is still tough), then remove the beef and vegetables with a slotted spoon and set aside.

5 Discard the onion, celery and parsley, squeezing their juices so all their flavour and goodness leach into the soup. Slice the carrot into strips and shred the beef, then add it to the chicken, cover and refrigerate.

6 Strain the broth through a sieve or muslin into a separate saucepan. Taste and add more salt if necessary. If you are eating the soup immediately, try to remove as much fat as you can from the surface of the broth with a skimmer slotted spoon or baster.

7 If you are cooking the soup ahead of time (preferred), leave it to rest after straining until it reaches room temperature, then refrigerate. The next day, remove any fat that has set on the surface using a slotted spoon.

8 When ready to serve, bring the broth back to the boil and add the sliced carrots and the shredded beef and chicken that you plan to eat with the soup. Add the pasta, if using, and cook according to the packet timings.

9 Serve hot.

Zuppa Imperiale di Pesach

PASSOVER 'IMPERIAL' SOUP

*I*mperial soup, which has another, equally elevated name, zuppa *reale or royal soup, is a typical dish from the Emilia Romagna region, and is also found in Le Marche on the Adriatic Coast. It is a rich first course of cheesy semolina cubes in a meat broth, which Italians often serve at Christmas. The Jews of these regions substituted matzah meal and olive oil for the non-kosher mix of ingredients, turning it into a perfect dish for their annual Passover family meals.*

This recipe was kindly given to me by Claudia Finzi Orvieto, an old family friend who is originally from Bologna and now lives in Rome.

You can prepare both the broth and the matzah cubes well in advance and keep them in the fridge. This will mean the soup can be assembled in a matter of minutes.

1   Prepare the broth as described on page 71, or use any meat or chicken broth of your choice.

2   Preheat the oven to 200°C (180°C fan/400°F/gas mark 6).

3   To prepare the matzah cubes, whisk the eggs in a medium bowl until fluffy, then add the oil, salt and nutmeg. Stir and slowly add the matzah meal, continuing to stir until well combined.

4   Pour the mixture into the prepared oven dish to make a layer about 1cm (½in) thick and cook in the oven for 18–20 minutes until just golden on top. Remove from the oven, leave to cool, then transfer onto a chopping board and cut into 1cm (½in) cubes.

5   When you are ready to eat, bring the broth to the boil, add the matzah cubes, stir and cook for 2–3 minutes. Serve hot.

Preparation:
15 minutes
Cooking:
20 minutes for the matzah cubes, or 3 hours if also making the broth

SERVES 6–8

Ingredients
BROTH
See ingredients for *Brodo di Carne* (see page 71),
or use 4 litres (135fl oz/17 cups) meat or chicken broth of your choice

MATZAH CUBES
4 large eggs
4 teaspoons extra virgin olive oil
¼ teaspoon sea salt
¼ teaspoon ground nutmeg
80g (2¾oz/generous 1 cup) medium matzah meal

You will also need a small oven dish or baking tray (about 20 x 30cm/8 x 12in) lined with lightly oiled baking parchment.

Cugoli in Brodo

VENETIAN MATZAH BALLS

Preparation:
20 minutes
Cooking:
10 minutes, or
3 hours if also
making the broth

**MAKES 22–24
CUGOLI**

Ingredients

BROTH
See ingredients for *Brodo
di Carne* (see page 71),
or use 4 litres (135oz/
17 cups) meat or
chicken broth of your
choice

CUGOLI
4 tablespoons extra virgin
olive oil, or fat from the
meat in the soup, or a
mix of both
1 onion (I like to use red,
but white is also good),
very finely chopped
1 garlic clove, crushed
2 tablespoons finely
chopped fresh
flat-leaf parsley
200g (7oz/4 cups)
medium matzah meal or
dried breadcrumbs
2 large eggs
sea salt and black pepper,
to taste

*T*his dish, also called gnocchi all'ebraica or Jewish-style dumplings, comes from Venice, where there was once a thriving Ashkenazi community. The word cugoli comes from the German word kugel (ball). Matzah balls are typical of the cuisine of Jews from northern and eastern Europe, and are added to chicken soup for Sabbath or festive meals. They are usually made of eggs and matzah meal, however, unless they are made for Passover, Italian Jews like to replace the matzah meal with breadcrumbs. We also make a soffritto of onion, garlic and parsley, which is then mixed with the matzah meal to give it a lovely kick. In Venice, cugoli were adapted to Italian tastes again and served not just in soup but also boiled in water and served with tomato sauce or ragù, rather like a gnocchi dish.

This recipe for a dish that perfectly marries Ashkenazi and Italian cuisine is inspired by Joan Rundo's La Cucina Ebraica in Italia.

1 Prepare the broth as described on page 71, or use any meat or chicken broth of your choice.

2 To make the *cugoli*, heat the oil or fat in a small frying pan over a low to medium heat, then add the onion together with a couple of tablespoons of warm water, stir and cook for 4–5 minutes. The water allows the onion to soften while still cooking, and will evaporate after a few minutes.

3 Add the garlic, parsley and a pinch each of salt and pepper. Stir and leave to cook for a few minutes until the onion starts to turn golden, then remove from the heat and transfer to a heatproof bowl. Add the matzah meal or breadcrumbs and mix well. Beat the eggs in a small bowl, then add them to the matzah mixture and mix again until all the ingredients are well combined. Now wet your hands with water and roll the mixture into dessertspoon-sized oblongs.

4 Bring the broth to the boil, add the *cugoli*, stir and cook for about 10 minutes, then serve them together. The *cugoli* keep well in the broth (in the fridge) for the following day.

Minestra di Pesce

FISH SOUP

Preparation: 15 minutes
Cooking: 1–1½ hours

SERVES 4–6

Ingredients

3 litres (102fl oz/12¾ cups) water
heads and bones of 2–3 whole sea bass, hake, red snapper or sea bream, or a mix
1 slice lemon
1 bay leaf
1 carrot, peeled and cut into chunks
1 celery stick, cut into chunks
1 onion, peeled and halved
bunch of fresh flat-leaf parsley, half kept whole, half finely chopped
1 teaspoon coarse or kosher salt
3 tablespoons extra virgin olive oil
2 garlic cloves, crushed
pinch of dried chilli flakes or chilli powder
3–4 anchovy fillets in oil
splash of white wine
100g (3½oz) passata or **1 tablespoon tomato paste or purée**
½ head of Romanesco broccoli, separated into florets (optional)
100g (3½oz) spaghetti, broken into 2cm (¾in) pieces, or small pasta shapes
2–3 boneless fillets of your chosen fish, skinned and cut into thin strips
pecorino or Parmesan, freshly grated (optional)
sea salt and black pepper, to taste

A traditional Italian fish soup contains shellfish, which is *not kosher. This version, using only kosher fish, is another example of the way Italian Jews have adapted a local recipe to their dietary restrictions. If you would like to further extend their inventiveness and make this a thrifty recipe, as at the time of the ghetto, use only fish heads and bones, keeping the fillets for another dish. Here, I use all parts of the fish and cook the fillets in the soup just before serving, which is a more contemporary approach.*

Roman Jews often add a few florets of Romanesco broccoli to the soup and make it quite spicy. My preference is to add just a pinch of chilli flakes, but to otherwise stick to the pure fish flavour.

1. Fill a large saucepan with the cold water. Add the fish heads and bones along with the lemon slice, bay leaf, carrot, celery, onion, the unchopped parsley plus 1 teaspoon of the coarse or kosher salt. Cover with a lid and bring to the boil over a medium heat. Once it is boiling, turn the heat down to low. Skim off any scum and leave the stock to cook, partially covered with a lid, for about 1 hour, stirring occasionally and skimming regularly.

2. Meanwhile, in another saucepan, heat the oil, garlic, chilli, anchovy fillets, a pinch of salt and pepper and most of the chopped parsley over a low heat. Let it sizzle, then add the wine. Once the wine has evaporated, add the passata or tomato paste or purée. Stir and cook, uncovered, over a low heat for 10 minutes. This base gives a wonderful extra flavour to the soup.

3. Pass the fish broth through a sieve or muslin straight into the saucepan containing the tomato base (discarding the bones and vegetables). Bring to the boil, taste and add more salt if needed. Add the Romanesco broccoli, if using, and simmer, uncovered, over a medium heat for about 15 minutes.

> **TIP:** You can cook the soup to this stage, including the addition of the broccoli, up to one day ahead and keep it refrigerated.

4. When you are ready to eat, bring the soup to the boil and add the pasta. Cook it according to the packet timings, plus a further 2 minutes.

5. If you are not planning to eat all the soup immediately, cook only as much pasta and soup as you need. Cook new pasta in the remaining soup when you next serve it.

6. Add the sliced fish fillets to the simmering soup 2–3 minutes before the pasta is ready.

7. Serve the soup hot on its own, or with a sprinkle of of parsley and grated pecorino or Parmesan.

Minestrone

VEGETABLE SOUP

Preparation:
20 minutes
Cooking:
1½ hours

SERVES 6

Ingredients

- 4 tablespoons extra virgin olive oil, plus extra for optional drizzling
- 1 onion, finely chopped
- 1 celery stick, finely chopped
- 3–4 carrots, peeled, 1 finely chopped and 2–3 cut into 1cm (½in) cubes
- 2 garlic cloves, crushed
- 2 anchovy fillets in oil (optional)
- pinch of dried chilli flakes or chilli powder (optional)
- 4 leaves of cavolo nero or Savoy cabbage, thinly sliced
- 1 waxy potato, peeled and cut into 1cm (½in)cubes
- 1 courgette, cut into 1cm (½in) cubes
- 100g (3½oz) fine green beans, cut into 1cm (½in) lengths
- 200g pumpkin or butternut squash, peeled and cut into 1cm (1/2in) cubes
- 400g (15½oz) tin borlotti beans, drained
- 400g (14½oz) tin peeled plum tomatoes
- 2.5 litres (85fl oz/10½ cups) boiling water
- 2 teaspoons coarse or kosher salt
- 100g (3½oz) frozen or fresh peas
- Parmesan cheese (optional)
- sea salt and black pepper, to taste

My family eats this soup so often we consider it one of our classics. The *perfect* minestrone *requires good-quality, fresh and seasonal ingredients, lots of chopping and some patience. All you need to add to that is water, olive oil and salt – you don't even need any stock. As a purely vegetarian first course, minestrone goes with a meat or dairy meal and is ideal in winter, though my family also likes it lukewarm on a summer's day, so feel free to be creative and vary the vegetables according to the season. Spinach, chard, broccoli and sweet potatoes are all great additions or alternatives to any of the vegetable listed. I like to change them regularly. However or whenever you serve it, it tastes even better by the second day, so make it in advance. It is also perfect for freezing.*

1 Heat the oil in a large saucepan over a low heat, then add the onion, celery, finely chopped carrots and a pinch each of sea salt and pepper. Cook gently, stirring occasionally, for about 10 minutes, until softened.

> **TIP:** *The onion, celery and carrots can be chopped by hand or pulsed a few times in a food processor until fine but not mushed! I usually use the machine.*

2 Add the garlic, and the anchovy fillets and chilli, if using. Cook this base, or *soffritto*, for a further 5 minutes, until softened and lightly browned. This is fundamental to making tasty *minestrone*, so don't rush it!

3 Once the *soffritto* has softened, add all the remaining vegetables except the peas, then add the tinned beans and tomatoes, crushing the tomatoes by hand or with a fork as you add them. Rinse out the tomato tin with a little water and add the liquid to the pan. Cook for 5 minutes over a medium heat, uncovered, then add the boiling water and the coarse or kosher salt.

4 Leave the soup to simmer, partially covered and stirring occasionally, for about 1 hour. Add the peas in the final 10 minutes. Taste and add more salt or chilli, if desired.

5 Turn off the heat and leave to rest for at least 10 minutes before serving.

6 Serve hot, topping each portion with some grated Parmesan, if you like, or a drizzle of extra virgin olive oil.

Minestra di Pasta e Patate

PASTA AND POTATO SOUP

Preparation:
10 minutes
Cooking:
45 minutes

SERVES 4–6

Ingredients

3–4 tablespoons extra virgin olive oil, plus extra for drizzling
1 onion, finely chopped
1 celery stick, finely chopped
1 carrot, peeled and finely chopped
2 garlic cloves, crushed
pinch of dried chilli flakes or chilli powder
2 anchovy fillets in oil (optional)
200g (7oz) tinned peeled plum tomatoes
3 waxy potatoes (about 300g/10½oz), peeled and cut into 1½cm (½in) dice
1.5 litres (50fl oz/ 6¼ cups) boiling water
2 teaspoons coarse or kosher salt
100g (3½oz) small pasta shapes of your choice
4 or 5 fresh basil leaves
Parmesan or pecorino cheese (optional)
sea salt and black pepper, to taste

I grew up with this chunky, thick soup and I love it. The recipe is from my late maternal grandmother, Nonna Emma, who used to make it without a soffritto as my late grandfather Nonno Sandro liked neither onion nor garlic. It was simply delicious so you can try leaving it out if you like. Here, I propose my slightly richer version.

I was so thrilled when Lisa Goldberg from the Monday Morning Cooking Club in Australia asked me to contribute a few of my recipes to their gorgeous books, and even more delighted when she chose this as one of the recipes, as it's quite off-stream and great comfort food. It's the perfect combination of potatoes and pasta for carb-lovers like me!

1. Heat the oil in a medium saucepan over a low heat, then add the onion, celery and carrot. Cook gently, stirring occasionally, for about 10 minutes until softened, then add the garlic, chilli, anchovies and a pinch each of salt and pepper. Simmer the *soffritto* for 5–7 minutes, then add the tomatoes (crushing the tomatoes by hand or with a fork as you add them).

2. Rinse the diced potatoes, then add them to the pan. Stir well and sauté over a medium heat for a couple of minutes, then add the boiling water and coarse or kosher salt and stir again. Partially cover with a lid and cook over a low heat, stirring occasionally, for about 30 minutes or until the potatoes are cooked – a fork should easily break a piece. You can either cook the pasta straight away in the boiling soup or keep the potato soup as it is, even for a day or two covered in the fridge, until you are ready to cook the pasta in it and serve.

3. If re-heating, bring the soup back to the boil. If too thick, add a ladle of water. Add the pasta and cook, stirring occasionally, according to the packet timings, plus an extra 2 minutes as the pasta absorbs water more slowly in a thick soup than in plain salted water. The pasta should still be al dente. Add the basil, taste and add more seasoning if desired. Grate some Parmesan or pecorino over the soup, if you like, and serve hot with a drizzle of extra virgin olive oil.

Pasta e Fagioli

BORLOTTI BEAN SOUP

I love this soup. It is a hearty and warming Italian classic which is popular in Rome. In the original recipe the soffritto, the slow-cooked base which gives the soup its deep flavour, includes a cut of cured pork belly called pancetta. Roman Jews leave out the bacon and, personally, I like to add rosemary to it. A drizzle of extra virgin olive oil gives it a tasty final touch.

You can make pasta e ceci (pasta soup with chickpeas) by following almost exactly the same method as below, and using the same weight of chickpeas as beans, just leaving out the tomato.

Preparation:
10 minutes with tinned beans, or minimum 8 hours if using dried beans
Cooking:
1¼ hours (plus 1½–2 hours if using dried beans)

SERVES 4–6

Ingredients

300g (10½oz/1½ cups) dried borlotti beans or **2 x 400g (15½oz) tins borlotti beans**, drained
4 tablespoons extra virgin olive oil for cooking, plus extra for drizzling
1 onion, finely chopped
1 celery stick, finely chopped
1 carrot, peeled and finely chopped
2 garlic cloves, crushed
pinch of dried chilli flakes or chilli powder
2–3 sprigs of rosemary
200g (7oz) passata
1.2 litres (40fl oz/5 cups) boiling water
1 teaspoon coarse or kosher salt
100g (3½oz) small pasta shapes of your choice
sea salt and black pepper, to taste

1. If you are using dried beans, soak them in cold water overnight, or for at least 8 hours. Drain, place in a large saucepan filled with fresh cold water and bring to the boil. Cover with a lid and simmer for 1½–2 hours until fully cooked. Drain and set aside, covered, until ready to use.

2. Heat the oil in a medium saucepan over a low heat, then add the onion, celery and carrot. Cook, stirring occasionally, for about 10 minutes, until softened but not browned, then add the garlic, chilli, rosemary (leaves and stalks) and a pinch each of salt and pepper. Cook the *soffritto* for 5–7 minutes, then add the passata.

3. Stir well and cook for a further 5 minutes, add the beans, stir and cook for a few minutes, then add the boiling water and stir again. Leave to cook, partially covered, for about 30 minutes, stirring occasionally.

4. After this time, remove and discard the rosemary sprigs and add the coarse or kosher salt. Spoon out half the soup into a small, deep heatproof bowl or jug (making sure you have a good mix of beans and liquid) and blend with a stick blender to create a smooth 'cream'. Add this back into the unblended mixture and stir to mix the different consistencies together. Cook for a final 10–15 minutes, taste and add more seasoning if needed.

5. If you don't want to add pasta, you can serve the soup at this stage, with a drizzle of extra virgin olive oil on each portion. However, to follow the Italian version, add the pasta to the boiling soup and cook, stirring occasionally, for 4–5 minutes longer than instructed on the packet. (Because the soup is chunky, the pasta absorbs liquid more slowly than in plain salted water.) The final consistency should be quite thick, with some beans and pasta still whole. If you are not planning to eat all the soup immediately, cook only as much pasta and soup as you need. Cook new pasta in the remaining soup when you next serve it.

Gnocchi di Nonna Bianca

NONNA BIANCA'S GNOCCHI

T *hese are the gnocchi my grandmother Bianca would make for the memorable large family lunches of my childhood, maintaining the Roman tradition that Thursday is gnocchi day. They are light and delicious. Make a tomato sauce of your choice (see pages 84–85) or fresh basil pesto (see page 87) and dress each portion separately so you cut down the amount of stirring and the gnocchi don't break up or stick together. A potato ricer is handy for the gnocchi as it makes the potato fluffy and easy to knead – a potato masher works, however it doesn't give quite the same result. This is one of those recipes where it's hard to be prescriptive with the quantities: your hand, eye and taste buds, and a bit of practise, will tell you when you've got it right.*

Preparation:
30 minutes
Cooking:
45 minutes

SERVES 4–6

Ingredients
1kg (2lb 4oz) floury potatoes such as King Edward, Maris Piper or Desirée
250–300g (9–10½oz/ scant 1⅔–scant 2½ cups) plain white flour (ideally '00' type) **mixed with 1 teaspoon sea salt**, plus extra flour for dusting
2 tablespoons coarse or kosher salt (1 for the potatoes, 1 for the gnocchi water)

1 Wash the potatoes, leaving the skin on, add them whole to a large saucepan of cold water with a tablespoon of the coarse or kosher salt, then cover and bring to the boil over a medium heat. Once the water has reached boiling point, remove the lid, reduce the heat and keep an eye on the potatoes as you don't want them to cook so fast that the skins break. After about 25 minutes, check for doneness with a fork – they are cooked when the fork slides out easily. A general rule of thumb is 30 minutes cooking time, but that depends on the size, age and quantity of the potatoes in the pan.

2 Once the potatoes are cooked, drain and peel them while still warm. This step is important, as the potato flesh will stay dry and flaky if the skin is still warm. Press them through a potato ricer (or you can use a potato masher).

3 Dust the work surface with flour and knead the still-warm potatoes with the salted flour, adding a little at a time. The aim is to have a soft, light mixture that is neither too sticky nor too dry. Some varieties of potato absorb more flour than others, so don't tip all the flour in at once but keep a bit aside. If the dough is still sticky once all the flour has been added, add a little more, but don't overwork it. The less the dough is handled, the lighter the result.

4   Divide the dough into 4–6 pieces and roll each piece on a floured surface into a long cigar shape, then cut those into 2cm (¾in) pieces. Gently press your finger, or the handle of a teaspoon, into the middle of each gnocco to form a little ridge where the sauce will nestle. Be quick and handle the pieces lightly. Put them on a flour-dusted tray or cloth ready to be cooked.

5   Bring a large saucepan of water to the boil. When it boils, add the remaining tablespoon of coarse or kosher salt and drop in a few handfuls of gnocchi without overcrowding the pan. Cook them for a couple of minutes, until they rise to the surface, then lift them out with a slotted spoon and put them straight into a serving bowl or directly onto individual plates. Repeat the process until all the gnocchi are cooked.

6   Pour the tomato sauce, pesto or dressing of your choice over the top, add some Parmesan, if you like, and stir gently. Serve immediately and enjoy!

Pesto alla Genovese

FRESH BASIL PESTO

Preparation:
10 minutes

SERVES 4

Ingredients

**80ml (2¾fl oz/⅓ cup)
extra virgin olive oil**,
plus extra for drizzling

**50g (1¾oz) fresh
basil leaves**

**20g (¾oz/2 tablespoons)
pine nuts**

1 small garlic clove, peeled

**1 tablespoon freshly grated
pecorino cheese**

**4 tablespoons freshly
grated Parmesan cheese**

¼ teaspoon sea salt

*A*nother of Nonna Bianca's specialities was her fresh basil pesto. She usually served it with linguine pasta – and added a generous knob of butter – but any pasta shape is good. Alternatively, serve it with fresh gnocchi: the gnocchi and pesto go together extremely well. It is incredibly easy to make and so delicious, and freezes well, too. Once you learn how to make it, you'll probably never consider a shop-bought jar again. If you don't have pecorino cheese, just add one more tablespoon of Parmesan cheese instead.

1 Put all the ingredients in a blender or food processor and pulse a few times (be careful – you don't want to overheat the blades and 'cook' the basil). Add more oil if it looks too dense, taste, and adjust the seasoning accordingly. You can also use a mortar and pestle, which is the traditional tool used to make pesto and results in a coarser mixture: crush the basil, garlic, pine nuts and salt together in the mortar with the pestle, then gradually add the oil. Finally, stir in the cheeses.

2 To avoid the pesto oxidising and becoming dark in colour, as soon as it is ready, transfer it into a sterilised glass jar and drizzle a little extra virgin olive oil on top. Sealed, the pesto will keep in the fridge for up to 5 days, or alternatively it can be frozen in a freezer-proof container for up to 1 month.

TOMATO SAUCE

T omato sauce, *salsa* or *sugo*, is a serious business for Italians, and Italian Jews are no exception, especially as tomatoes seem to have been first introduced from the New World into Livorno, on the Tuscan shores, through the Marranos and Jewish traders in the 16th century. Initially, tomatoes were mostly grown for use as ornaments, as many people believed them to be poisonous because they belong to the nightshade family. Jews, however, seem to have eaten and appreciated them from quite early on, in dishes such as *pesce alla Livornese*. Once tomatoes won over the general Italian palate, they became incredibly popular, and it is difficult to think of Italian cooking today without tomatoes, and in particular tomato sauce.

As with so many things, the keys to a good tomato sauce are simplicity and quality ingredients. Unless it is summer and you are in a hot climate with wonderful, tasty, ripe tomatoes, I suggest using tinned tomatoes for their consistency and depth of flavour. Peeled plum tomatoes in tomato juice are my favourite: I simply crush the whole fruits with my hands while tipping them into the pan. You can also use *passata* (sieved tomatoes), which has quite a smooth texture or, if you can find it, *passata rustica*, which is a little thicker with more body to it. When I'm making large quantities of sauce, I sometimes like to mix plum tomatoes and passata (I recommend this in a few recipes in the book). Avoid tinned or bottled tomatoes with added flavours like basil or onion.

Fresh onion, celery or carrots are wonderful additions to tomato sauce and each gives extra and different flavours. There are also many ways of adding garlic: some people like to leave it whole (skin on or off) which gently releases flavour, then remove it once cooked, others like it sliced, chopped or crushed to infuse the sauce with a deeper garlic flavour. Many believe that you should use either garlic or onion as a base

but never both, as they give contrasting flavours: garlic sharper and onion sweeter. Others like stronger flavours and use them together. Some people would never serve Parmesan over a garlic-based tomato sauce, but if it's made with onions, they do! A few years back, on a visit home, there was a lovely bowl of pasta with tomato sauce for lunch. I asked for some Parmesan. My dad looked at me and said, 'You've been away from Italy for way too long. This is a garlic-based tomato sauce and it calls for no Parmesan.' End of conversation! For me, however (perhaps indeed because I have been away from Italy for too long), I feel you can cook the way that tastes best to you, not necessarily how something is 'supposed to be'. Don't tell my dad, but when I'm in England, I do put cheese on my garlic-based tomato sauce, as I like it that way.

Tomato sauce is also the first recipe I ever cooked on my own. I was 11 and staying with an English family in a small town on the east coast of England while doing an English language summer course. One day they asked if I would like spaghetti for dinner and I happily said yes, naively expecting pasta like at home. What was served was tinned mushy spaghetti hoops in an orange sauce – I had no idea they even existed! It only took a phone call home for me to have written down my mum's recipe for a proper tomato sauce. The next day I conjured up an easy sauce from olive oil, garlic and tinned tomatoes and cooked proper pasta. My hosts loved it.

You can make a tomato sauce in as little as 15–20 minutes in a frying pan over a medium heat, or you can simmer it in a saucepan for a few hours (I like to use a terracotta saucepan when I make my slow-cooked sauces, but other heavy pans that conduct heat evenly work just as well). Each version is delicious and will result in a different flavour and consistency. A general rule of thumb is that the longer you cook it for, the sweeter and more intense the flavour will be, and larger quantities benefit from longer cooking. Personally, I don't add sugar to any of my sauces as I like the slightly sharp flavour, however, if you prefer it less tart, do feel free to add a pinch of sugar or bicarbonate of soda when the tomato sauce starts bubbling. You can also sweeten it naturally by adding grated carrot to the *soffritto*. Once the sauce has cooked, I always add fresh basil, tearing the leaves into it at the very end so the flavour bursts out (the leaves should not cook). Dried basil is no good for

this so if you don't have fresh leaves, just serve the sauce without. Finally, if you like to add a kick to the sauce, add chilli (fresh or dry) to make an *arrabbiata* sauce. Should you wish to add some texture to a quick tomato sauce, a few good cherry tomatoes, halved and added in the last 5 minutes of cooking, will brighten both the look and taste of the sauce.

A natural extension to a good tomato sauce is a scrumptious *ragù*, the classic meat sauce of the centre-north of Italy. There are more than 20 versions of the sauce, some made with or without tomato, but they all recall the most famous, originally from Bologna – hence it's often called Bolognese sauce. Italian Jews adapted the dish to leave out pork and to avoid mixing meat and dairy, both of which are usually found in most versions. My own take on Bolognese sauce combines beef with lamb and veal and uses tomato sauce. You can, of course, just use one type of meat, preferably beef, which will result in a lighter sauce. Sometimes sausages are added for flavour, either in chunks or crumbled, so if you find good beef sausages, do go for them. The sauce can be used to dress tagliatelle (its original partner), to make meat lasagne, or served with polenta. The flavours deepen if you make the sauce a day in advance and it will keep for a few days in the fridge – it also freezes well.

THREE TOMATO SAUCES AND A CLASSIC RAGÙ

Here are three types of tomato sauce, based on garlic, onion, or a richer *soffritto* of onion, celery and carrots, with or without garlic. The garlic-based sauce is sharper – and perhaps my favourite. It's also the quickest and easiest to make. Alternatively, the base of onions or mixed celery and carrots comes out naturally sweet. I then propose one *ragù*. The quantities I give here are generous and designed for serving with 500g (1lb 2oz) dried pasta, as I like my pasta with plenty of sauce. If you are using egg pasta (fresh or dried), you may want to make more, as it absorbs more sauce. All versions can be prepared in advance, refrigerated and reheated at the last minute. They also freeze well.

Onion-based Tomato Sauce

Preparation:
10 minutes
Cooking:
1 hour+

SERVES 4–6

Ingredients
4 tablespoons extra virgin olive oil
1 onion, finely chopped
2 x 400g (14½oz) tins peeled plum tomatoes or passata, or a mix of both
4–5 fresh basil leaves
sea salt and black pepper, to taste

1 Heat the oil in a frying pan or saucepan over a medium heat, then add the onion. Cook for a minute, then add a couple of tablespoons of warm water to help the onion to soften. The water will evaporate after a few minutes. Cook for 10–12 minutes over a low heat, uncovered, until the onion softens and turns lightly golden.

2 Add the tomatoes or passata (crushing the plum tomatoes by hand or with a fork as you add them to the pan) and a good pinch of salt, and a pinch of pepper. Simmer, partially covered, over a low to medium heat for 40–45 minutes, or fully covered for an 1 hour or longer over a low heat – the longer you cook it, the more intense and sweet the flavour will be. Stir the sauce occasionally. Remove from the heat, tear in the basil leaves and stir to combine.

Rich Soffritto-based Tomato Sauce

Preparation:
10 minutes
Cooking:
1 hour+

SERVES 4–6

Ingredients
4 tablespoons extra virgin olive oil
1 onion, finely chopped
1 carrot, peeled and finely chopped
1 celery stick, finely chopped
2 garlic cloves, thinly sliced
2 x 400g (14½oz) tins peeled plum tomatoes or passata, or a mix of both
4–5 fresh basil leaves
sea salt and black pepper, to taste

1 Heat the oil in a saucepan over a medium heat, then add the onion, carrot and celery. After a minute of cooking, add a couple of tablespoons of warm water to help the vegetables soften, then simmer for 10 minutes, uncovered.

2 Add a good pinch of salt, and a pinch of pepper, then add the garlic and cook for a couple of minutes until softened but not browned. Add the passata or tinned tomatoes (crushing the plum tomatoes by hand or with a fork as you add them to the pan) and cook over a low to medium heat, partially covered, for about 45 minutes or fully covered for about 1 hour or longer, over a low heat – the longer you cook it, the more intense and sweet the flavour will be. Stir the sauce occasionally. Remove from the heat, tear in the basil leaves and stir to combine.

Garlic-based Tomato Sauce

Preparation: 5 minutes
Cooking: 25 minutes–
1 hour+

SERVES 4–6

Ingredients

**4 tablespoons extra virgin
olive oil**
2 garlic cloves, whole, thinly
sliced or crushed, as you wish
**2 x 400g (14½oz) tins peeled
plum tomatoes or passata**,
or a mix of both
4–5 fresh basil leaves
sea salt and black pepper,
to taste

1 Warm the oil together with the garlic in a medium frying pan or saucepan over a low heat. For a delicate flavour, keep the garlic whole and remove either before adding the tomatoes or once the sauce is ready. For a stronger flavour, thinly slice or crush the garlic cloves.

2 Just before the garlic turns golden, add the passata or tinned tomatoes (crushing the plum tomatoes by hand or with a fork as you add them to the pan) and a good pinch of salt, and a pinch of pepper. Cover with a splatter guard (or partially cover with a lid) and cook over a low to medium heat for 20 minutes, stirring occasionally. Alternatively, cook it for about 1 hour or longer, fully covered over a low heat – the longer you cook it, the more intense the flavour will be. Stir the sauce occasionally. Remove from the heat, tear in the basil leaves and stir to combine.

Ragù di Carne

BOLOGNESE SAUCE

Preparation: 15 minutes
Cooking: 1–1½ hours+

SERVES 4–6

Ingredients

**4 tablespoons extra virgin
olive oil**
1 onion, finely chopped
1 celery stick, finely chopped
1 carrot, peeled and
finely chopped
3 garlic cloves, crushed
**600g (1lb 5oz) minced beef,
veal or lamb,** or a mix
**100ml (3½fl oz/scant
½ cup) red wine**
**70g (2½oz) tomato paste
or purée**
**400g (14½oz) tin peeled
plum tomatoes or passata**
5–6 fresh basil leaves
sea salt and black pepper,
to taste

1 Heat the oil in a large frying pan or saucepan over a low to medium heat and add the onion, celery and carrot (I usually chop them in a food processor). After a minute, add a few tablespoons of warm water to allow the vegetables to soften, then cook the *soffritto* for 10–12 minutes, stirring occasionally.

2 Once the water has evaporated, add the garlic and a pinch each of salt and pepper. Cook for a couple of minutes, then add the minced meat and stir to break up any lumps. Cook over a medium heat, uncovered, for about 5 minutes, then add the wine and cook for a further 5 minutes.

3 Add the tomato paste or purée (diluted in 100ml water) and the passata or tinned tomatoes (crushing them by hand or with a fork as you add them to the pan). Rinse out the tin with a little water and add the liquid to the pan. Stir and cook for about 45 minutes over a low to medium heat, partially covered, stirring occasionally. For a more intense flavour, cook the sauce, fully covered, over a low heat for 1½ hours or longer. Tear in the basil and stir to combine.

Frittata di Spaghetti di Nonna Emma

NONNA EMMA'S SPAGHETTI FRITTATA

*T*his recipe is very dear to me. My grandmother Emma used to make it every Friday night for dinner to welcome the Sabbath. The key is to make the frittata thin and crispy and to use only as much egg as is needed to bind the spaghetti together. I like to serve it at room temperature, as Nonna Emma did. She would make one for each of us – which I really like – but it can be time-consuming to cook them individually, so I sometimes cook larger frittatas and serve them sliced to share.

Preparation:
10 minutes
Cooking:
45 minutes

**SERVES 4 AS
A STARTER, OR
2 AS A MAIN**

Ingredients
1 garlic clove, halved
**4 tablespoons extra virgin
olive oil**
**300g (10½oz/
1¼ cups) passata**
**1½ tablespoons coarse or
kosher salt** for the
pasta water
150g (5½oz) spaghetti
1 large egg
sea salt and black pepper,
to taste
3–4 basil leaves

1. Put the garlic and half the oil in a frying pan. Place over a low heat and as soon as the garlic starts turning golden, add the passata and season with salt and pepper. Stir, partially cover, and cook over a low heat for about 20 minutes, stirring occasionally. Once the sauce is ready, remove the garlic halves and add the basil leaves.

2. Meanwhile, bring a medium saucepan of water to the boil. When it boils, add the coarse or kosher salt and the spaghetti. Stir and cook, uncovered, over a medium heat, according to the packet timings (or until al dente).

3. Drain the spaghetti and stir it into the tomato sauce, then leave to cool for at least 5 minutes. Gently beat the egg in a small bowl with a pinch each of salt and pepper, add to the spaghetti and tomato and toss well.

4. Heat 1 tablespoon of the remaining oil in two non-stick frying pans 23–25cm (9–10in) in diameter (or in one larger pan) and, when it is hot, add the spaghetti mixture to the pan(s). If you only have one small pan, and would like to make small frittatas, you will need to do this in two batches.

   TIP: *The great thing about this frittata is that it is very thin and crispy so you can almost see through it.*

5. Cook the frittata(s), uncovered, over a low heat for 10–15 minutes, then use a flat lid or plate to flip over and cook the other side(s) for 5 minutes. Both sides should be golden and crispy. Serve warm or at room temperature.

Ravioli di Zucca con Burro e Salvia

PUMPKIN RAVIOLI WITH BUTTER AND SAGE

Preparation:
1 hour, plus 30 minutes resting time for the pasta dough
Cooking:
30 minutes

SERVES 4

Ingredients
DOUGH
400g (14oz/2½ cups) plain white flour, 'oo' type
4 large eggs
pinch of salt
semolina to sprinkle

FILLING
3 tablespoons extra virgin olive oil
1 garlic clove, crushed
2 sprigs of fresh rosemary
500g (1lb 2oz) deseeded, peeled pumpkin, cut into 1.5cm (5/8in) cubes

20g (¾oz) *frutta di mostarda* or 1 teaspoon Dijon mustard
20g (¾oz) Parmesan cheese, freshly grated, plus extra to serve
2 small dry Amaretti biscuits
sea salt and black pepper, to taste

SAUCE
100g (3½oz) salted butter
5–6 fresh sage leaves
1 tablespoons coarse or kosher salt for the pasta water
Parmesan cheese, freshly grated or shaved
2 teaspoons roughly chopped toasted hazelnuts (optional)
sea salt and black pepper, to taste

I love making fresh pasta. I don't do it often enough, but whenever I do, I get a real kick out of it. Pumpkin is a popular ingredient in Italian Jewish cuisine from the centre-north of Italy. In Mantua, where this dish was born, they make delicious tortelli with it. I use the same filling but make ravioli in the Roman style, a slightly simpler pasta shape.

The authentic recipe calls for frutta di mostarda, a condiment of crystallised fruit preserved in spiced mustard oil, which you may not find so easily outside Italy. You can replace it with Dijon mustard. I like to sauté the pumpkin, but you can also roast it or boil and drain it well instead, both options giving a lighter result.

I do recommend using a pasta machine to roll out the pasta as it will make easier work of getting the thinness needed for ravioli, but you can use a rolling pin instead, which is fun and also brilliant if you want to make a long pasta like fettuccine. Now, let's roll up our sleeves and make delicious fresh pasta!

MAKING THE DOUGH

1 Pour out the flour in a circle on a clean flat surface, such as a large board or worktop, and make a well in the middle. Break the eggs into the well, making sure there is enough flour around the edge to keep them inside (the larger the well, the easier it is to mix the eggs). Add the salt and gently beat the eggs with a fork or small whisk. Continue whisking and slowly start tossing the flour into the well. When everything comes together and the mixture has a dense and manageable consistency, clean any residual dough from the fork or whisk and continue working the dough with your hands. Incorporate the rest of the flour until the dough is malleable (you may not need to mix in all the flour).

2 Knead the dough with the heel of your hand for 8–10 minutes, pushing it away from you, rotating and folding it each time, until you have a smooth and elastic consistency, adding more flour if it gets sticky. You can never knead the dough too much, so don't worry! When it is smooth and elastic, wrap the dough in clingfilm and set it aside for at least 30 minutes at room temperature.

PREPARING THE FILLING

3 Heat the oil, garlic and rosemary (leaves and stalks) in a large, non-stick frying pan over a low heat and cook for a couple of minutes (the garlic should soften but not brown), then add the pumpkin cubes with a pinch each of salt and pepper. Cover and simmer for 15 minutes, stirring occasionally. Once the pumpkin is softened, remove the lid and cook for a further 8–10 minutes over a medium heat until the pumpkin turns light golden on the outside.

4 Remove the rosemary stalks and put the pumpkin in a shallow heatproof bowl. Mash with a fork, then add the *frutta di mostarda* or Dijon mustard and Parmesan and crush in the Amaretti biscuits. Mix well and adjust the seasoning to taste.

ROLLING THE PASTA

5 Attach the pasta machine firmly to a table or work surface and cut the dough you prepared earlier into six equal pieces.

6 Pass one piece of dough twice through the pasta machine on its widest setting, covering the other pieces with clingfilm so they don't dry out. Continue to pass the dough through the machine, each time on a finer setting. Stop at the penultimate gauge, or the one before that, depending which pasta machine you are using (each make is slightly different). You should now have a long, thin, elastic sheet of pasta. Leave it to dry slightly for a few minutes (on a clean surface sprinkled with semolina or hanging on a pasta drying rack) while you pass a second piece of dough through the machine, following the same process as above. Repeat with the remaining dough.

MAKING THE RAVIOLI

7 Place 1 teaspoon of filling onto one end of a pasta sheet – about 4cm (1½in) in from the end. Repeat along the length of the sheet, leaving 5cm (2in) between each teaspoon. Brush a little water along the edges and between each portion and place a second pasta sheet on top. Cut into squares using a pastry wheel.

8 Press the edges together with your fingertips to seal the ravioli and expel any air, then place them on a dry tray or surface sprinkled with semolina. Repeat the process with the remaining dough and filling.

MAKING THE SAUCE

9 Melt the butter with a pinch each of salt and pepper, and the sage, in a large frying pan over a low heat. As soon as the butter melts, take the pan off the heat and keep covered until ready to use.

COOKING THE RAVIOLI

10 Bring a large saucepan of water to the boil. When it boils, add the coarse or kosher salt and gently lower in the ravioli, a few at a time. Leave to cook for about 5 minutes.

11 Reheat the sauce, then, when the ravioli are ready, lift them out of the water with a slotted spoon and transfer them straight into the hot sauce. Sauté for 1 minute and stir. If the sauce appears dry, add a little cooking water from the ravioli to the pan. Toss well and serve immediately with a generous amount of grated or shaved Parmesan and a sprinkle of chopped hazelnuts, if using, to taste.

Spaghetti con la Bottarga

SPAGHETTI WITH CURED FISH ROE

*T*his is a delicious and super-quick pasta dish which I sometimes make for lunch. Spaghetti con la bottarga *is often found on kosher restaurant menus in Rome, where it's almost as common as it is in Sicily and Sardinia. I like to think that perhaps the Jews of the southern islands took cured fish roe with them when they were forced northwards at the time of the Spanish Inquisition, which is how this dish ended up being part of the Roman Jewish repertoire. Mullet and tuna – the most common of the kosher fish varieties – both work well for this recipe. Outside of Italy, bottarga may be available through specialist Italian delicatessens or online. I get mine from the kosher delis in Rome whenever I am there.*

Preparation:
10 minutes
Cooking:
15 minutes

SERVES 4–6

Ingredients
1½ tablespoons coarse
  or kosher salt for the
  pasta water
500g (1lb 2oz) spaghetti
100ml (3½fl oz/scant
  ½ cup) extra virgin
  olive oil
4 garlic cloves, crushed
80g (2¾oz) bottarga
  (cured fish roe), most
  grated, and the rest
  shaved, to serve
2–3 tablespoons finely
  chopped fresh
  flat-leaf parsley
sea salt and black pepper,
  to taste

1 Bring a large saucepan of water to the boil. When it boils, add the coarse or kosher salt and the spaghetti. Stir and cook, uncovered, over a medium heat according to the packet timings (or until al dente).

2 Meanwhile, warm the oil in a large, non-stick frying pan over a low heat together with the garlic. After a couple of minutes add half the grated bottarga, half the parsley and a pinch each of salt and pepper. Cook over low heat for 2–3 minutes.

3 Just before draining the spaghetti, remove about 1 cup of cooking water from the pan and set it aside in case it is needed to keep the final mixture moist.

4 Drain the spaghetti and add it to the frying pan (heat off) with the rest of the parsley and grated bottarga. Toss well. If the dish seems dry, add some of the reserved water and toss again. If the pan is too small to mix the spaghetti and sauce comfortably, do this in a large heatproof bowl.

5 Serve immediately, topping each portion with the shaved bottarga.

Carbonara di Zucchine

COURGETTE CARBONARA

*T*he classic Italian carbonara *recipe from Rome is made with pancetta, eggs and lots of Parmesan cheese. Roman Jews took out the original recipe's forbidden pork and avoided the meat-dairy combination by substituting the pancetta with courgette. The result is this delicious vegetarian carbonara. In Rome, it is also possible to make this a meaty dish, with local varieties of carne secca or coppiette (cold cuts of dried beef) that are sold by the city's kosher butchers. Cheese is omitted from the meat version, but the eggs still give it a wonderful 'creamy' consistency. You can, of course, substitute kosher salami from anywhere in the world, but to my Roman taste buds, it's just not the same.*

Preparation:
10 minutes
Cooking:
30 minutes

SERVES 4–6

Ingredients
4–5 tablespoons extra virgin olive oil
3 garlic cloves, crushed
2 anchovy fillets in oil (optional)
pinch of dried chilli flakes or chilli powder
splash of white wine
1kg (2lb 4oz) courgettes, sliced into thin rounds
1 tablespoon coarse or kosher salt for the pasta water
500g (1lb 2oz) pasta of your choice
2 large eggs
grated zest of ½ lemon
Parmesan cheese, freshly grated, to taste
sea salt and black pepper, to taste

1 Warm the oil in a large, non-stick frying pan over a low heat together with the garlic, anchovy fillets (if using) and chilli. Cook for 1 minute until the garlic softens (it should not brown), then add a splash of wine. Let the wine evaporate, then add the courgettes with a good pinch each of salt and pepper. If the pan is too crowded, split them between two frying pans. Stir well, partially cover and cook over a low heat, stirring occasionally, for 10 minutes until the courgettes soften. Remove the lid, slightly increase the heat to medium and cook, stirring occasionally, for a further 15–20 minutes, until golden.

2 While the courgettes are cooking, bring a large saucepan of water to the boil. Add the coarse or kosher salt and the pasta. Stir and cook, uncovered, over a medium heat, according to the packet timings (or until al dente). Before draining the pasta, remove 1 cup of cooking water from the pan and set aside in case it is needed to keep the final mixture moist.

3 Drain the pasta, add it to the frying pan of courgettes and toss through over a medium heat. If the pan is too small, remove from the heat and transfer everything to a large heatproof bowl. Mix thoroughly and slowly add some of the water you set aside earlier. You will see that the pasta absorbs the liquid as you stir. If it looks dry, add a little more water – you may not need all the liquid.

4 Gently beat the eggs in a serving bowl, then add the lemon zest and a couple of tablespoons of grated Parmesan. Add the pasta and courgettes and toss thoroughly.

5 Serve immediately, with plenty of extra Parmesan.

Pasta alla Norma

PASTA WITH AUBERGINES, TOMATO AND SALTED RICOTTA

Preparation:
15 minutes
Cooking:
45 minutes

SERVES 4–6

Ingredients
3 tablespoons extra virgin olive oil
3 garlic cloves, crushed
2 x 400g (14½oz) tins peeled plum
tomatoes or passata, or a mix
of both

500ml (17fl oz/generous 2 cups)
light olive or sunflower oil for
frying the aubergines
600g (1lb 5oz) aubergines (about 2),
cut into 1.5cm (5/8in) cubes
5–6 fresh basil leaves
1 tablespoon coarse or kosher salt
for the pasta water
500g (1lb 2oz) short pasta
of your choice
salted ricotta, pecorino or Parmesan
cheese, freshly grated
sea salt and black pepper, to taste

*T*his is one of my favourite dishes – a classic mix of pasta with
aubergines and tomato sauce, originally from Catania in
Sicily. The story goes that Nino Martoglio, a 19th-century Sicilian
writer, tasted it and exclaimed, 'È una vera Norma!', claiming it to
be as delightful and perfect as Vincenzo Bellini's opera of the time,
Norma. The name lives on in this delectable dish.

The traditional recipe calls for deep-fried aubergines, but if you
prefer yours lighter, you can shallow-fry them. Try to source salted
ricotta made from ewe's milk – it's a delicious hard cheese. If you
can't find it, use pecorino or Parmesan. This dish also makes one
of the best pasta bakes; just add some mozzarella and bake it in
an oven set at 220°C (200°C fan/425°F/gas mark 7) for 20 minutes.
The sauce can be prepared a day ahead, and it also freezes well.

1   First, prepare the tomato sauce. Gently heat the extra virgin
olive oil and garlic in a medium frying pan or saucepan over
a low heat for a couple of minutes, making sure the garlic
doesn't burn, then add the passata or tinned tomatoes
(crushing them by hand or with a fork as you add them), plus
a pinch each of salt and pepper. Rinse out the tin with a little
water and add the liquid to the pan. Cook over a low to medium
heat for 20–25 minutes, partially covered, stirring occasionally.

2   Meanwhile, heat the light olive or sunflower oil in a large, deep frying pan or saucepan. When it is hot enough to start popping, add some of the cubed aubergines.

TIP: *You may need to fry the aubergines in 3–4 batches to avoid overcrowding the pan. It fries more evenly and faster this way and absorbs less oil.*

3   Fry the aubergine cubes over a high heat, turning occasionally, until golden. This may take about 5 minutes per batch. Remove them from the oil with a slotted spoon and place them in a sieve to drain the oil. Just before the next batch is ready, transfer them to a plate lined with kitchen paper to help absorb any excess oil.

4   Add the fried aubergines to the cooked tomato sauce, add another pinch of salt and cook for a further 10 minutes, uncovered, over a low to medium heat. Remove from the heat and tear in the basil leaves.

5   Meanwhile, bring a large saucepan of water to the boil. When it boils, add the coarse or kosher salt and the pasta. Stir and cook, uncovered, according to the packet timings (or until al dente).

6   Drain the pasta and ideally add it to the frying pan or saucepan containing the aubergine and tomato sauce and warm through, over a medium heat, for 1 minute. If the pan is too small, transfer everything to a large heatproof serving bowl or platter. Toss well to coat the pasta with the sauce.

7   Sprinkle the salted ricotta or your cheese of choice over the top and serve.

Pasta alla Puttanesca

PASTA WITH TOMATOES, OLIVES AND CAPERS

This is the pasta of my student days in Israel. I became known amongst my friends for my puttanesca and also my tiramisù. I love tomatoes and olives so this sauce ticks all the boxes for me. You can easily make the sauce a day in advance, and it freezes well.

Preparation:
15 minutes
Cooking:
1 hour

SERVES 4–6

Ingredients

4 tablespoons extra virgin olive oil
1 onion, finely chopped
3 garlic cloves, crushed
2 anchovy fillets in oil (optional)
pinch of dried chilli flakes or chilli powder (or to taste)
2 x 400g (14½oz) tins peeled plum tomatoes or passata, or a mix of both
30g (1oz/3 tablespoons) capers
150g (5oz/1 cup) pitted black or green olives, or a mix of both
5–6 fresh basil leaves
1 tablespoons coarse or kosher salt for the pasta water
500g (1lb 2oz) pasta of your choice
Parmesan cheese, freshly grated (optional)
sea salt and black pepper, to taste

1 Heat the oil in a large frying pan or saucepan over a low heat, add the onion and cook for 1 minute, then add a couple of tablespoons of water and cook for 5–7 minutes. Once the water has evaporated, add the garlic, anchovy fillets (if using), chilli and a pinch each of salt and pepper and cook for a couple of minutes over a low to medium heat.

2 Add the plum tomatoes (crushing the tomatoes by hand or with a fork as you add them) and/or passata and stir well. Rinse out the tin with a little water and add the liquid to the pan, then add the capers, olives and another pinch each of salt and pepper. Cook over a low to medium heat, partially covered, stirring occasionally, for 45–50 minutes.

> **TIP:** *You can also cook the sauce for 1½–2 hours – fully covered – over a low heat, stirring occasionally. Using this method, the flavour will be more intense.*

3 While the sauce is cooking, bring a large saucepan of water to the boil. When the water boils and the sauce is nearly ready, add the coarse or kosher salt and the pasta. Stir and cook, uncovered, over a medium heat, according to the packet timings (or until al dente).

4 Drain the pasta and add it to the pan containing the sauce. Warm through over a medium heat and toss well. If the pan is too small to mix the pasta and sauce comfortably, do this in a large heatproof bowl.

5 Serve individual portions with grated Parmesan sprinkled on top, if you like.

Spaghetti con Ricotta, Zucchero e Cannella

SPAGHETTI WITH RICOTTA, SUGAR AND CINNAMON

This is one of the strongest 'flavour memories' of my childhood, with an interesting mix of savoury and sweet flavours. Being a Roman dish, it is usually made with ewe's milk ricotta, but if you can't find this then cow's will do. It is very quick to make and you will either love it or hate it, and for those who like it, like me, it can become quite addictive... You can also add the grated zest of half a lemon to the ingredients listed here; try both versions and see which you prefer.

Preparation:
5 minutes
Cooking:
15 minutes

SERVES 4–6

Ingredients
1 tablespoon coarse or kosher salt for the pasta water
500g (1lb 2oz) spaghetti
500g (1lb 2oz/2 cups plus 2½ tablespoons) ricotta cheese
1–1½ teaspoons ground cinnamon, to taste
2 tablespoons granulated sugar
¼ teaspoon sea salt

1 Bring a large saucepan of water to the boil. When it boils, add the coarse or kosher salt and the spaghetti. Stir and cook, uncovered, according to the packet timings (or until al dente).

2 Meanwhile, mix the ricotta in a heatproof serving bowl with the cinnamon, sugar and salt.

3 Just before draining the spaghetti, remove 1 cup of cooking water from the pan and set it aside in case it is needed to keep the final mixture moist.

4 Drain the spaghetti and add it to the bowl containing the ricotta, cinnamon, sugar and salt and mix well. If it looks and feels dry while stirring, add the reserved water, a little at a time, until the dish has a creamy consistency – you may not need all the liquid.

5 Serve immediately and adjust the seasoning to taste, with more salt, cinnamon or sugar.

Bigoli in Salsa

SPAGHETTI WITH ONION AND ANCHOVY SAUCE

*T*his recipe is a staple of Venetian Jewish cooking, even if its Jewish origins are often forgotten. It reminds me of my own roots in the city of canals, where my father's father, Nonno Bino, was born. Bigoli is pasta from the Veneto region originally made with buckwheat flour. It is a little thicker than traditional spaghetti, with a rough texture that allows the sauce to be more easily absorbed. I usually make this dish with wholewheat spaghetti which has a nutty flavour that works well with the anchovies. You may find that even people who say they aren't a fan of anchovies often like this dish – somehow the combination of onions, parsley and the unrefined pasta balances the fish out.

Preparation:
15 minutes
Cooking:
30 minutes

SERVES 4–6

Ingredients
100ml (3½fl oz/scant ½ cup) extra virgin olive oil
3 onions, finely chopped
100g (3½oz) anchovy fillets in oil, roughly chopped
4 tablespoons finely chopped fresh flat-leaf parsley
1 tablespoon coarse or kosher salt for the pasta water
500g (1lb 2oz) bigoli buckwheat or wholewheat spaghetti
black pepper, to taste

1   Heat the oil in a large frying pan over a low heat and add the onions and a couple of tablespoons of water. Cover and cook for 15–20 minutes, until the water has evaporated and the onion is softened, then add the anchovies, half the parsley and a pinch of black pepper. Stir and cook over a low heat for 5–8 minutes, adding the rest of the parsley at the last minute.

2   While the sauce is cooking, bring a large saucepan of water to the boil. When it boils, add the coarse or kosher salt and the pasta. Stir and cook, uncovered, according to the packet timings (or until al dente). Just before draining the pasta, remove 1 cup of boiling water from the pan and set it aside in case it is needed to keep the final mixture moist.

3   Drain the pasta and add it to the pan containing the onion and anchovy sauce and toss through over a medium heat for about a minute. If the pan is too small, remove from the heat and transfer everything to a large heatproof bowl. Mix thoroughly until the pasta is completely covered with sauce.

4   If it looks and feels dry while stirring, slowly add some of the water you set aside earlier. You will see that the pasta absorbs the liquid as you stir. Add just enough water for it to be creamy – you may not need all the liquid.

5   Serve immediately, adding black pepper to taste.

Tagliolini Freddi per Shabbat

COLD TAGLIOLINI FOR SHABBAT

*V*inegar, sugar, chilli and lemon give a twist to the tomato sauce in this great pasta dish, which is ideal served at room temperature for a summer Shabbat meal. It may seem as if you have too much sauce when you first mix the pasta into it, but it will be absorbed as it cools and you will end up using it all. The dish tastes slightly different when warm rather than cold, but it is delicious either way. The tomato sauce can be prepared in advance, and it's actually better used cold.

Preparation:
10 minutes, plus cooling time
Cooking: 45 minutes

SERVES 6

Ingredients

100ml (3½fl oz/scant ½ cup) extra virgin olive oil, plus extra for drizzling

3 garlic cloves, crushed

1kg (2lb 4oz) passata or tinned peeled plum tomatoes, or a mix

3 tablespoons cider vinegar or white wine vinegar

2 tablespoons granulated sugar

pared rind of 1 lemon

pinch of dried chilli flakes or chilli powder

6 tablespoons finely chopped fresh flat-leaf parsley

1 tablespoon coarse or kosher salt for the pasta water

500g (1lb 2oz) tagliolini, linguine or other long pasta

sea salt and black pepper, to taste

1. First, prepare the tomato sauce. Heat the oil in a medium frying pan or saucepan over a low heat and add the garlic together with a pinch each of salt and pepper. Cook for a couple of minutes, being careful not to let the garlic brown, then add the passata and/or plum tomatoes (crushing the tomatoes by hand or with a fork as you add them). Rinse out the tin with a little water and add the liquid to the pan, then add the vinegar, sugar, lemon rind, chilli and a good pinch of salt. Stir, and cook over a low heat, partially covered, for about 40–45 minutes, stirring occasionally.

2. Remove the lid, add 4 tablespoons of the parsley and cook over a medium heat for a further 5 minutes. Remove the lemon rind and leave it to cool down, uncovered, or transfer to a heatproof bowl.

3. Meanwhile, bring a large saucepan of water to the boil. When it boils, add the coarse or kosher salt and the pasta. Stir and cook, uncovered, according to the packet timings (or until al dente).

4. Drain the pasta and place in a large, shallow bowl. Pour over most of the tomato sauce, hot if you have just made it, or cold if prepared earlier, and toss well. Reserve a couple of ladles of tomato sauce for adding to the pasta just before serving. This gives it a fresher taste.

5. Partially cover the pasta and leave to cool, before serving at room temperature. You can also chill it in the fridge overnight; just remove it from the fridge about an hour before serving.

6. Add the tomato sauce you set aside and the remaining parsley and drizzle a little oil over the top. Stir before serving.

TIP: *The easiest way to cut the lemon rind into long strips is with a potato peeler, but be careful just to remove the rind, not the white pith beneath (as it tastes bitter).*

Ruota di Faraone or Frisinsal

PHARAOH'S WHEEL

Preparation: 15 minutes
Cooking: 30 minutes

SERVES 4–6

Ingredients

200ml (7fl oz/scant 1 cup) *sugo d'arrosto* (cooking juices from roast beef, veal, lamb or chicken) **or** *soffritto* (see right)
50g (1¾oz/scant ½ cup) pine nuts
50g (1¾oz) raisins or sultanas, soaked in warm water for 5 minutes, then drained
250g (9oz) goose sausage, rolled into bite-sized balls, **or beef sausage, hot dog, salami or salted beef**, diced

2 litres (68fl oz/8½ cups) boiling water or meat stock for cooking the pasta
1 tablespoon coarse or kosher salt for the pasta water (if using water)
250g (9oz) tagliatelle

SOFFRITTO (if using)
100ml (3½fl oz/scant ½ cup) extra virgin olive oil
2 garlic cloves, crushed
2 sprigs of fresh rosemary
6 fresh sage leaves, roughly chopped
sea salt and black pepper, to taste
generous splash of white wine

You will also need a large, shallow round oven dish

*T*his dish, popular in the Jewish communities of northern Italy, most particularly in Venice, Trieste and Ferrara, has a colourful, if perhaps macabre, story behind it. A perfect fusion of Ashkenazi, Sephardi and Italian Jewish ingredients, it is traditionally made for Shabbat Beshelach (around the time of Tu BiShvat), when the story is told of the Jews' exodus from Egypt. Italian Jews' three traditions have different names for it: Frisinsal, hamin, or ruota di faraone (pharaoh's wheel). According to the Bible, after God parted the Red Sea to liberate the Israelites from slavery, the waters closed again, swallowing the Egyptians. The tagliatelle is meant to represent the waves, and the goose, pine nuts and raisins the heads, bodies and horses of the drowning Egyptians… (I did say it was macabre!).

Baked in the oven, this dish calls for fresh goose sausages or salami, which can be hard to find kosher. You could try it with good beef sausages, or sometimes I mix the salami with a little salted beef. The best flavour will come from using sugo d'arrosto (leftover cooking juices from roast meat) but if you don't have this, you could make an aromatic soffritto instead. Some traditional recipes use goose fat, but I don't particularly like it and much prefer the sugo d'arrosto or soffritto.

1 Preheat the oven to 220°C (200°C fan/425°F/gas mark 7).

2 If you are using the *sugo d'arrosto*, heat it in a large, non-stick frying pan over a medium heat and, when sizzling, add the pine nuts, drained raisins or sultanas and sausage or salami. Reduce the heat to low and cook, covered, for 5 minutes.

3 Alternatively, make a soffritto by heating the olive oil in a large, non-stick frying pan with the garlic, rosemary, sage and a pinch each of salt and pepper. Cook over a low heat, uncovered, for a couple of minutes, making sure the garlic doesn't burn, then add the wine and cook for another couple of minutes. Add the pine nuts, raisins or sultanas and sausage or salami and sauté over a low to medium heat for a further 5 minutes.

4 Meanwhile, pour the water or stock into a large saucepan and bring to the boil – stock will give extra flavour to the dish (add coarse or kosher salt if you are using water) – then add the tagliatelle. Stir and cook, uncovered, over a medium heat, for just a couple of minutes as the pasta will continue cooking in the oven.

5 Drain the pasta and mix it with the meat juices or soffritto. Transfer everything into the oven dish.

6 Bake in the oven for about 15–20 minutes until the top is light golden.

7 Serve hot or warm for a Friday night meal, or at room temperature or warm from a hot-plate, for Shabbat lunch.

TIP: *Set aside a few tablespoons of the meat, pine nut and raisin or sultana mixture to sprinkle over the top for an attractive crispy topping.*

Lasagne al Sugo

TOMATO AND CHEESE LASAGNE

Preparation:
30 minutes
Cooking:
1 hour

SERVES 6

Ingredients
4 tablespoons extra virgin olive oil
3 garlic cloves, crushed
700g (1lb 9oz/scant 3 cups) passata
6–7 fresh basil leaves, plus extra to garnish
10–12 fresh or dried egg lasagne sheets
400g (14oz) mozzarella cheese (ideally the semi-hard cooking type, as it is less watery than a ball) or a mix of cheeses of your choice, finely diced, or shredded in a food processor
40g (1½oz/¾ cup) freshly grated Parmesan cheese
sea salt and black pepper, to taste

BÉCHAMEL
500ml (17fl oz/generous 2 cups) milk
30g (1oz/2 tablespoons) butter
30g (1oz/3 tablespoons) plain white flour
¼ teaspoon ground nutmeg
¼ teaspoon sea salt

You will also need a rectangular oven dish, about 35 x 25cm (14 x 10in).

*T*raditional Italian lasagne is not an option for Jews who respect the rules of kashrut, as the sauce mixes meat with béchamel and cheese. Consequently, Italian Jews have created their own versions, including this one, with a plain tomato sauce instead of a Bolognese sauce. Its simplicity is its greatest asset. I love it and encourage you to try this recipe first and then experiment with variations. You could, for instance, strengthen the flavours by adding a mix of cheeses, or perhaps add roast vegetables to the tomato sauce, or go lighter by using ricotta and spinach instead of the béchamel and cheeses. Do use thick egg lasagne sheets (fresh or dry) if you can as they have more flavour and will give the dish a better consistency. For a shortcut, you can also simply use 150ml (5fl oz/²/₃ cup) of double cream instead of making a béchamel sauce – it is a bit of a cheat, but it works quite well! You can make the lasagne a day or two ahead and simply reheat it before serving. It also freezes well.*

1   Preheat the oven to 200°C (180°C fan/400°F/gas mark 6).

2   First, prepare the tomato sauce. Warm the oil with the garlic in a large saucepan over a low to medium heat and cook for a couple of minutes until the garlic has softened but not browned. Add the passata, then rinse out the passata container with a little water and add the liquid to the pan. Add a good pinch of salt and a pinch of pepper. Leave to cook, partially covered, for about 30 minutes, stirring occasionally. Remove from the heat and tear in the basil.

3   While the tomato sauce is cooking, prepare the béchamel. Heat the milk in a small saucepan over a medium heat until almost boiling. In a separate medium saucepan, melt the butter over a low heat. As soon as it has melted, stir in the flour with a wooden spoon. Cook the flour and butter gently for a minute until it forms a

roux. Gradually pour the hot milk onto the roux, stirring constantly, this time with a hand whisk. Initially you may see small lumps, but they should disappear as you whisk. Continue cooking, stirring, until the hot blend of milk, butter and flour has a creamy, custardy consistency, adding the nutmeg, salt and a pinch of pepper, and reducing the heat to low once it reaches boiling point. Continue whisking for a further minute, then remove from the heat and keep covered.

TIP: *If your béchamel is too thick, add more milk to make a smoother consistency. If it is too runny, gradually add more flour, whisking it in bit by bit, to thicken it. For this recipe it is good to have a smooth, slightly runny béchamel.*

4 To assemble the lasagne, spread a thin layer of tomato sauce over the base of the oven dish, then lay some of the lasagne sheets on top in a single layer, trimming them to fit the dish. Cover this with about a third each of the tomato sauce, béchamel, mozzarella and Parmesan. Add another layer of lasagne sheets, then another third of the other ingredients in the same order. Top with a final layer of lasagne sheets, tomato sauce, a thinner covering of béchamel, and the remaining mozzarella and Parmesan. Bake in the oven for 20–25 minutes, until golden and bubbling on top. Garnish with basil leaves.

5 Remove from the oven and leave to rest for 5 minutes before serving hot.

THE FASCINATION WITH MATZAH

The fascination with matzah is an interesting one and it goes back a long way. Its origins are, of course, in the rushed exodus of the Israelites from Egypt, and not having enough time to leaven the bread. To remember this, Jews eat matzah every year during the festival of Passover. One hasty night and we still eat matzah 3,000 years later!

Ariel Toaff, professor at Bar-Ilan University and son of Rome's late former Chief Rabbi, the much-loved Elio Toaff, describes in an engaging way in his book *Mangiare alla Giudia* (Eating Jewish-style) how in Italy, during the time of the ghetto and beyond, matzah was seen as Jewish food 'par excellence'. Christians would make special trips into the ghettos to buy and eat all types of food, and matzah with its many variations was very popular, and a particular source of fascination to non-Jews.

Part of this fascination was perhaps because Christians were prohibited from eating it. As Toaff explains, an edict issued by the ruling Church in Reggio Emilia in 1701, and again in 1745, forbade Christians to 'receive and eat matzah from the Jews'. In Mantua, three separate warnings and edicts were issued as early as 1619, then again in 1740 and 1755, when the bishop warned his followers 'not to eat alongside Jews and not to eat the matzah made by them'. Other similar warnings were given in Massa, Carrara, Guastalla and other cities in the centre-north of Italy.

In Rome, where the Catholic Church was the strongest, the warnings were even more severe, with a ruling in 1775 by Pope Pius VI stating that heavy fines would be given to both Jews and Christians if they sold or bought matzah bread to or from each other. In real terms, the limitations were wider, including milk and cheese as well as other types of food. It was simply forbidden for Jews and Christians to share meals both privately and in public places, since sharing food was seen as 'harmful and censurable'.

This prohibition somehow made the forbidden matzah even more delectable, and Cardinals themselves would send messengers out in secret to buy food from the Roman ghetto.

Other cities across the Italian peninsula were also well-known for their delicious matzah, in particular Ancona on the Adriatic Coast and Venice. Toaff describes the different types of matzah in detail: there was a plain one, *shmura* – produced for the Seder following careful kosher overseeing – and, most famously, the *mazza ashira* (ashira means 'rich' in Hebrew) with the addition of eggs, sugar, anise, wine and goose fat, which was particularly appreciated. No surprise then that its popularity reached beyond the gates of the ghettos. Interestingly, a sweet version of the matzah (*azzime dolci*) is still made and sold at Panificio Volpe in Venice today.

Another famous matzah dish was fritters from Ferrara, made with honey, cinnamon, pine nuts and raisins. A close parallel in contemporary Roman Jewish cooking is *pizzarelle col miele* – delicious matzah fritters dipped in honey. Both my mother and sister organise *pizzarelle* evenings during Passover and many of their enthusiastic guests are their non-Jewish friends, who wait patiently every year to come and eat the delicious 'exotic' matzah fritters. Thankfully, there is no prohibition or a fine here, and the sharing of food is joyous and genuine, although the element of fascination with the 'different' is perhaps still there.

Matzah is also popular in savoury dishes such as *scacchi* – layers of matzah, meat, artichokes and vegetables – and is used nowadays to make 'pizza' and 'lasagne', too. Finally, of course, there's matzah meal that can be used instead of breadcrumbs or sometimes flour.

Pizza d'Azzima

MATZAH PIZZA

*P*assover, or Pesach, the spring festival celebrating the Israelites' biblical Exodus *from Egypt, throws up all sorts of challenges for the cook. The kosher rules tighten further for eight days, making it forbidden to eat leavened bread or any food that has risen or fermented. To Italians, who are used to eating pasta, bread or pizza daily, it is even more challenging. In my family, we therefore created our own special pizza – we just make it from matzah!*

When I was growing up, Pizza d'Azzima was one of our Passover treats. It's quick and simple and I still make it today with my daughters. I'm a purist when it comes to pizza and Margherita, the simplest tomato and mozzarella topping, is my favourite. You can, of course, add extra toppings if you want to.

Preparation:
10 minutes
Cooking:
10 minutes

SERVES 2

Ingredients

8 tablespoons passata or ready-prepared tomato sauce (see pages 92–93)

¼ teaspoon dried oregano, plus extra for garnishing (optional)

2 teaspoons extra virgin olive oil, plus extra for drizzling

2 whole sheets matzah

2 tablespoons pitted olives, black or green (optional)

1 mozzarella ball (about 100g/3½oz), drained and sliced

5–6 fresh basil leaves

sea salt and black pepper, to taste

You will also need an oven tray lined with baking parchment.

1   Preheat the oven to 200°C (180°C fan/400°F/gas mark 6).

2   Mix the passata, oregano, oil and a pinch each of salt and pepper in a small bowl, or, if you're using tomato sauce, just add the oregano.

3   Cover the lined oven tray with the matzah sheets and spread the tomato mixture over them (adding the olives, if using).

4   Bake for 5–7 minutes, then remove from the oven and add the sliced mozzarella with a final drizzle of olive oil. Turn on the grill and cook for 2–3 minutes or until the cheese has melted, bearing in mind that all grills are different! The topping should be neither too wet with liquid cheese nor grilled too much. Keep an eye on it so that it does not burn.

5   Scatter the basil over the matzah pizza and serve.

Lasagne di Matza di Carne

MEAT MATZAH LASAGNE

Preparation:
20 minutes
Cooking:
1 hour

SERVES 4–6

Ingredients

4 tablespoons extra virgin olive oil
2 onions, finely chopped
2 carrots, peeled and finely chopped
2 celery sticks, finely chopped
1kg (2lb 4oz) minced meat (beef, veal, or a mix of any)
100ml (3½fl oz/scant ½ cup) red wine
150–200g (5½–7oz) fine matzah sheets
2 tablespoons finely chopped fresh flat-leaf parsley
sea salt and black pepper, to taste

PARVE (DAIRY-FREE) BÉCHAMEL
40g (2½ tablespoons) dairy-free spread or margarine
40g (1½oz/⅓ cup) potato flour
700ml (24fl oz/scant 3 cups) homemade meat or vegetable stock or stock made with 1 teaspoon bouillon dissolved in boiling water
¼ teaspoon ground nutmeg
¼ teaspoon sea salt

You will also need a rectangular oven dish, about 30 x 25cm (12 x 10in).

*T*his dish is a family favourite for Passover and my sister Simona is the best at making it. It's put together in a similar way to a typical 'lasagne', but uses matzah instead of lasagne sheets.

The béchamel is both dairy-free and flour-free to keep the kosher for Passover rules and I make it quite loose so it moistens the matzah, as there is no tomato sauce or other liquid. I usually use potato flour, meat or vegetable stock and a good-quality dairy-free spread, but olive oil can also be used instead (same weight). I like a combination of minced meats, such as beef and veal, which is widely used in Italian cooking, but you can, of course, use just one if you prefer.

A similar version of this dish with the addition of vegetables such as artichokes (my favourite!), spinach and peas, is called *scacchi* and resembles the more widely known Sephardi dishes *mina* or *maiena*.

The lasagne keeps well for a couple of days in the fridge.

1 Heat the 4 tablespoons of olive oil in a large, non-stick frying pan over a low heat and add the onions, carrots and celery with a good pinch of salt and a pinch of pepper. Cook, partially covered, for about 10 minutes, stirring occasionally, until softened and light golden, then add the minced meat. Cover and cook over a medium to high heat for 10 minutes, stirring occasionally and breaking up the mince with a wooden spoon or spatula, then remove the lid and add the wine. Stir well and cook, uncovered, for another 5 minutes. The meat should still be a little wet and moist. Remove from the heat, cover and set aside until ready to use.

2 While the meat is cooking, prepare the parve béchamel. Heat the dairy-free spread or margarine in a small to medium saucepan over a low heat, then add the potato flour. Stir well with a spatula or wooden spoon and cook for a minute to create a roux. Gradually add the stock, and start stirring with a hand whisk. Gently bring to the boil, then add the nutmeg and salt, and continue to stir. You may have a few lumps

but don't worry, if you keep on stirring vigorously after it reaches boiling point, they will eventually dissolve. Don't rush this stage (and don't give up in stirring with the whisk!), as amalgamating these ingredients well is key to a smooth béchamel. The béchamel should be quite loose – when ready remove from the heat and keep covered.

3   Preheat the oven to 220°C (200°C fan/425°F/gas mark 7).

4   To assemble the matzah lasagne, spread half a ladle of béchamel and half a ladle of the minced meat mixture over the base of the oven dish and mix, then distribute over one layer of the matzah sheets, trimming them to fit the dish. Cover with 2 ladles of minced meat, followed by 2 ladles of béchamel and a sprinkle of parsley on top. Add a second layer of matzah sheets, then 2 ladles of meat, 2 ladles of béchamel and a little parsley. Top with a final layer of matzah and the remaining béchamel, minced meat and parsley. Bake in the oven for 20 minutes.

5   Remove from the oven and leave to rest for 5 minutes before serving hot.

Pomodori col Riso

STUFFED TOMATOES WITH RICE

I *talian Jews adopted this classic Italian dish for its sheer versatility. It is an ideal choice for Shabbat, especially in the summer, because it can be prepared in advance and is usually served at room temperature. It is also popular during Passover when Italian Jews, the Italkim, unlike Ashkenazi Jews, eat rice. We usually have it as part of our Seder night menu.*

Our family loves the tasty rice around the tomatoes so my mother's version, which I've included here, has much more rice than the traditional pomodori col riso, which is mostly stuffed tomatoes with just a hint of rice around them. My Nonna Bianca used to add potatoes to the rice as well. If you would like to try that, simply peel and par boil a medium to large waxy potato, dice it and mix with the tomato rice, then bake it all together. I find this dish comes out differently every time, depending on the kind and size of tomatoes you use and how the rice absorbs the liquid – no exact quantities ever seem to determine a consistent outcome. It is always good though!

Preparation:
30 minutes, and ideally
2 hours (optional)
in the fridge
Cooking:
1¼ hours minimum

SERVES 4

Ingredients
**200ml (7fl oz/scant
1 cup) extra virgin olive
oil**, plus extra for
drizzling
3 garlic cloves, crushed
**500g (1lb 2oz/generous
2 cups) passata**
5–6 fresh basil leaves
4 large vine tomatoes
**10g (¼oz) fresh
flat-leaf parsley**
2–3 ladles of water
**250g (9oz/1¼ cups)
Arborio or Carnaroli
risotto rice**
sea salt, to taste

You will also need an oven
dish (of any shape) large
enough to fit 4 large tomatoes
with space between them.

1 Put 50ml (1¾fl oz/3½ tablespoons) of the oil and 2 of the garlic cloves in a saucepan over a low heat and, just before the garlic turns golden, add the passata and a pinch each of salt and pepper and cook over a low to medium heat, partially covered, for 25–30 minutes, stirring occasionally. Remove from the heat and tear in a couple of the basil leaves. Transfer to a large heatproof bowl and allow to cool.

TIP: *The sauce is even better made in advance and used cold or at room temperature.*

2 Meanwhile, slice the tops off the tomatoes and scoop out the insides. Set the tops aside for later. Place the tomato pulp and juice from the insides in a food processor and add the parsley, remaining garlic clove, 1 teaspoon of salt, 100ml (3½fl oz/ scant ½ cup) of the oil and the remaining basil leaves. Pulse until finely blended.

3 Pour this tomato and herb mixture into the bowl with the cooked tomato sauce, add 2 ladles of water and finally stir in the rice.

4 Arrange the hollow tomatoes in the oven dish and sprinkle a pinch of salt inside each one. Drizzle the remaining 50ml (1¾fl oz/3½ tablespoons) of oil over the tomatoes and the base of the dish.

5 Fill the tomatoes with the rice and tomato mixture and gently pour the remainder around them. Cover with clingfilm and ideally place in the fridge for a couple of hours, or longer. This resting time is not essential, but it does allow extra time for the flavours to develop.

TIP: *Plenty of olive oil is the key to a tasty and moist outcome for this dish.*

6 Preheat the oven to 200°C (180°C fan/400°F/ gas mark 6).

7 Take the dish out of the fridge (if chilling it). There should still be a thin layer of liquid above the rice. If it looks dry, gently stir in another ladle of water, mixed with a tablespoon of oil and a pinch of salt. Cover each tomato with the reserved tops, add a generous drizzle of oil and cook on the middle shelf of the oven, uncovered, for about 45 minutes.

TIP: *After 15 minutes, take the dish out of the oven, carefully swap the rice inside the tomatoes for the rice around them, then put back in the oven for the remaining cooking time. This is not essential, but it helps to cook all the rice evenly and ensures a fuller flavour.*

8 After this time, if the top is not golden, turn on the grill and cook for a few more minutes.

9 Eat warm or at room temperature.

Riso Giallo del Sabato

'YELLOW' SAFFRON RICE FOR SHABBAT

Preparation:
10 minutes
Cooking:
30 minutes

SERVES 4–6

Ingredients

½ teaspoon saffron
threads or powder
1 litre (34fl oz/4½ cups)
chicken or
vegetable stock
100ml (3½fl oz/scant
½ cup) meat cooking
juices (from leftover
roast chicken or beef)
or extra virgin olive oil
1 onion, finely chopped
(optional or for the
vegetarian version)
360g (12½oz/2 cups)
Carnaroli, Arborio or
Vialone Nano risotto rice
120ml (4fl oz/½ cup)
white wine
sea salt and black pepper,
to taste

TIP: *If you make
the vegetarian/dairy
version and plan to
eat it immediately,
more like a risotto,
then add a knob of
butter and grated
Parmesan cheese just
before serving.*

*T*he beauty of this old rice dish from Venice and Ferrara is in
its simplicity, versatility and delicate flavour. Fragrant golden
saffron, a precious spice that reached Venetian shores thanks to the
Levantine Jewish traders of the Renaissance period, contributes much
of this delicacy.

Originally made with long-grain rice and called pilaf, this saffron
rice dish evolved into different versions, reflecting the cosmopolitan
nature of Venice at the time of the formation of the ghetto in the early
1500s. It uses local short-grain rice, typically used for risotto, but
cooks it in the style of long-grain rice: in contrast to the classic risotto,
where stock is added slowly throughout the cooking process, with
this recipe, the stock is added all at once and the rice is left to cook,
covered, without stirring.

This dish, as its name conveys, was created with Shabbat in mind,
so it could be made on a Friday and eaten either for the evening meal or
the next day. Its sheer versatility means that a variety of vegetables are
either added to the rice or served alongside, such as mushrooms, peas or
artichokes, and a sweeter version with raisins is served for Hanukkah.

A good chicken stock makes all the difference to the flavour (for a
vegetarian version, use a rich, flavourful vegetable stock) as does a good
saffron. Originally, goose fat was used to coat the rice in the initial cooking
stage, but I suggest using chicken or meat juices instead, or simply olive
oil. You could also make it into a classic dairy rice by adding onion in the
initial stages, and butter and grated Parmesan at the end – this is not, of
course, suitable for the meaty version due to the kosher restriction of not
mixing dairy and meat, so for this version use only vegetable stock.

1   Place the saffron in a small bowl with 4 tablespoons of warm water and set
aside for at least 15–20 minutes while the rice cooks (if you leave it soaking
at room temperature for a few hours or overnight this will give the rice a
more intense orange colour and deeper flavour).

2   Place the stock in a saucepan over a medium heat and bring to the boil,
then keep it simmering on the hob. In a separate shallow (ideally non-stick)
saucepan (with matching lid), heat 4 tablespoons of the meat cooking
juices or olive oil over a low heat. If you are using onion, add it to the hot
juices or oil with a pinch each of salt and pepper and cook for about 10
minutes, until softened and pale golden.

3   Add the rice to the saucepan of juices or oil and stir well for a couple of minutes until the grains are coated and becoming translucent, then add both the boiling stock, the wine and half a teaspoon of salt all at once. Stir well, cover with a lid, and leave it to simmer gently – without stirring – for 20–25 minutes until the rice is cooked and the liquid has been absorbed. The consistency should be slightly runny and moist, not dry.

4   Once cooked, switch off the heat and add the saffron with its coloured soaking water,

along with the remaining meat juices or oil. Stir well until the rice becomes yellow in colour, then taste to adjust the seasoning and keep it covered for 5 minutes to let all the flavours blend.

5   The rice can be eaten straight away or served the next day (ideally warmed on a hot-plate or in a Shabbat oven).

Risotto ai Funghi Porcini

PORCINI MUSHROOM RISOTTO

Preparation:
15 minutes
Cooking:
45 minutes

SERVES 4

Ingredients
20g (¾oz) dried porcini mushrooms, roughly chopped
150ml (5fl oz/⅔ cup) hot water or milk
4 tablespoons extra virgin olive oil
1 onion, finely chopped
3 garlic cloves, crushed
small bunch of fresh flat-leaf parsley, finely chopped
small bunch of fresh thyme **or lemon thyme**, stalks on
50ml (1¾fl oz/3½ tablespoons) white wine
500g (1lb 2oz) chestnut mushrooms, washed and thinly sliced, **or frozen mushroom medley**
1.2–1.5 litres (40–50fl oz/5–6¼ cups) vegetable stock, either homemade (see page 66) or made with 1 tablespoon vegetable bouillon or a stock cube
360g (12½oz/2 cups) Carnaroli, Vialone Nano or Arborio risotto rice
30g (1oz/2 tablespoons) butter
Parmesan cheese, freshly grated
sea salt and black pepper, to taste

*W*hen I was a child, my father was very keen on mushrooms. Mycology became his passion and he kept a microscope and dozens of slides and samples in a room we were not allowed to play in. He would go out mushroom picking almost every weekend, particularly in the autumn. In fact, mushroom picking in the woods outside Rome often became a family outing; the ultimate prize was porcini, cep mushrooms with their wonderfully refined flavour. We would eat them simply sautéed with garlic and parsley; I strongly recommend you doing the same if you can get hold of fresh porcini, or use them for this risotto! Otherwise, dried porcini are fine for this recipe. I combine them with chestnut mushrooms, which hold their shape, have a delicate flavour and are easily available. You can also use a mixture of wild European mushrooms or a frozen mushroom medley instead, if you wish.

1 Put the dried porcini in a small heatproof bowl, cover with the hot water, or with milk for a creamy consistency. Set aside.

2 Heat the oil in a large, shallow saucepan over a low heat, add the onion and cook for 10 minutes, uncovered, until the onion has softened and is lightly golden, then add the garlic, half each of the parsley and thyme, and a pinch each of salt and pepper. Add a splash of the wine and cook for 1 minute, then add the chestnut mushrooms or frozen medley. Cook over a medium to high heat, uncovered, for 10–15 minutes, stirring occasionally, until all the liquid has evaporated and the mushrooms start turning golden. Remove the thyme stalks but leave in any loose leaves.

3   Meanwhile, bring the stock to the boil in a separate large saucepan and leave to simmer over a low heat.

4   Once the chestnut mushrooms are cooked, remove a couple of tablespoons and reserve them for later, then add the rice and stir for a minute until coated. Add the rest of the wine and cook for a couple of minutes, stirring, until the wine has been absorbed and the rice is translucent. Add 3–4 ladles of the hot stock initially, as this will get absorbed quickly, stir until the liquid has almost been absorbed, then add another ladle of stock. Repeat the process, adding the stock one ladle at a time, stirring often.

5   Drain the porcini mushrooms and reserve the liquid, passing it through a sieve to remove any dirt or grit.

6   After the risotto has been cooking for 10 minutes, about halfway through the cooking time, add the porcini mushrooms, together with the reserved soaking liquid.

7   The risotto should take 18–20 minutes in total to cook. The rice should be tender but firm to the bite, and the risotto should be slightly runny.

8   Remove from the heat, add the butter, the remaining parsley and thyme leaves and a couple of tablespoons of grated Parmesan. Stir well and cover, allowing it to rest for a couple of minutes. This is called *mantecare* and is the key to a smooth and creamy texture. Taste and season with more salt if necessary.

9   Top each portion with the cooked mushrooms, sprinkle over black pepper, parsley and Parmesan to taste, and serve immediately.

Risotto con la Zucca

PUMPKIN RISOTTO

Preparation:
15 minutes
Cooking:
1 hour

SERVES 4–6

Ingredients

4 tablespoons extra
   virgin olive oil
1 onion, finely chopped
3 garlic cloves, crushed
2–3 sprigs of fresh
   rosemary
pinch of dried chilli
   flakes or chilli
   powder (optional)
50ml (1¾fl oz/3½
   tablespoons) white wine
1kg (2lb 4oz) pumpkin
   or butternut squash,
   peeled, deseeded and cut
   into 1.5cm (5/8in) cubes
1.2–1.5 litres (40–50fl oz/
   5–6¼ cups)
   vegetable stock, either
   homemade or made
   with 1 tablespoon
   vegetable bouillon or
   a stock cube
360g (12½oz/2 cups)
   Carnaroli, Vialone
   Nano or Arborio
   risotto rice
30g (1oz/2 tablespoons)
   butter
small bunch of fresh
   flat-leaf parsley,
   finely chopped
2 dry Amaretti
   biscuits, crumbled
Parmesan cheese,
   freshly grated
sea salt and black pepper,
   to taste

Perhaps it's thanks to this dish that I met my husband, Marc. We met at Limmud, the annual learning conference on all things Jewish, when he came to see my cookery demonstration and lecture on the history of Italian Jewish cuisine. The dish I was demonstrating was pumpkin risotto, however, the electric hob that I was given was not working properly, so I played down the tricky situation by imagining cooking the risotto and cracking a few jokes. I ended up serving an uncooked risotto to 100 people, and was pretty embarrassed, but apparently, I still managed to impress Marc. This wonderful autumnal dish benefits from the sweet, deep orange flesh of the pumpkin, but you can easily replace it with its cousin, the butternut squash. For a parve version, use a dairy-free spread and leave out the Parmesan.

1   Heat the oil in a large, shallow saucepan over a low heat, add the onion with a pinch each of salt and pepper and cook for 10 minutes, uncovered, until softened but not browned. Add the garlic, rosemary, chilli (if using) and a splash of the wine and cook for a further 5 minutes, then add the pumpkin or squash and cook over a low to medium heat, partially covered, for 15–20 minutes until the pumpkin/squash has softened. Remove the lid, increase the heat to medium to high, and cook for a final 5 minutes, uncovered, until the pumpkin/squash turns golden. Remove a couple of tablespoons and reserve for later.

2   Meanwhile, bring the stock to the boil in a separate large saucepan and leave to simmer over a low heat.

3   Add the rice to the pumpkin/squash and stir over a medium heat. Add the rest of the wine and cook for a couple of minutes, stirring, until the wine has been absorbed and the rice is translucent. Add 3–4 ladles of hot stock initially and stir until the liquid has almost been absorbed, then add another ladle of stock. Repeat the process over a low heat, adding the stock one ladle at a time, stirring often. The risotto should take 18–20 minutes in total to cook. The rice should be tender but still firm to the bite, and the risotto should be creamy.

4   Remove from the heat and add the butter, most of the parsley, 1 crumbled Amaretti biscuit and a couple of tablespoons of Parmesan. Stir well and cover, allowing it to rest for a couple of minutes. This is called *mantecare* and is the key to a smooth, creamy texture. Taste and season with more salt if the risotto tastes bland. Top each portion with the reserved cooked pumpkin/squash, the remaining crumbled Amaretti biscuit, and more Parmesan and parsley, and serve immediately.

Pappa al Pomodoro

TUSCAN TOMATO AND BREAD MASH

Preparation:
10 minutes
Cooking:
1 hour

SERVES 4–6

Ingredients

3 garlic cloves, crushed
150ml (5oz/⅔ cup) extra virgin olive oil,
   plus extra for drizzling
splash of white wine
2 x 400g (14½oz) tins peeled plum tomatoes
200g (7oz /4–5 slices) hard or stale brown or white sourdough bread or ciabatta
5–6 fresh basil leaves,
   plus extra to garnish
sea salt and black pepper,
   to taste

This Tuscan classic is cucina povera at its best, one of those 'poor food' peasant dishes that makes sure nothing is wasted. It is ideal when you have stale ends of bread that are too hard to eat (sourdough or ciabatta are ideal, but any other bread is also good, except challah), preferably kept in a paper bag or closed basket. If you don't have any old bread, simply toast a few fresh bread slices in a warm oven and leave them there with the heat switched off until hard.

Pappa al Pomodoro is usually eaten in summer and served at room temperature or cold. However, it is no less lovely served warm. My family cooks it for Shabbat, as it is great made in advance. A drizzle of extra virgin olive oil over each portion finishes it off perfectly; I sometimes also add diced buffalo mozzarella on top. The dish keeps well for a few days in the fridge.

1 Put the garlic and oil in a large saucepan over a low heat and cook for a couple of minutes. When the garlic starts sizzling, add the wine, then once it has evaporated, add the ½ teaspoon of salt and a pinch of pepper. Add the tinned tomatoes, crushing them by hand or with a fork as you add them so they are evenly-sized and cook more uniformly, then rinse out the tins with a little water and add the liquid to the pan. Cover the pan and cook over a low to medium heat for 25–30 minutes, stirring occasionally.

2 Fill a medium bowl with cold water. Break the bread into 2–3cm (¾–1¼in) chunks and soak them in the water for about a minute, then drain and add them to the tomato sauce. Add a ladle of hot water or vegetable stock, a pinch of salt and stir well.

3 Cover and simmer, stirring occasionally, for a further 30 minutes. The bread should mop up most of the tomato sauce. If it appears too dry, add half a ladle of warm water while it is cooking. Taste and adjust the seasoning if needed.

4 Remove from the heat, tear in the basil leaves and stir.

5 Serve warm or at room temperature with a couple or so basil leaves and a drizzle of oil on top of each portion.

CHAPTER 2

Meat, poultry and fish

Meat, poultry and fish represent main courses in most cultures, and Italian Jewish cuisine is no exception. In the past, they would be cooked only for family celebrations and Shabbat, or on holidays, but nowadays (fortunately or unfortunately) we have easy access to relatively cheap fresh meat, poultry and fish, so for many of us they have become part of our daily diet. I am a carnivore and I love my meat; however, I would never encourage excessive consumption of it and feel strongly that everyone should cook and eat meat and fish in moderation, respecting, whenever possible, the welfare of the animals.

The kosher rules here are more important than ever, as not all animals are regarded as pure and allowed – be they from land, sky or sea – and there are strict laws on how to butcher an animal. In addition, meat cannot be cooked with, or eaten alongside, milk or dairy products. To read more about kosher rules, see pages 38–41.

rop capsrved for special occasions, inventive thrift has been a common thread throughout Jewish communities over the centuries as means were often limited, especially at the time of the ghettos and up until after World War II. Minced meat, tougher cuts of beef and small bony fish were popular and affordable, and the Jews of Rome and Venice in particular, managed to create delicious dishes from them, some eaten hot and others cold, ideal for Shabbat. This chapter celebrates such creativity with recipes like *stracotto*, *zucchine ripiene di carne*, *sarde in saor*, and, of course, *polpettoni* (both meat and fish varieties), not only from my family but also from the wonderful Yotam Ottolenghi who has kindly shared a recipe from his Italian Jewish grandmother.

Lamb is popular in Roman Jewish cooking, especially for Passover, and veal was and still is widely cooked. Should you wish to use veal, I've mentioned where it can be used instead of (or alongside) beef or chicken in specific recipes.

Poultry is particularly popular in the north of Italy within the Ashkenazi community, although it was at one time more expensive than other meats. For centuries, goose was the domestic fowl of choice for Ashkenazis, but it was gradually replaced by turkey and then chicken. I've not included goose recipes as mains, as they are seldom made today and it is almost impossible to find kosher goose. If you do, it usually comes in the form of cold cuts rather than fresh meat (see my recipe for *ruota di faraone* made with goose salami). Instead, I've included chicken recipes, which are still traditional, easy to make, and are more suitable for use in today's kitchen. These include a delicious *pollo Ezechiele*, *pollo coi peperoni*, and a dish featuring pomegranate that my family created to celebrate Rosh Hashanah – *scaloppine di pollo al melograno*. For me, these dishes represent continuity in tradition, adapting to what is available today and reflecting a constantly evolving community. Hence, I have also included two of my favourite meat and fish dishes from Libyan Jewish cuisine, which has only been introduced in Italy in the last 60 years but is having a delicious and long-lasting impact on Italian Jewish cuisine: *haraimi* and *lubia bel cammun*.

Abbacchio al Forno con Patate

ROASTED LAMB CUTLETS WITH POTATOES

*L*amb is the classic Passover Seder main course eaten by many Roman Jews, my family included. It represents the Paschal sacrifice, or Korban Pesach, a ritual that came to an end with the destruction of the Second Temple in Jerusalem in 70CE. Many Italian and Sephardi Jews eat lamb on Passover's first night, keeping alive a tradition that Jews took with them 2,000 years ago. Interestingly, Ashkenazi Jews do not eat lamb for the Seder precisely because it reminds them that the Temple was destroyed.

Abbacchio (baby lamb) is especially tender and is popular in Roman cooking. Catholics also eat baby lamb at Easter, which occurs around the same time as Passover, so this is a perfect marriage of Jewish and Catholic Italian cooking. You can use cutlets or chops; either work beautifully with roast potatoes. The meat keeps well in the fridge for a few days and freezes well, but don't freeze the potatoes.

 Preparation:
15 minutes, plus
30 minutes–12 hours
marinating time
Cooking:
1 hour, plus
10 minutes resting

 SERVES 4

Ingredients
12 lamb cutlets or chops
4 garlic cloves, halved
4 sprigs of fresh rosemary
juice of 2 lemons
120ml (4fl oz/½ cup)
extra virgin olive oil
8–10 King Edward, Maris
Piper or Desirée
potatoes, peeled
and cut into 2cm
(¾in) cubes
100ml (3½fl oz/scant ½
cup) white wine
sea salt and black pepper,
to taste

1 Place the lamb in a non-metallic, ovenproof dish and add 2 garlic cloves, 2 rosemary sprigs, the lemon juice, ¼ teaspoon of salt, ¼ teaspoon of pepper and 4 tablespoons of the oil. Mix well, cover with clingfilm and leave to marinate for 30 minutes at room temperature or up to 12 hours in the fridge, turning the pieces once or twice during the process to evenly distribute the marinade.

2 Preheat the oven to 200°C (180°C fan/400°F/gas mark 6) and remove the lamb from the fridge so it reaches room temperature before cooking.

3 Rinse the cubed potatoes, then add to a large saucepan of salted boiling water. Bring to the boil again and cook for 5 minutes – they should be parboiled, not cooked through. Drain well, transfer to a shallow roasting tin or tray and add the 2 remaining garlic cloves and sprigs of rosemary, ½ teaspoon of salt, a pinch of pepper and the rest of the oil. Mix well.

4 Put the lamb in the oven on one shelf and the potatoes on another. Roast for 40–50 minutes, depending on the size of the cutlets or chops, and how well-cooked you like your lamb. Halfway though cooking, stir the potatoes and add the wine to the meat and stir. Five minutes before the end of the cooking time, turn on the grill to lightly brown the lamb, then remove everything from the oven and let the meat rest, covered, for 5 minutes before serving.

5 To serve, mix the potatoes with the lamb and its juices, or serve separately. Mixing them may crush the potatoes slightly and look less pretty, but they definitely gain in flavour! Serve hot.

Abbacchio Brodettato

BRAISED LAMB WITH EGG AND LEMON SAUCE

Preparation:
10 minutes
Cooking:
1¼ hours

SERVES 4

Ingredients
3 tablespoons extra virgin olive oil
1 onion, finely chopped
about 100ml (3½fl oz/scant ½ cup) white wine
1.2kg (2lb 12oz) lamb cutlets, cut into large chunks
2 egg yolks
juice of 2 lemons
1 tablespoon finely chopped fresh flat-leaf parsley
sea salt and black pepper, to taste

*T*his delicious lamb dish with a flavoursome sauce is popular in Rome and the surrounding Lazio region. Jews traditionally make it for Passover using olive oil, and Catholics have it at Easter with butter and ham. The recipe is best made with abbacchio (baby lamb) but ordinary lamb can be used, too.

I love meat on the bone, so I tend to use lamb cutlets for this dish, which are tender and have just enough fat. I then cut the cutlets into chunks, but you can leave them whole, if you prefer. Diced boneless lamb makes a more traditional stew, or you could use diced shoulder meat, which is fattier. Either of these would need to be cooked for up to an hour or two longer, depending on the cut – the meat should be tender and easily fall apart with a fork when it is done. Add more wine and water to the meat while it's cooking, as necessary, to keep it moist.

The egg yolk and lemon mixture added at the end is a simple way to make a tasty 'creamy' sauce, and it gives a tangy edge to the rich lamb. This dish may not win a beauty competition, but it certainly pleases the palate. It can easily be prepared ahead of time, even a day in advance, as it stays delicious. It also freezes well.

1   Heat the oil in a large, high-sided, non-stick frying pan or heavy-based saucepan over a low heat, then add the onion and let it sweat, covered, for 10–12 minutes, adding a pinch each of salt and pepper, and a splash of the wine halfway through.

2   Increase the heat to medium to high, add the lamb cutlets and sauté, uncovered, for a few minutes until seared and lightly golden. Stir and reduce the heat, then cover and cook over a low heat for about 1 hour, or until the meat is tender. Add the remaining wine after 30 minutes, and a few tablespoons of water if the pan is dry – every pan cooks its contents differently.

3   When the lamb is cooked, remove from the heat. Mix the egg yolks with the lemon juice in a small bowl and add a pinch of salt and most of the parsley. Pour over the hot lamb and stir well for about a minute until the lemony egg turns creamy.

4   Garnish with the rest of the parsley, serve hot and enjoy the tangy taste!

TIP: *If you have prepared this in advance, or to warm up any leftovers, add 3–4 tablespoons of water, then heat, covered, over a medium heat on the hob or at 180°C/350°F in the oven, stirring occasionally, for 10–15 minutes.*

Ngozzamoddi

MEATBALLS IN CELERY AND TOMATO SAUCE

Preparation:
20 minutes
Cooking:
1 hour

**SERVES 4
(MAKES 8
LARGE
MEATBALLS)**

Ingredients
TOMATO SAUCE
**120ml (4fl oz/½ cup)
olive oil**
2 celery sticks, peeled
and cut into long,
thin strips
**700g (1lb 9oz/scant
3 cups) passata or 2 x
400g (14½oz) tins
peeled plum tomatoes**

MEATBALLS
**100g (3½oz/1½ cups) soft
breadcrumbs** (made
from stale or old bread,
if you like)
**300g (10½oz)
minced chicken**
300g (10½oz) minced veal
1 large egg
**1 teaspoon dried
breadcrumbs**, plus
extra for coating
**a pinch of ground
cinnamon**
sea salt and black pepper,
to taste

*T*he origin of this curiously-named, delicious dish goes back to
the time of the Roman ghetto, when crushed bones were added
to chicken meat to give it more volume and flavour (an inventive way
of being thrifty with ingredients, which was typical of this time). Its
name comes from the Hebrew word for bones, azamot, which with
time has been moulded into Italian through the Giudaico Romanesco
dialect to create ngozzamoddi.

   This recipe has been kindly given to me by Micaela Pavoncello
(pictured here), a most wonderful guide who runs the successful
Jewish Roma Walking Tours, and whom I've known for many years.
This dish has been part of the Pavoncello family celebrations for
as long as Micaela can remember. Micaela's grandmother, Rosina,
would traditionally use a linen handkerchief to shape the meatballs
into an oval shape. On Rosh Hashana many years ago, when
Micaela first tried to make this dish, she glimpsed her father getting
very emotional: the taste and the look of the ngozzamoddi took
him back to his childhood. Now they are part of her tradition too,
together with many other Roman Jewish families, mine included.

1 Prepare the tomato sauce by placing the oil, celery and passata
or plum tomatoes, (crushing the tomatoes by hand or with a fork as
you add them), all from cold, in a large saucepan and bring to the
boil over a medium to high heat. Reduce the heat to low and cook for
about 20 minutes, partially covered, until the sauce is reduced.

2 Meanwhile, prepare the meatballs. Soak the soft breadcrumbs in
water for around 30 seconds, then squeeze out as much liquid as
possible. Place the minced meats, egg, moistened breadcrumbs, dried
breadcrumbs, cinnamon and a pinch each of salt and pepper in a
large bowl and mix well. Form the mixture into 8 large oval meatballs
and place on a plate dusted with dried breadcrumbs. Gently roll the
meatballs in the breadcrumbs.

3 Carefully place your meatballs in the sauce, cover and cook gently
for 35–40 minutes, turning them occasionally. Taste and adjust the
seasoning if necessary. Serve hot.

Polpettone in Tegame

CLASSIC MEATLOAF

Preparation:
15 minutes
Cooking:
1 hour, plus
cooling time

SERVES 4–6

Ingredients
3 tablespoons extra virgin
    olive oil
1 onion, finely chopped
3 garlic cloves, thinly sliced
pinch of dried chilli flakes
    or chilli powder
    (optional)
1 bay leaf
2 dried juniper berries
about 200ml (7fl oz/scant
    1 cup) white wine
100g (3½oz/1½ cups) dried
    breadcrumbs (or medium
    matzah meal if for Passover)
150ml (5fl oz/⅔ cup) water
    or vegetable stock
2 large eggs
¼ teaspoon ground cinnamon
¼ teaspoon ground
    nutmeg
800g (1lb 12oz) minced
    beef or lamb, or a mix
    of both
sea salt and black pepper,
    to taste

My mother taught me to mix cinnamon and nutmeg into the meat for this family classic, which is perhaps a Sephardi influence. Unlike northern European versions which go in the oven, ours is cooked on the hob, which lets the meat cook slowly and absorb the flavour and moisture of the white wine. We serve it at room temperature with hot gravy, and when Passover falls on Shabbat, this polpettone is our choice of main course, as it can be prepared ahead of time, and is simultaneously uncomplicated and delicious.

I like to use a mixture of beef and lamb, but you can make it using one or the other, if you prefer. It is easier to slice the polpettone *at room temperature or cold from the fridge, so the recipe is best made in advance. The cooked dish keeps well in the fridge for a few days, and also freezes well.*

1 Heat the oil in a large, shallow saucepan over a low heat, then add the onion with a couple of tablespoons of warm water to help it soften. Cook for about 5 minutes, until the water has evaporated, then add the garlic, chilli (if using), bay leaf, juniper berries and a pinch each of salt and pepper. Splash in some of the wine and cook for a further minute or so.

2 Soak the breadcrumbs (or matzah meal) in the water or vegetable stock for 5 minutes, or until the water has been fully absorbed.

3 While the onion is cooking and the breadcrumbs are soaking, prepare the meatloaf mixture. Gently beat the eggs with the cinnamon, nutmeg and a good pinch of salt in a bowl. Add the moistened breadcrumbs, mix well, then tip in the minced meat and mix again. Ideally blend it in a food processor using a few brief pulses for an even consistency – don't overmix it – or mix it together by hand (using either your hand or a spoon).

4 Using your hands, press the mixture into a big, thick, compact oval (about the size of a small loaf – roughly 20 x 10cm/8 x 4in). Lift it gently into the saucepan containing the onion, cover and cook over a low heat for about 45 minutes, gently turning it from time to time. Every now and then, add more wine and, if the pan is still dry after all the wine has been added, a little water.

5 When the cooking time is up, remove the meatloaf from the heat. Insert a long skewer or thin knife – if the juices run clear, the meatloaf is cooked.

Carefully lift the meatloaf out of the pan onto a heatproof plate, wrap in foil or baking parchment to keep the juices in, and allow to cool. Reserve the meat juices in the pan to serve with the meatloaf.

6 To serve, cut the *polpettone* into slices (remember it is easier to slice from cold or at room temperature, otherwise it may fall apart!) and pour the reserved meat juices (reheated to hot) over each slice, discarding the bay leaf and juniper berries. If you serve it cold, make sure the gravy is hot.

7 If there is too little gravy or it is too thick, add a couple of extra tablespoons of wine and 2 tablespoons of water and simmer, uncovered, for a couple of minutes.

Polpettone di Yotam Ottolenghi

YOTAM OTTOLENGHI'S MEATLOAF

Preparation:
40 minutes, plus 3–4 hours draining and cooling time
Cooking: 2 hours

SERVES 8

Ingredients
3 eggs
1 tablespoon finely chopped fresh flat-leaf parsley
2 teaspoons olive oil
500g (1lb 2oz) minced beef
100g (3½oz/1½ cups) dried breadcrumbs (or medium matzah meal if for Passover)

60g (2¼oz) whole shelled pistachios
80g (2¾oz) gherkins, cut into 1cm (½in) pieces
200g (7oz) ox tongue, thinly sliced
1 large carrot, peeled and cut roughly into chunks
2 celery sticks, cut roughly into chunks
sprig of fresh thyme
2 bay leaves
½ onion, thinly sliced
1 teaspoon powdered chicken stock
sea salt and black pepper, to taste

SALSINA VERDE
50g (1¾oz) fresh flat-leaf parsley, stalks and leaves, chopped
1 garlic clove, crushed
1 teaspoon capers
1 teaspoon lemon juice
1 tablespoon white wine vinegar
1 hard-boiled egg, cooled and peeled
150ml (5fl oz/⅔ cup) olive oil
3 tablespoons dried breadcrumbs (or medium matzah meal if for Passover)
sea salt and black pepper, to taste

*T*his polpettone recipe was kindly given to me by the wonderful London-based Israeli chef Yotam Ottolenghi a few years ago, when we met for a coffee at his restaurant NOPI and discussed some ideas for my book. I asked him if there was a recipe which was dear to him from his Italian Jewish family, the Ottolenghis, and which I might include in my own recipe collection when the time came. I became pregnant with twins so my book went on the backburner for a while, and Yotam's recipe was subsequently published in Jerusalem, his own book with Sami Tamimi, but I'm delighted to have kept Yotam's recipe for inclusion here. Thank you, Yotam!

This great family recipe is from Yotam's father, Michael, who was born in Florence. Before Michael, his Nonna Luciana, who was originally from Rome, would serve it at their Passover Seder.

I particularly love the different textures and the flavour combination in this recipe. My mum used to make a similar dish called galantina di pollo, enclosing cold cuts of cured kosher beef and pitted olives with minced chicken: utterly delicious and indeed a labour of love. Nowadays, she buys a tasty veal roast stuffed with different cuts of kosher salamis from the kosher butcher in Rome – a real treat!

1 Start by making a flat omelette. Whisk 2 of the eggs in a bowl with the chopped parsley and a pinch of salt. Heat the oil in a large frying pan (about 28cm/11in in diameter) over a medium heat and pour in the eggs. Cook for 2–3 minutes, without stirring, until the eggs set into a thin omelette. Remove from the pan and set aside to cool.

2 In a large bowl, mix together the minced beef, breadcrumbs (or matzah meal), pistachios, gherkins, the remaining egg, 1 teaspoon of salt and ½ teaspoon of pepper. Take a large, clean tea towel (you may want to use an old one you don't mind getting rid of; cleaning it will be a slight menace) and lay it over your work surface. Now take the meat mix and spread it on the tea towel, shaping it with your hands into a 1cm (½in)-thick rectangle roughly 30 x 25cm (12 x 10in). Keep the edges of the cloth clear.

3 Cover the meat with the sliced ox tongue, leaving a 2cm (¾in) border around the edge.

4 Cut the omelette into four wide strips and spread them evenly over the tongue.

5 Lift the tea towel to start rolling the meat from one of its long sides. Continue using the tea towel to roll the whole piece tightly into a large sausage shape, with the mince on the outside and the omelette in the centre. Cover the meatloaf with the tea towel, wrapping it up well so it is sealed inside. Tie the ends with string and tuck any excess cloth underneath the log so you end up with a tight bundle.

6 Place the bundle inside a large saucepan or lidded casserole dish. Throw the carrot, celery, thyme, bay leaves, onion and powdered stock around the loaf, then pour in boiling water from the kettle to almost cover it. Cover the pan or dish with a lid and simmer over a low heat for 2 hours.

7 After 2 hours, remove the loaf from the pan and, still in its cloth, place it on a wire rack over a dish to drain off some of the liquid (the poaching stock would make a great soup base). After about 30 minutes, place something heavy on top of the loaf to remove more of the juices. Once it reaches room temperature, put the meatloaf in the fridge, still covered in cloth, until it's properly chilled, 3–4 hours.

8 For the sauce, pulse together all the ingredients in a food processor (or, for a more rustic look, chop the parsley, capers and egg by hand and stir together with the rest of the ingredients). Taste and adjust the seasoning.

9 To serve, remove the loaf from the cloth, slice into 1cm (½in)-thick pieces, lay on a serving plate and serve the sauce on the side.

Zucchine Ripiene di Carne

COURGETTES STUFFED WITH MEAT

Preparation:
40 minutes
Cooking:
1¼ hours

SERVES 4

Ingredients
12 **Romanesco courgettes**
   or 6 regular
   courgettes, rinsed
1 **onion**, finely chopped
2 **garlic cloves**, crushed
6½ tablespoons **extra**
   virgin olive oil
6 tablespoons **dried**
   breadcrumbs (or
   medium matzah
   meal if for Passover)
80ml (2¾fl oz/⅓ cup)
   water
500g (1lb 2oz) **minced beef**
1 large **egg**
¼ teaspoon **ground**
   cinnamon
¼ teaspoon **ground**
   nutmeg
700g (1lb 9oz/scant
   3 cups) **passata**
5–6 fresh **basil leaves**
sea salt and black pepper,
   to taste

You will also need
an oven dish just big
enough to hold the
courgettes in a single
layer, at least 30 x 30cm
(12 x 12 in).

*T*his dish is typical of the Roman Jewish community's
cucina povera *and is popular for Shabbat. The minced
meat is 'stretched' with courgette to help it feed more people.
It is traditionally made with the small tender zucchine
romanesche (Romanesco courgettes), which don't need
par boiling, but these are not easy to find outside Rome,
especially abroad; fortunately, classic green courgettes work
just as well.*

*A courgette corer is a handy tool, as it has a pointed tip
which makes it easy to pierce and scoop out the flesh.
I recommend having a couple of extra courgettes in reserve,
in case they split while coring, especially if you are a beginner!*

*As the recipe is a little laborious, I like to prepare two or
three times the quantity, stuffed and cooked, so I have them
in the freezer for a future occasion. The dish can easily be
made a few hours or even a day ahead and kept refrigerated.*

1 Trim off the ends of the courgettes and cut each courgette in
half crossways to create two cylinders. Pierce each cylinder
with a courgette corer and scoop out the tender flesh.

2 If you are using regular courgettes, soften the cored courgettes
slightly by cooking them in a saucepan of salted simmering
water for 5 minutes; they will then take less time to cook in
the oven. Lift them out of the water with a slotted spoon and
cool under cold running water to stop them cooking further.

3 Finely chop the scooped-out courgette flesh and mix it in a bowl
or mixer with the onion, garlic and a pinch each of salt and pepper.

> **TIP:** *To save time, use a food processor to chop the courgette
> flesh and mix it with the onion, garlic and seasoning. It combines
> the mixture perfectly with just a few pulses – don't overmix or it
> will become watery.*

4 Heat 2 tablespoons of the oil in a non-stick frying pan over a medium heat and add the chopped courgette mixture. Cook for 10–12 minutes, uncovered, and stirring occasionally, until all the liquid evaporates. Remove from the heat and leave to cool for 5 minutes.

5 While the mixture is cooling, soak the breadcrumbs (or matzah meal) in the water for 5 minutes, or until the water has been fully absorbed.

6 Preheat the oven to 200°C (180°C fan/400°F/gas mark 6).

7 Mix the cooked courgette mixture with the meat and add the soaked breadcrumbs (or matzah meal), the egg, cinnamon, nutmeg and a pinch of salt. Ideally, blend everything in a food processor using a few brief pulses so it combines perfectly, or mix it together by hand (using either your hand or a spoon).

8 Fill each courgette cylinder with some of the raw meat mixture and place them in a single layer, in an oven dish just big enough to hold them. Roll any remaining meat mixture into small balls and place them around the courgettes.

9 Mix the passata in a jug with ½ teaspoon of salt and a pinch of pepper. Tear the basil leaves and add them to the passata with the remaining 3½ tablespoons of oil, mix well and pour over the stuffed courgettes and meatballs to at least half-cover them – if there isn't enough, add a little water. Drizzle the remaining tablespoon of oil on top.

10 Bake in the oven, uncovered, for about 1 hour, turning the courgettes and meatballs halfway through cooking. The dish is ready when the courgettes are coloured and soft when tested with a fork, and the tomato sauce is thick.

11 Remove from the oven, cover with foil, and allow to stand for 10 minutes before serving.

Peperoni Ripieni di Carne

PEPPERS STUFFED WITH MEAT

Peperoni ripieni di carne *is the sister recipe of* zucchine ripiene di carne *(courgettes stuffed with meat). It is faster to prepare and one of my favourite classics. It can be made a day ahead so is ideal for Shabbat. In Italy, we eat it with bread, but you can serve it with plain rice or couscous instead. The cooked dish keeps well for a few days in the fridge, and also freezes well.*

Preparation:
20 minutes
Cooking:
1½ hours

SERVES 4

Ingredients
80g (2¾oz/generous 1 cup)
   dried breadcrumbs
   (or medium matzah
   meal if for Passover)
100ml (3½fl oz/scant
   ½ cup) **water**
2 large **eggs**
¼ teaspoon
   ground cinnamon
¼ teaspoon
   ground nutmeg
600g (1lb 5oz) **minced beef
   or lamb,** or a mix
   of both
4 yellow, orange,
   red or green **peppers**
700g (1lb 9oz/scant
   3 cups) **passata**
3½ tablespoons
   extra virgin olive oil,
   plus extra for drizzling
5–6 fresh **basil leaves**
sea salt and **black pepper,**
   to taste

You will also need an
oven dish about 35 x 25cm
(14 x 10in).

1 Preheat the oven to 200°C (180°C fan/400°F/gas mark 6).

2 Soak the breadcrumbs in the water for 5 minutes, or until the water has been fully absorbed. Mix the eggs in a bowl with the cinnamon, nutmeg and a pinch of salt. Add the moistened breadcrumbs and stir. Add the minced meat and mix again. Ideally, blend everything in a food processor using a few brief pulses so it combines perfectly, or mix it together by hand, (using either your hands or a spoon).

3 Cut the peppers in half lengthways for large portions, or in thirds or quarters lengthways for smaller servings. Remove the stems, white membranes and seeds, and rinse the pieces. Fill each pepper piece with the meat mixture and roll any remaining mixture into small balls. Place the filled peppers and meatballs in a single layer in the oven dish.

4 Mix the passata in a jug or bowl with a good pinch of salt, a pinch of pepper and the oil. Mix well and pour over and around the peppers. Tear the basil leaves, add them to the dish and drizzle with a little more oil.

5 Cover the dish with foil and cook in the oven for 30 minutes. Remove the foil, gently stir the sauce and cook, uncovered, for 45 minutes– 1 hour until the peppers are softened and slightly browned and the sauce has thickened. Serve hot.

Cotolette al Limone di Shabbat

COLD LEMON SCHNITZELS

*M*y dear childhood friend Deborah Romano, who lives in Bologna, introduced me many years ago to this recipe for cold lemon schnitzels, something rather unusual, which captured my curiosity straight away. It was an immediate hit in my family, and I have been making it ever since. This recipe is from Deborah's aunt, Jose Romano Levi, who lived for most of her life in Ferrara, home to a fascinating Jewish community. She married into the Bonfigliolis, a Jewish family of long standing in Ferrara. This is the Bonfiglioli family recipe, and I am grateful to Jose for sharing it.

Best made ahead of time, this dish is ideal for a summer Shabbat meal as it is eaten cold or at room temperature. Variations include using veal instead of chicken, and chicken or vegetable stock instead of water. The cooked dish keeps for a few days in the fridge, and also freezes well.

Preparation:
15 minutes
Cooking:
45 minutes, plus
cooling time

SERVES 4

Ingredients
2 large eggs
50g (1¾oz/⅓ cup)
   plain white flour
150–200g (5½–7oz/
   generous 2–3 cups) dried
   breadcrumbs or panko
600g (1lb 5oz) skinless,
   boneless chicken breasts
   or veal escalopes
100ml (3½fl oz/scant
   ½ cup) light olive oil
   or sunflower oil
2–3 tablespoons extra
   virgin olive oil
juice of 3–4 lemons, to taste
about 600ml (20fl oz/2½
   cups) water or chicken/
   vegetable stock
sea salt and black pepper,
   to taste

1 Break the eggs into a shallow bowl and beat them with a pinch each of salt and pepper. Put the flour, seasoned with a pinch of salt, in a second shallow bowl, and the breadcrumbs, also seasoned with a pinch of salt, in a third shallow bowl. Slice the chicken or veal lengthways into thin goujons, or if you prefer, keep the meat pieces whole and pound them to make them thinner, forming large escalopes. Coat each piece first with flour, then dip into the egg mixture and then coat with breadcrumbs.

2 Heat the light olive or sunflower oil in a large frying pan over a medium heat and shallow-fry the schnitzels in batches, uncovered, for 3–4 minutes on each side. Drain the schnitzels on kitchen paper, leave to cool for a few minutes, then pat them to remove the remaining excess oil.

3 In a separate large, high-sided frying pan, warm up the extra virgin olive oil over a medium heat to coat the pan, then, when hot, add the schnitzels. Add the lemon juice and enough water or stock to cover the schnitzels, then cover the pan with a lid. Bring to the boil and simmer, covered, for 35–40 minutes. Turn the schnitzels just once half way through the cooking, doing this gently to avoid breaking them.

4 Remove from the heat and leave to cool completely (although we end up eating them warm sometimes and they are also delicious!). Served at room temperature, the lemon sauce will thicken to a jelly-like consistency. If made a day or so in advance, remove from the fridge about 1 hour before serving.

Scaloppine di Pollo al Melograno

CHICKEN ESCALOPES WITH POMEGRANATE

My family created this dish many years ago for Rosh Hashanah as it contains pomegranate, the deep-coloured Biblical fruit that is a symbol of abundance, procreation and prosperity. In the early autumn, pomegranates may be a little sour, so we sometimes sweeten the dish with honey, another symbol of good things for the Jewish New Year.

Margarine – or a dairy-free spread if, like me, you aren't a fan of man-made butter substitutes – is essential to keep the chicken breasts moist, along with the flour coating. This is the only savoury recipe in the book where I don't use extra virgin olive oil, so trust me on this alternative! If you don't have a hand-press juicer to make fresh pomegranate juice, look for a good-quality 100 per cent pomegranate juice made from concentrate, without added sugar.

Veal escalope is a great alternative to chicken breast and can be cooked in the same way. The dish keeps well in the fridge for a couple of days, even if it won't look as vibrant as when freshly cooked.

Preparation:
15 minutes
Cooking:
10 minutes

SERVES 4

Ingredients
- 600g (1lb 5oz) skinless, boneless chicken breasts
- 3–4 pomegranates, or 250ml (8fl oz/1 cup) good-quality pomegranate juice from concentrate
- 1 tablespoon runny honey (optional)
- about 50g (1¾oz/⅓ cup) plain white flour
- 2 tablespoons dairy-free spread or margarine
- 2–3 tablespoons pomegranate seeds
- sea salt, to taste

1 Slice each chicken breast lengthways into 3 or 4 thin slices, or cut them in half, then pound each half breast flat.

2 To make pomegranate juice, cut the crown off each fruit, then cut in half and squeeze each half through a large hand-press juicer (alternatively, use shop-bought pomegranate juice).

3 Mix the pomegranate juice in a glass with the honey, if using. Place the flour in a shallow bowl, add a good pinch of salt, mix, then lightly coat each slice of chicken with the seasoned flour, shaking off any excess.

4 Heat the dairy-free spread or margarine in a large, non-stick frying pan over a medium to high heat. Add the chicken slices to the pan, taking care that they don't overlap (you may need to cook them in batches). Sauté for 1–2 minutes on each side, or until golden, adding more spread or margarine if they look dry.

5 Once the chicken is golden, add the pomegranate juice and a good pinch of salt and reduce the heat to low. Simmer, covered, for 5 minutes until just cooked through, turning each slice once carefully so it absorbs the sauce well. The sauce will thicken while cooking. Taste and adjust the seasoning if needed. Remove from the heat.

6 Garnish with the pomegranate seeds and serve immediately.

TIP: *If you make this dish in advance, use just half the pomegranate juice to cook the chicken. Keep the cooked dish covered and, when ready to serve, reheat it for a few minutes in the frying pan with the remaining juice diluted with about 3½ tablespoons of water.*

Pollo Ezechiele

CHICKEN EZEKIEL

*T*he name of the prophet Ezekiel in the title of this dish gives away its likely Jewish origins. *It's also quintessentially Italian, with tomatoes, olives, fresh herbs and red wine. I have barely changed the recipe from the version I first saw in* La Cucina nella Tradizione Ebraica *by the Giuliana Ascoli Vitali-Norsa and Jewish women's association Adei-Wizo from Padova, as it's just perfect. I have cooked this chicken endless times using fresh herbs from my garden, and I hope it becomes a classic in your repertoire, too – it is so tasty and so simple to make!*

I suggest using chicken on the bone here, but if you prefer it off the bone, I would go for boneless thighs as they are juicier and more tender than chicken breasts. Boneless thighs take 10–15 minutes less cooking time than that given below. The dish can easily be prepared ahead of time and reheated in the same pan, or transferred to the oven. Once cooked, it also keeps well in the fridge for a few days, and freezes well.

Preparation:
10 minutes
Cooking:
1 hour

 SERVES 4

Ingredients
**3 tablespoons extra virgin
  olive oil**
**4 chicken legs or a mix
  of 8 drumsticks and
  thighs,** skin on and
  excess skin trimmed
2 garlic cloves, crushed
**2 tablespoons good-quality
  pitted black olives,** such
  as Taggiasca or Kalamata
1 bay leaf
**2–3 sprigs of fresh
  rosemary**
5–6 fresh sage leaves,
  plus optional extra
  (chopped) to serve
**400g (14½oz) tin peeled
  plum tomatoes**
**100ml (3½fl oz/scant ½ cup)
  red wine**
5–6 fresh basil leaves, plus
  optional extra to serve
sea salt and black pepper,
  to taste

1 Heat the oil in a large, non-stick frying pan or casserole over a medium to high heat. Add the chicken and sauté for a few minutes until golden on all sides.

2 Add the garlic, olives, bay leaf, rosemary, sage and a pinch each of salt and pepper. Stir well and cook for a couple of minutes, then add the tomatoes (crushing the tomatoes by hand or with a fork as you add them). Rinse out the tin with a little water and add the liquid to the pan. Stir, reduce the heat to low and cover.

3 Cook the chicken for about 40 minutes until tender, turning occasionally. Check for doneness by piercing the thickest part of each leg, drumstick or thigh with a skewer or the tip of a sharp knife. If the juices run pink, cook for a further 5 minutes and then check again until the juices run clear.

4 Once the chicken is cooked, take the lid off the pan and add the red wine. Increase the heat to medium to high and cook for a final 5 minutes until the wine has evaporated and the sauce has thickened. Tear in the basil leaves, stir and remove from the heat.

5 Transfer to a warmed dish, discarding the rosemary sprigs and bay leaf, and sprinkle with more fresh herbs for garnish, if desired. Serve hot.

Pollo coi Peperoni

BRAISED CHICKEN WITH PEPPERS

*E*very time I cook this dish it reminds me that you don't need many ingredients or a complex method to create something delicious. Pollo coi Peperoni is typically Roman and popular everywhere, not only among Jews, and it's a classic in our family.

Such a simple dish underlines why good-quality ingredients are so important. Use free-range chicken if you can, and perhaps also make this in the summer or autumn when peppers are at their best. Use beautiful ripe tomatoes if you can find them, or tinned if not – the dish only needs a touch of their colour and flavour. The cooked dish keeps well for a few days in the fridge, and also freezes well.

Preparation:
15 minutes
Cooking:
1 hour

SERVES 4

Ingredients
3 tablespoons extra virgin
  olive oil
1 onion, thinly sliced
2 garlic cloves, crushed
**pinch of dried chilli flakes
  or chilli powder**
100–150ml (3½–5fl oz/
  scant ½–⅔ cup)
  white wine
200g (7oz) **tinned peeled
  plum tomatoes**,
  or 4 **ripe vine
  tomatoes**, diced
8 **chicken pieces on the
  bone**, skin on, fat and
  excess skin trimmed
3–4 **peppers of different
  colours**, deseeded and
  cut into long strips
5–6 **fresh basil leaves**
sea salt and black pepper,
  to taste

1 Heat the oil in a large non-stick frying pan or casserole over a low to medium heat, add the onion and cook for 5 minutes, stirring gently, until softened but not browned. Add the garlic, chilli, a good pinch of salt, a pinch of pepper and a splash of the wine and cook for a couple of minutes, then add the tinned tomatoes (crushing the tomatoes by hand or with a fork as you add them) or fresh diced tomatoes and stir well. Cook, uncovered, for 5 minutes, stirring occasionally.

2 Add the chicken pieces and stir to combine. Reduce the heat to low, cover and cook for about 10 minutes, adding more of the wine and turning the chicken pieces once. Now add the peppers, stir, add another pinch of salt and cook, partially covered, for a further 30–35 minutes, stirring occasionally and adding more wine from time to time (and a little water if it looks a touch dry).

> **TIP:** *The saucepan or frying pan will look pretty full once all the raw peppers are in, but they will soften and shrink while they cook. Just stir every 10–15 minutes or so to make sure the chicken and peppers cook evenly.*

3 Remove the lid for the last 10 minutes, inreasing the heat to medium to high, so the sauce thickens and the chicken and peppers become slightly golden. If after this time, the sauce still appears too liquid, simply increase the heat and simmer for a few more minutes. Add a last splash of wine and leave it to evaporate for a couple of minutes over a medium heat. Finally, tear in the basil, stir, remove from the heat and keep the dish covered until ready to eat.

4 Serve hot. This is equally delicious a day or two later.

GOOSE – THE 'PORK' OF THE JEWS

A s an old saying from Ferrara goes: 'Dell'oca non si butta via niente' (Nothing gets thrown away from the goose). However, the original saying actually reads 'Del maiale non si butta via niente' (Nothing gets thrown away from the pig)! It is no coincidence, therefore, that goose has been associated with Italian Jews for centuries, and even Pellegrino Artusi in his 1891 *La Scienza in Cucina e l'Arte del Mangiar Bene* called the goose 'the pork of the Jews'.

Captivated by these quotes, I started researching the story behind the fascination with goose and why it had been associated with the Jews in Italy for so long. Coming from Rome, goose had rarely been part of our culinary culture, Jewish or not, so I had to look to the north of Italy to find an answer...

A great source of information has been the wonderful book *Mangiare alla Giudia* (*Eating Jewish-style*) by historian and professor Ariel Toaff, who dedicates a whole chapter to goose, explaining how it played an essential role in the domestic economy of north-Italian Judaism from the late Middle Ages, through the Renaissance, up until modern times. During this period, goose was a common and inexpensive food for northern-Italian Jewish families, just as pork was for Italian Christians. There were several similar-sounding cold cuts of meat.

It's interesting to note the clear geographical demarcation drawn by the Apennine Mountains and the effect it had on culinary traditions: in the north and east of Italy (and in particular, in what is today Piedmont, Lombardy, Veneto, Marche and Emilia-Romagna), where there has been an Ashkenazi influence and it is the ideal climate for breeding geese, goose was extremely popular and commonly eaten mostly by Jews but also by other Italians. In the west and south (Liguria, Tuscany and Lazio – where Rome is), goose never gained much of a following and beef reigned supreme as an alternative to pork to create kosher cold cuts of meat (and still does today).

Where geese were abundant, Jews used to breed and feed them in their homes – in courtyards, terraces and basements. In Venice, there are several references from the time of the ghetto to geese roaming around in the main square, which served as a market. In *Venice and its Jews: 500 Years Since the Founding of the Ghetto*, historian Donatella Calabi describes the fascinating 1830s census of geese owned by the butchers in the ghetto at the time. They counted 1,580 geese, which was roughly the number of Jews living in the ghetto at the time, so one per head!

During the summer months, the geese were mostly left to grow. However, at the start of autumn, in October, the large-scale slaughter began, continuing right through until April. During that time, goose mainly appeared as carefully prepared cold cuts, the best and tastiest of which were kept and then eaten during Passover in the spring. An extract from an official 1596 document of Casale Monferrato in Piedmont states that: 'Jews in the winter months eat goose on a regular basis.'

Toaff explains how all parts of the goose were eaten. For example, its fat was widely used in cooking as it was full of protein and calories and was cheap to buy. Its meat was used to make prosciutti (literally 'ham', but not real ham, obviously!) – the ones made in Ferrara were particularly famous – or goose sausages and salami, such as the Venetian *luganegotti* (not to be confused with the famous pork sausage *luganega*), all in goose-skin casings. From the late 18th century, *foie gras* made from goose liver, originally from France, was also in demand, both inside and outside the Jewish communities.

Popular goose delicacies included *gribole* or *griboli*, small pieces of goose skin fried in its own fat with onions – these were either eaten on their own as a snack or added to focaccia to make a savoury Venetian *fugassa* snack. The Ashkenazi influence can be clearly seen in the name, which comes from the German *griben* or Yiddish *grebene*, meaning *ciccioli* (small pieces) of goose fat. There was then the Renaissance *hamin*, also called *frisinsal*, one of the oldest goose recipes – a pasta bake made with goose-ham and fat (and some people also add liver and eggs), which evolved over time to include pine nuts and raisins. Its third, and perhaps most common, name is *ruota di faraone* (see page 112). This is the only recipe using goose that I've included in the book, both because of its unusual tale and because it is still perhaps the most popular dish made with goose within the different Jewish communities in the north of Italy today, even if it is typically made only once a year for Tu BiShvat and its Shabbat Beshalach.

Over time, the consumption of goose dwindled and turkey became more popular, as the meat was more tender and also cheaper.

By the second half of the 18th century, turkey had already replaced goose in most of Europe. In northern Italy, the popularity of goose lasted for an extra century as it continued to be enjoyed by the different Jewish communities.

What was once a most common, unpretentious home-produced food has now become a delicacy that is quite hard to find. The last kosher butcher dealing with goose in the Venetian ghetto closed more than 30 years ago and just a handful of people, at least to my knowledge, still make goose charcuterie at home (although rarely). Besides being a laborious process, it is also very difficult to source fresh kosher goose, and it is usually imported from France at a hefty cost. Nowadays, I know of only one producer of kosher goose in the north of Italy – Jolanda de Colò. They distribute cold cuts to kosher butchers and delis throughout Italy and worldwide and make them to order for private clients and special events, such as wedding and bar/t mitzvah, for those goose-lovers for whom geese still represent Jewish tradition and heritage. There is also a wonderful revival, led by Anna Campos of the Venetian Jewish community, to learn and teach how to make kosher cold cuts of geese at home, so traditions are still alive.

Personally, although I like the occasional cold cut of goose, with its slightly sweet flavour, I'm not a big fan of goose fat as I find its flavour rather overpowering. I do, however, have to admit that I have a (unethical!) soft spot for goose liver, *foie gras*.

Stracotto

BEEF STEW WITH TOMATO AND RED WINE

*T*his slow-cooked beef is another signature dish that's typical of Roman Jewish cuisine. Here the stew is stracotto, i.e. cooked for a very long time, in a recipe with just a few simple and classically Italian ingredients. Cooked slow and low for several hours, the beef tenderises and the sauce takes on a most satisfying flavour. In the past, this was a way to make the most gristly meat palatable, but today we use more tender cuts with some fat in them so they stay moist while cooking.

Roman Jews love to serve this for a winter Friday night Shabbat dinner. Leftover sauce and meat pieces can be turned into a sauce for pasta, risotto or polenta. The dish keeps in the fridge for several days, and also freezes well.

Preparation:
10 minutes
Cooking:
3½–4 hours

SERVES 4

Ingredients
150ml (5fl oz/⅔ cup) extra virgin olive oil
2 onions, finely chopped
1.2kg (2lb 12oz) beef chuck, cut into 4–5cm (1½–2in) cubes
200ml (7fl oz/scant 1 cup) red wine
700g (1lb 9oz/scant 3 cups) passata
sea salt and black pepper, to taste

1 Heat the oil in a casserole or heavy-based saucepan over a low heat, then add the onions with a pinch each of salt and pepper and cook, covered, for 12–15 minutes, until softened but not browned.

> **TIP:** *150ml (5fl oz/⅔ cup) may seem a lot of oil, but you need it as the beef cooks for a long time and the oil will help to keep it moist.*

2 Add the beef and stir well. After a few minutes the meat will start to sweat. Leave it to cook in its liquid, partially covered, over a low to medium heat for about 30 minutes.

3 Increase the heat to medium, add the wine, stir and cook, uncovered, for 5 minutes. Add the passata, rinsing out the container with a little water and adding the water to the pan to incorporate all the residue. Stir, cover and bring to the boil. Once it starts boiling, reduce the heat to low. You can use a heat diffuser if you have one, to keep the heat even.

4 Leave the beef to simmer for at least 2½–3 hours, stirring occasionally. The cooking time will depend on the cut of meat and the pan you are using. Press the cubes with a fork to test them: the beef is ready when the meat feels tender and falls apart easily. Taste and adjust the seasoning if necessary.

5 *Stracotto* tastes even better made a few hours ahead of time, or a day ahead.

Arrosto di Manzo

ROAST BEEF

Preparation: 10 minutes
Cooking: 40 minutes for medium rare (up to 1 hour for well-done), plus 30 minutes to 1 hour resting

SERVES 4

Ingredients
½ **onion**, thinly sliced
½ **carrot**, peeled and cut into thin sticks
½ **celery stick**, cut into thin sticks
2 **garlic cloves**, thinly sliced
1 **bay leaf**
2 **sprigs of fresh rosemary**
1–1.2kg (2lb 4oz–2lb 12oz) **beef joint** suitable for roasting, such as prime bola or rib
4–5 **tablespoons extra virgin olive oil**
about 200ml (7fl oz/scant 1 cup) **white wine**
sea salt and black pepper, to taste
80g (2¾oz) **fresh rocket**, to serve (optional)

You will also need an oven dish just slightly bigger than the piece of beef, so it retains all its juices.

I love roast beef and make this dish all the time. White wine is commonly used in Italian cooking with red meat and makes a natural gravy with a wonderfully sharp flavour. I think the use of white wine, instead of red wine, is the secret of this recipe, as well as not overcooking the beef!

Kosher cuts of meat are limited for this dish; rib joint is the most usual cut, but I also like to use a long, thin prime bola joint, which is tender if it is not overcooked. If in doubt about which piece to use, ask your butcher.

My mother uses only garlic, bay leaves and a couple of dried juniper berries in her sauce. My version includes a few more ingredients. You will find the beef tender and easiest to carve at room temperature or when cold. This dish can be prepared a day in advance or a few hours before serving. It keeps well in the fridge for 2–3 days, and is also great in a sandwich.

1 Preheat the oven to 260°C (240°C fan/500°F/gas mark 10).

2 Use your hands to coat the meat with a good pinch of salt, a pinch of pepper and the oil. Place the onion, carrot, celery, garlic, bay leaf and rosemary in the oven dish. Position the joint on top of the vegetables and herbs. As well as giving it extra flavour and preventing it from burning, this will raise the meat

TIP: *The beef will continue cooking after you take it out of the oven, so factor this in when you are checking it for doneness. Remember that the longer you cook it, the tougher it gets!*

above the fat and stop it frying rather than roasting.

3 Roast the beef for 15 minutes, turning it once halfway through and splashing in some of the wine (over the meat), then reduce the heat to 200°C (180°C fan/400°F/gas mark 6) and continue to roast, turning the meat and adding a splash of wine every 10 minutes. At this stage, you can spread the vegetables around and on top of the meat to finish cooking and become golden. The cooking time at this lower temperature will be 20 minutes per 1kg (2lb 4oz) if you like your meat medium-rare. For medium, cook for a further 10 minutes, or for well-done, a further 20 minutes.

4 Remove the roast beef from the oven, cover with foil and leave to rest for at least 30 minutes before carving, ideally 1 hour. This resting time is important as it makes the meat more tender and easier to carve.

5 Once it has cooled, cut the roast beef into thin slices with a very sharp knife. It can be served warm or at room temperature but the gravy must be hot. I recommend not serving the beef hot, but if you must, then immerse the slices in half the gravy and heat them in the oven for 5 minutes, taking care not to cook it further.

6 Warm the remainder of the gravy separately on the hob and serve alongside. You can keep the chunks of vegetables from the oven dish in the gravy, or remove them and serve separately. This dish also looks lovely served on a bed of fresh rocket on a large plate.

Lubia bel Cammun

LIBYAN BRAISED BEEF WITH BEANS AND CUMIN

A popular dish for Shabbat and the High Holidays, this stew is one of my favourites from Libya's Jewish culinary repertoire. Although it means planning ahead, do try and use dried beans soaked in water for this recipe, as they are so much better than tinned ones; the beans slow-cook with the meat and the two marry perfectly with the spices.

This recipe has evolved a lot during the years I've been making it, with my Israeli-Libyan friends suggesting richer versions with plenty of spices and my Italian-Libyan friends insisting it be kept simple. I eventually settled for the latter, as it better reflects my pared-down cooking style, where each ingredient is celebrated. My version is inspired by one in La Cucina Ebraica Tripolina *by Linda Guetta Hassan, a gem of a book with wonderful traditional recipes. I like to add potatoes to it, as some other versions do, but try both options. Couscous is the perfect accompaniment.*

This rich and delicious braised meat (usually beef or veal) is good, if not better, prepared in advance. Once cooked, it keeps well in the fridge for 3–4 days.

Preparation:
10 minutes, plus minimum 8 hours soaking time
Cooking:
3½–4 hours

SERVES 4

Ingredients
100ml (3½fl oz/scant ½ cup) **extra virgin olive oil**
2 **onions**, finely chopped
4 **garlic cloves**, sliced
2 teaspoons **ground cumin**
½ teaspoon **chilli powder**
3 tablespoons **tomato paste or purée**
1kg (2lb 4oz) **chuck beef or veal**, cut into medium-sized chunks
200g (7oz/generous 1 cup) **dried white cannellini beans**, soaked in cold water overnight (minimum 8 hours) and drained
2 **waxy potatoes**, peeled and quartered (optional)
sea salt and black pepper, to taste

1 Heat the oil in a casserole or large, heavy-based saucepan over a low heat, then add the onions and cook, uncovered, for 10 minutes, until lightly browned. Add the garlic, 1 teaspoon of the cumin, the chilli powder, tomato paste or purée and a pinch each of salt and pepper. Stir and cook for a further 5 minutes, then add the meat and soaked, drained beans.

2 Increase the heat to medium to high and sear the meat, uncovered, for 10 minutes, then add enough boiling water from the kettle to almost cover the meat. Stir, cover, then reduce the heat to low and simmer, stirring occasionally, for about 3 hours or until the meat is tender. If you are using veal, it will take roughly 30–45 minutes less time than beef. The meat is ready when it feels tender and is easy to break with a fork.

3 After the meat has been cooking for 2½ hours, add the remaining teaspoon of cumin, a good pinch of salt and the potatoes, if using. If the meat is starting to look dry, add more water. Cook for another 30–40 minutes.

4 Taste and add more seasoning of salt, pepper or cumin to your liking. Remove from the heat and leave to rest for at least 15 minutes before serving.

5 Serve hot, ideally with couscous. As with most stews, this dish tastes even better when prepared ahead of time.

Sarde in Saor

VENETIAN SWEET AND SOUR SARDINES

Preparation:
15 minutes, plus 1–2
days marinating time
Cooking:
30 minutes

SERVES 4

Ingredients
3–4 tablespoons extra
  virgin olive oil
3 onions, thinly sliced
1 tablespoon sugar
250ml (8fl oz/1 cup) white
  wine vinegar or
  cider vinegar
30g (1oz/3 tablespoons)
  pine nuts
40g (1½oz) raisins
  or sultanas
3–4 bay leaves
grated zest of 1 small
  orange (optional)
600g (1lb 5oz) small
  butterflied fresh
  sardines (heads
  removed, deboned)
about 50g (1¾oz/⅓ cup)
  plain white flour
about 200ml (7fl oz/
  scant 1 cup) light olive or
  sunflower oil, for frying
sea salt and black pepper,
  to taste

You will also need a
non-metallic serving
dish, ideally a glass or
ceramic one.

*T*his sweet and sour staple of Venetian cuisine is usually served
  as cicchetti, a small appetiser enjoyed with an aperitif. Saor is
the Venetian dialect word for flavour, referring to the way that first
frying then marinating the sardines for a few days gives them such a
distinctive love-it-or-hate-it pungency.

  Pine nuts and raisins are typical ingredients of Italian Jewish cuisine
across Italy, Venice included, being a cosmopolitan port where Jews
have played an important role in overseas trade for centuries. Vinegar
helps preserve the dish as the fish marinates. I love fresh sardines but
you could also use fish like plaice or sole instead, for a milder taste; the
method is the same. The dish calls for deboned and butterflied sardines
– this is rather fiddly, so ask the fishmonger to do it.

  This dish can be eaten cold or at room temperature, is ideal for
Shabbat and is a classic way to break the fast after Yom Kippur in Venice.

1 Heat the extra virgin olive oil in a non-stick frying pan over a low heat and
stir in the onions. Add the sugar, a pinch each of salt and pepper and a
couple of tablespoons of water. Cover and gently sweat the onions for
about 20 minutes until softened and translucent, stirring occasionally.

2 Once the onions have softened, remove the lid and add the vinegar.
Don't be concerned if it looks like a lot, it will all be mopped up by the
onions and fish. Cook, uncovered, for a further 5 minutes, then add the
pine nuts, raisins or sultanas, bay leaves and orange zest (if using).
Increase the heat to medium to high, stir and cook for a further couple
of minutes, then remove from the heat.

3 Meanwhile, rinse the sardines in fresh water and pat dry with kitchen
paper. Place the flour in a shallow bowl, season it with salt, then lightly
dust the sardine fillets with the flour, tapping off any excess.

4 Heat the light olive or sunflower oil in a separate frying pan over
a medium to high heat and fry the sardines in batches for about 2
minutes on each side until lightly golden. Remove them from the oil
with a slotted spoon and place in a sieve to drain. Just before the next
batch is ready, transfer them to a plate lined with kitchen paper to help
absorb any excess oil, then sprinkle with salt.

5 Assemble the dish by creating layers of sardines and onions in your chosen non-metallic dish. Start with a thin layer of onions, then add a layer of sardines, another layer of onion mixture and a bay leaf. Repeat until you have just enough of the onion mixture to make the top layer. Pour over any remaining juices from the pan.

6 Cover with clingfilm or a tight lid and leave in the fridge to marinate ideally for a day or

two. Or, if you are like my husband Marc, you might want to eat them straight away; try it both ways and see which you prefer. The dish keeps well in the fridge for up to a week.

7 Serve at room temperature or cold, but never hot!

Triglie con Pinoli e Passerine

RED MULLET WITH PINE NUTS AND RAISINS

Preparation:
10 minutes
Cooking:
15 minutes

 SERVES 4

Ingredients
8 small to medium whole
  or filleted red mullet
3–4 tablespoons extra
  virgin olive oil
2 tablespoons pine nuts
2 tablespoons raisins
  or sultanas
3½ tablespoons white
  wine vinegar or cider
  vinegar
splash of white wine
  (about 3½ tablespoons)
sea salt and black pepper,
  to taste

You will also need an
oven dish or baking tray
about 35 x 25cm (14 x 10in)

*M*y mother serves this classic Roman Jewish dish every year
  before the 25-hour Yom Kippur fast. She likes to use very
small red mullet. It also appears on our family's Seder plate at
Rosh Hashanah, as fish is one of the festival's nine symbolic foods,
suggesting proliferation. If you follow the tradition not to use vinegar
at New Year because of its sourness, leave it out on this occasion and
use more white wine instead.

Personally, I always struggle with the tiny bones in red mullet, but
if you don't mind them, then do try the original recipe with whole
fish. Alternatively, you can use fillets instead, if you prefer.

Rather than roasting, as I suggest here, some Roman Jews cook
the fish on the hob in a covered non-stick frying pan over a low to
medium heat for 10–12 minutes. You get more juice this way and the
fish stays a touch moister. Try it both ways.

1 Preheat the oven to 200°C (180°C fan/400°F/gas mark 6).

2 Rinse the fish in fresh running water, pat dry, then place them in the oven
  dish or baking tray. Drizzle the oil on top and sprinkle with salt, pepper
  and half the pine nuts and raisins or sultanas. Gently rub the ingredients
  around the fish and arrange in one layer (skin-side up if using fillets).

> **TIP:** *Soaking the raisins or sultanas in warm water for 5 minutes before adding
> them to the fish makes them softer and juicier.*

3 Roast in the oven for 10–12 minutes for whole fish or 5 minutes for fillets.
  Add the remaining pine nuts and raisins or sultanas along with the
  vinegar and wine, and then place under a hot grill for a final 3–5 minutes,
  until light golden.

4 Remove from the grill and serve hot, warm or at room temperature.

Baccalà alla Romana

SALT COD WITH TOMATO AND CINNAMON

Preparation:
15 minutes
Cooking:
45 minutes–1 hour

SERVES 6

Ingredients

1kg (2lb 4oz) pre-soaked
salt cod (ready to cook)
or 6 fresh cod loins,
filleted, with the skin
left on

3–4 tablespoons extra
virgin olive oil

2 onions, thinly sliced

400g (14½oz) tin
peeled plum tomatoes

500g (1lb 2oz/generous
2 cups) passata

¼ teaspoon ground
cinnamon

splash of white wine

a handful of fresh
basil leaves

100ml (3½fl oz/scant
½ cup) light olive or
sunflower oil, for
shallow-frying the fish

about 50g (1¾oz/⅓ cup)
plain white flour, mixed
with a pinch of sea salt
(if using fresh cod)

sea salt and black pepper,
to taste

I have been cooking this fish dish since I first saw it many years ago in Bruna Tedeschi's book, La Mia Cucina Ebraico Romanesca. I was fortunate enough to meet Bruna and she is one of the people who inspired me to specialise in Italian Jewish cuisine when I first started cooking professionally.

I like the way the tomato combined with cinnamon adds a little sweetness to the salty cod. Baccalà has a strong taste, which I love, but it may be too strong for some and it is not always easy to source already soaked and ready to cook. I often use fresh cod as a good (though slightly different) alternative, which results in a dish with a more delicate flavour. Whether you use fresh or salt cod, the cooking method is the same, although salt cod is unlikely to need extra salt and it will take a little longer to cook. Buy pre-soaked, deboned salt cod, so it is ready to cook, and leave the skin on, as that helps prevent the fillets from falling apart.

This dish keeps well in the fridge for a couple of days. Any leftover sauce is a great accompaniment to cooked rice – I usually sauté them together in a frying pan.

1 Rinse the fish in fresh running water and pat it dry. Remove any bones.

> **TIP:** *The easiest way to extract bones from raw fish is with fish tweezers. These are wider and sturdier than cosmetic tweezers and enable you to pull the bones away from the flesh with greater force.*

2 Heat the extra virgin olive oil in a large, non-stick frying pan over a low heat, add the onions and cook, covered, for 12–15 minutes, until softened and lightly browned.

3 Add the tomatoes, crushing them by hand or with a fork as you add them, and the passata. Rinse the containers out with a little water and add the liquid to the pan. Stir, then add a good pinch of salt, a pinch of pepper and the cinnamon. Stir again, partially cover, and cook over a low to medium heat for 20–25 minutes, adding the wine halfway through. Tear in most of the basil leaves once the sauce is cooked.

> **TIP:** *Some Roman Jews like to add pine nuts and raisins to the dish, towards the end of cooking.*

4 Meanwhile, heat the light olive or sunflower oil in a separate non-stick frying pan over a medium to high heat. Place the flour in a shallow bowl and gently coat the fish fillets, shaking off any excess. Place, flesh-side down, into the hot oil. Do not overcrowd the pan (fry in batches if necessary). Shallow-fry over a medium to high heat for a couple of minutes on each side until they are just golden on the outside but not yet fully cooked inside.

5 Drain the fish fillets on kitchen paper and keep covered while the tomato sauce continues to cook. Once the sauce is ready, add the fish fillets to the pan, skin-side down. Spoon the tomato sauce over each fillet and finish by cooking them over a low to medium heat, partially covered, for 15–18 minutes for salted cod or 5–7 minutes for fresh cod.

6 Arrange a couple of the remaining basil leaves on top of each fillet and serve hot.

THE CURIOUS STORY OF THE DELICIOUS FISH HEAD

The head of a fish is its tastiest part, or so they say. I have clear memories of my grandfather, Nonno Bino, eating whole fish heads, whatever the size, during my favourite Thursday lunches at his and Nonna Bianca's home. He came from a humble background in Venice, but fish was abundant and he appreciated them in their entirety. He had a great sense of humour and he was always looking for ways to make everyone laugh. He used to grab everyone's attention by holding a fish head and gulping it down, eyes included, as if it was the most natural thing to do! We children, meanwhile, all sat there with our eyes tight shut, but in reality were sneaking quick peeks and laughing our heads off, as we were too curious to see what was happening!

My father is also not squeamish about eating fish heads, and neither, funnily enough, is my husband Marc. Together, they once gave a crash course to my daughters while eating mixed fried fish, *pescetti fritti*, teaching them that the best way to eat them is whole, and that they are 'deliciously crunchy!' My daughters seem to have inherited the Nacamulli fish-head-eating genes, at least as far as small fried fish is concerned and they are a pleasure to watch as they do. This love of fish heads clearly missed a generation, as I am unable to even attempt to eat one. What I can eat, however,

and always look out for, are delicious fish cheeks. The only time I use whole heads is to make my fish soup.

That fish heads are a delicacy is no novelty – the appreciation of them dates back to the Middle Ages. Large heads were particularly sought after, so much so that in the main fish market in Rome, La Pescheria, which was once at Portico d'Ottavia, one of the ghetto's gates, near the banks of the Tiber, there were two plaques that reminded vendors of their importance. One is still clearly visible on the right-hand side of the Portico and the other, which is bigger and also shows a large sturgeon, was carved in 1581 and can now be found in the Musei Capitolini in Rome (above).

The plaques state in Latin 'Capita piscium hoc marmoreo schemate longitudine majorum usque ad primas pinnas inclusive conservatoribus danto,' which translates as

'The heads of fish longer than the markings [about 1m] on this marble shall be given to the Conservatori [magistrates under the Pope] up to and including the first fins.' So the best and most sought-after part of the fish for the magistrates was not its tender fillets but rather its large head, as it made the most delicious soup.

A line behind the first fin of the large sturgeon on the plaque at the Musei Capitolini indicates where the fish should be cut in order to remove the head. The fish head functioned as a tax to be paid to the magistrates and the plaque clearly specifies, 'Fraudem ne committito ignorantia excusari ne credito', or 'Commit no fraud, ignorance is no excuse.' This tax was only lifted in 1798.

The leftover fish and any small fish went to the 'people', the poor and the Jews, who were, of course, never magistrates or officials. Perhaps as a result, and mostly

because the Jews in Rome were particularly poor, a variety of dishes using small inexpensive fish like anchovies and sardines became traditional in the ghettos. We have dishes such as *aliciotti con l'indivia*, *fritto misto* and one of my favourite soups, *minestra di pesce*, made with just fish heads and bones (not sturgeon, as it is not kosher!).

Even outside Rome, popular Italian Jewish fish dishes tend to contain small bony fish, be it the red mullet from Livorno (*pesce alla Livornese*) or the Venetian *sarde in saor* (sweet and sour sardines). The emphasis in all these dishes is on their flavour rather than their boniness. The use of fish fillets in Italian Jewish cuisine is relatively new and also quite a privilege that, for centuries, most Jews could not afford. Nowadays, most people can thankfully pay for a beautiful sea bass, sole or bream, and many would throw the head and bones away!

Aliciotti con l'Indivia

FRESH ANCHOVY AND CURLY ENDIVE BAKE

Preparation:
15 minutes
Cooking:
50 minutes

SERVES 6

Ingredients
700g (1lb 9oz) butterflied fresh anchovies (heads removed, deboned)
500g (1lb 2oz) curly endive, trimmed (about 1kg/ 2lb 4oz before trimming)
extra virgin olive oil
sea salt and black pepper, to taste

You will also need an oven dish about 35 x 25cm (14 x 10in).

A real classic of Roman Jewish cuisine, this dish is witness to the cucina povera of Rome's Jews, who made a meal out of small bony fish and widely available vegetable leaves. Curly endive is a kind of frizzy chicory which is easy to find in Rome but less so elsewhere. You could try replacing it with curly kale but it won't be quite the same, as curly kale is tougher.

It is worth asking your fishmonger to prepare the fresh anchovies for you, as the job of deboning and butterflying them can be tricky. The finished dish, I have to admit, is not one of my personal favourites, as the leaves are rather bitter, but everyone else in my family loves it, and it is such a classic at my parents' dinner table and among Roman Jews that I couldn't leave it out!

1 Preheat the oven to 200°C (180°C/400°F/gas mark 6).

2 Rinse the anchovies under fresh running water and leave to drain. Roughly chop the trimmed curly endive.

3 Create layers of endive and anchovies in the oven dish. Start with a thin layer of oil over the base, then place slightly less than half the endive in the bottom to make the first layer, sprinkle with salt and pepper and add a drizzle of oil over the top. Cover with about half the anchovies and season again with salt, pepper and oil.

4 Add a second layer of endive, leaving just a handful of leaves for the very top. Season with salt and pepper and drizzle with oil, then add the final layer of anchovies. Scatter the remaining handful of endive on top, seasoning again with salt, pepper and oil.

5 Cover with foil and bake on the bottom shelf of the oven for 15 minutes, then remove the foil and bake for a further 30 minutes. Turn on the grill to high, then place the dish under the hot grill for the last 5 minutes or until golden.

6 Serve hot, warm or at room temperature. The flavour is different at each temperature, so try the different options and see which you like best.

Pesce alla Livornese

LIVORNESE FISH WITH TOMATO AND CHILLI

*T*his dish is a staple of Livorno and its other name, pesce alla mosaica, *is another reference to Jews, the people of the Mosaic faith. It's a classic dish for the Jewish New Year and Passover and uses whole red reef mullet which are plentiful on the rocky shores of northern Tuscany. These small fish, which are not the same as the paler red mud mullet, are delicious but full of bones. If you are someone who feels comfortable handling fish from head to tail and can source red reef mullet, then I suggest you try the classic version, as the whole fish gives an unrivalled depth of flavour. But if, like me, you don't particularly relish small bones, you can use red mullet fillets instead – just make sure your fishmonger debones them well! I usually choose whichever fish looks freshest on the day, and I have made this with sea bass, sea bream and red snapper, all delicate and slightly different in flavour. The dish keeps well for a couple of days in the fridge, although most fish dishes are better eaten freshly made. If there are leftovers, I like to break the fish into the tomatoes to create a second-day pasta sauce – perfection.*

Preparation:
10 minutes
Cooking:
35–40 minutes

SERVES 4

Ingredients

3 tablespoons extra virgin olive oil
2 garlic cloves, thinly sliced
1 fresh mild red chilli, thinly sliced and partially deseeded, **or a pinch of dried chilli flakes or chilli powder**
400g (14½oz) tin peeled plum tomatoes
10 cherry tomatoes, halved
1 generous tablespoon of fresh flat-leaf parsley, finely chopped, plus extra to garnish
8 red mullet, whole or filleted, or 4 fillets of sea bass, sea bream or red snapper
sea salt and black pepper, to taste

1 Heat the oil, garlic and chilli in a large, non-stick frying pan over a low heat. If you are using fresh chilli and like it spicy, then finely chop the seeds and add them, too, otherwise – for a milder sauce – remove all the seeds. When the garlic starts sizzling, add the plum tomatoes (crushing them by hand or with a fork as you add them). Rinse out the tin with a little water and add the liquid to the pan. Season with a good pinch of salt and a pinch of pepper and cook over a low to medium heat, covered, for about 20 minutes.

2 Once the sauce has thickened, add the cherry tomatoes and parsley and cook over a medium heat, uncovered, for 5 minutes.

3 While the sauce is cooking, rinse the fish under fresh running water and pat dry. Add the whole fish or fillets to the pan, skin-side down if using fillets, taking care not to let them overlap. Sprinkle a pinch each of salt and pepper over the fish.

4 Gently take spoonfuls of tomato sauce from the pan and cover the fish with them. Cover, and leave to cook over a low to medium heat for 10 minutes for whole fish, or 5 minutes for fillets. Do not turn the fish as it may break.

5 Sprinkle more parsley on top to garnish and serve hot.

Carpaccio di Trota e Orata

TROUT AND SEA BREAM CARPACCIO

Preparation:
15 minutes, plus 30 minutes–2 hours marinating time

SERVES 4

Ingredients
400g (14oz) skinned and deboned fresh trout fillets
400g (14oz) skinned and deboned fresh sea bream fillets
small bunch of chives, finely chopped
salad cress, to garnish (optional)
grated zest of ½ orange

DRESSING
juice of 2 lemons
½ teaspoon sea salt in the dressing, plus sea salt flakes when serving
¼ teaspoon black pepper
80ml (2¾fl oz/⅓ cup) extra virgin olive oil, plus extra for drizzling

You will also need two shallow, non-metallic dishes, preferably glass or ceramic.

We often have this refreshing dish for a summer Friday night meal or Shabbat lunch as it can be prepared in advance and the fish takes its time to 'cook' in the lemon juice. We really like the delicate flavour of trout, but I would only recommend using trout if you can get deboned fillets or if you have good fish tweezers and patience, as its bones are small and plentiful! My preference is to combine trout with sea bream, or you could make it with sea bass and salmon. Whatever you choose, always go for the freshest fish you can find – ideally use sushi-grade fish.

The simple dressing of lemon juice, extra virgin olive oil and salt and pepper allows the flavour of the fish to shine through, and I like to add chives, flaked sea salt and orange zest just before serving. The dish keeps for up to a day in the fridge, and I love how both the taste and colours change as the marinade takes effect.

1 Check the fish for bones, rinse under fresh running water and pat dry. With a large sharp knife, slice the fillets diagonally into 5mm (¼in)-thick slices. Place the trout in one non-metallic dish and the sea bream in the other.

2 To make the dressing, mix the lemon juice, salt, pepper and oil in a jar. Shake well and pour three quarters over all the fish. Stir gently, cover with clingfilm and place in the fridge to marinate for 30 minutes to 2 hours.

3 When ready to serve, remove the fish from the fridge, add the remaining quarter of the dressing and stir well. Add more seasoning to taste.

4 If you want to serve this for a crowd, it looks good on a large plate either with the fish types mixed up, or with the pink trout on one half of the plate and the white sea bream on the other. Starter portions on individual plates also look great.

5 Sprinkle the chopped chives and cress over the fish, add a good pinch of sea salt flakes, a little grated orange zest and a drizzle of extra virgin olive oil.

6 Serve cold on its own, or with some bread, crackers or grissini.

TIP: *Don't worry if some of the fish breaks into slivers. Once laid out on the plate, all the slices will look and taste great.*

Pesce Finto

FAKE 'FISH'

Preparation:
30 minutes
Cooking:
20 minutes

SERVES 6

Ingredients
THE 'FISH' MIXTURE
1 tablespoon coarse or
  kosher salt
500g (1lb 2oz) King Edward,
  Maris Piper or Desirée
  potatoes, peeled and cut
  into large chunks
400g (14oz) tin tuna in
  olive oil
½ teaspoon sea salt

MAYONNAISE
1 egg or 2 egg yolks
½ teaspoon lemon juice
250ml (8fl oz/1 cup)
  sunflower oil
1½ teaspoons Dijon
  mustard (optional)
¼ teaspoon fine sea salt
½ teaspoon white wine
  vinegar or cider vinegar

TO GARNISH
cucumber slices
carrot slices/strips
yellow and red pepper
  slices
pitted olives
capers

You will also need a large
oval dish, ideally about
45 x 30cm (17¾ x 12in).

This is another recipe from my late grandmother, Nonna Bianca, who would often make fake 'fish' for her memorable Thursday lunches. She would garnish it with olives and a few carrots, which we all loved. Nowadays, I like to take the time to present it as a proper pretend fish with all its scales and fins – you can be as creative as you like! This makes a great dish for Shabbat lunch as it is eaten cold.

If you are new to making mayonnaise, I recommend giving it a go as it may be easier than you think. Or you can use 150g (5oz) of shop-bought mayonnaise instead – my favourite variety is Japanese mayonnaise, even if it is not very Italian Jewish! Note that this recipe contains raw eggs.

1 Bring a large saucepan of water to the boil and add the coarse or kosher salt. When it boils, add the potatoes and cook for about 15–20 minutes over a low to medium heat, partially covered, until soft when pierced with a fork. Drain and leave to cool for 5 minutes.

2 Mash the cooled potatoes with a potato ricer or masher. I prefer to use a ricer as it gives the potatoes a light, fluffy consistency.

3 Mix the mashed potatoes in a bowl with the tuna (with all the olive oil from the tin) with your hands or with a large fork and add the salt. Don't use a food processor as this will just turn the mixture into a thick, hard lump. Cover and keep to one side.

> **TIP:** *You can prepare the recipe up to this stage up to one day ahead and keep it in the fridge. The mayonnaise can also be prepared a day in advance.*

4 Make the mayonnaise using a hand whisk (keeping the bowl steady on a folded towel) or with an electric hand mixer. Whichever method you choose, the key is to add the oil very gradually, especially the first 100ml (3½fl oz/scant ½ cup). Begin by whisking the whole egg (or 2 yolks) in a bowl with a couple of drops of lemon juice. While whisking continuously by hand or on medium speed of the electric mixer, start adding the oil in a thin, steady stream.

5 The first half of the oil should take just a few minutes to incorporate and the mixture should emulsify and thicken. From time to time stop mixing and check. Add the mustard (if using), salt, vinegar and the remaining

lemon juice, then slowly add the second half of the oil while whisking continuously. This will take about 5 minutes in total. By the end, you should have a thick, shiny mayonnaise.

6 Taste and adjust the flavour and seasoning with more salt, mustard or lemon.

7 To make the 'fish', cover the surface of your chosen dish with the potato and tuna mixture. Model it with your hands into the shape of a fish, roughly 2–3cm (¾–1¼in) thick.

8 Spread the mayonnaise on top. About 150g (5½oz) should be enough to cover the top and sides of the whole fish, so you may not need all of the amount you just made, but it depends on your taste. Any remaining mayonnaise can be served in a bowl next to the 'fish' or kept in a sealed glass jar in the fridge for up to a week.

9 There are no fixed rules when it comes to garnishing the 'fish'. I like to use cucumber slices as 'scales', cutting each slice in half so they don't overlap too much. Carrot or pepper slices are great for the 'tail', 'mouth' and 'fins', and I like to use sliced olives and whole capers for the 'eye' and to garnish the sides. You can be as creative as you like and add more or omit any of the garnishing ingredients. Try not to use watery vegetables like tomato.

10 Place the dish in the fridge to firm up, but remove it 20 minutes before serving. The 'fish' can be garnished up to 3 hours ahead.

Polpettone di Tonno

SIMONA'S TUNA LOAF

Preparation: 20 minutes
Cooking: 1 hour

SERVES 4

Ingredients
5 large eggs
5 tablespoons dried breadcrumbs
5 tablespoons freshly grated
   Parmesan cheese
grated zest of 1 lemon

500g (1lb 2oz) tinned tuna in
   olive oil, drained
80g (2¾oz) fresh rocket (optional)
sea salt and black pepper, to taste
lemon wedges, to serve

DRESSING
juice of ½ lemon
100ml (3½fl oz/scant ½ cup)
   extra virgin olive oil
sea salt and black pepper, to taste

I 've made this tuna loaf countless times with my sister
Simona during shared summer seaside holidays, when
all 15 members of my close family gather and share many
tasty meals. We aim for dishes that are quick to make,
can be prepared in advance, don't force you to stand over
a hot stove, feed a large crowd and can be eaten at room
temperature, including for Shabbat. This tuna loaf ticks all
the boxes, and kids love it because it tastes so mild.

Simona makes a delicate olive oil and lemon dressing,
but feel free to use mayonnaise or any other dressing. For
mayonnaise, see the recipe on page 178. The salsina verde
of Yotam Ottolenghi's polpettone (see page 142) also works
well here. The proportions are 1:1, so you can change the
size of the loaf by increasing or decreasing the quantity of
ingredients to the same degree. The loaf keeps well in an
airtight container in the fridge for 3–4 days.

1   Mix the eggs, breadcrumbs, Parmesan, lemon zest, ½ teaspoon
    of salt and a pinch of pepper in a food processor. Add the
    drained tuna and pulse a few times until just evenly combined
    (don't overdo it). Alternatively, mix everything together in a
    bowl with a fork or, better still, with your hands. The mixture
    will feel very soft but should be just firm enough to hold a loaf
    shape; if it is still too soft, then add a further tablespoon or
    two of breadcrumbs and/or Parmesan.

2 Lay a sheet of baking parchment (about 40 x 30cm/16 x 12in) on top of a piece of foil the same size. Place the tuna mixture in the middle of the baking parchment and shape it into a loaf, first by lifting the paper up around it, and then again with the foil to make a firm shape. You can also shape it into two smaller tuna loaves, depending on the size of your saucepan.

3 Take a large oval or round saucepan and place the wrapped tuna loaf/loaves in it, then fill the pan with just enough cold water to cover. Cover and cook over a low to medium heat for 1 hour.

4 Remove the loaf (or loaves) from the water, with the wrapping still on. Most of the foil will be black, but that's normal, so don't worry! Leave to drain and cool down for at least 30 minutes, ideally in a colander. I find a large oval sieve works well, or you can simply place it on a large plate and discard any water.

5 Once it has cooled to room temperature, put it in the fridge with the wrapping still on, until ready to serve. To make the dressing, either combine and shake all the ingredients well in a jar, or mix the lemon juice, salt and pepper together, then slowly add the oil, stirring continuously with a small whisk to create an emulsion.

6 Unwrap and serve the tuna loaf cold or at room temperature, cut into 1cm (½in)-thick slices arranged on a serving dish, either alone or on a bed of rocket. Serve with the lemon dressing (or mayonnaise) on the side.

Buricche

TRIO OF SAVOURY PARCELS

 Preparation:
20 minutes
Cooking the meat parcels:
50 minutes
Cooking the tuna parcels:
30 minutes
**Cooking the aubergine and
tomato parcels:**
1 hour 10 minutes

 MAKES 20–22 PARCELS

Ingredients
PASTRY
100ml (3½fl oz/scant ½ cup) light
    olive or sunflower oil
80ml (2¾fl oz/⅓ cup) tepid water
1 teaspoon sea salt
250g (9oz/scant 1⅔ cups)
    plain white flour

PASTRY GLAZE
1 egg, beaten
sesame or poppy seeds (optional)

MEAT FILLING
3 tablespoons extra virgin olive oil
1 onion, finely chopped
pinch of ground cinnamon
pinch of ground nutmeg
200g (7oz) minced chicken (or other
    minced meat of your choice)
splash of white wine
30g (1oz/½ cup) soft breadcrumbs,
    moistened with 3 tablespoons
    stock or hot salted water
sea salt and black pepper, to taste

TUNA FILLING
150g (5½oz) tinned tuna in olive oil –
    weight includes the oil
3 anchovy fillets in oil, finely chopped

**50g (1¾oz) good-quality pitted
    black olives**, such as Taggiasca
    or Kalamata, chopped
**20g (¾oz/2 tablespoons)
    capers**, chopped
1 soft-boiled egg, cooled, peeled and
    chopped (optional)
grated zest and juice of 1 lemon

**AUBERGINE AND
TOMATO FILLING**
4 tablespoons extra virgin olive oil
1 onion, finely chopped
pinch of chilli powder (optional)
1 aubergine (about 200g/7oz), cut
    into 1cm (½in) cubes
200g (7 oz/scant 1 cup) passata,
sea salt and black pepper, to taste

*T*hese traditional Italian Jewish pastries from Ferrara and Emilia-Romagna (also known in Venice as burriche) come in both a savoury and sweet form with a dozen different types of filling, especially as savoury options – the sweet versions are usually made with almond paste. Sometimes leftovers such as shredded chicken or vegetables are used in savoury versions. The three I've included here are among my favourites and are filled with meat, tuna, and aubergine and tomato. They are great as an appetiser, a starter or as party food and popular for the festival of Purim.

The name and shape remind us of Turkish börek but the pastry is more like that of empanadas from Spain. Indeed, the many varied fillings of these small bites come from all three of Italy's Jewish traditions – Ashkenazi, Sephardi and Italian – reflecting the true marriage of cultures and culinary traditions that both Ferrara and Venice have witnessed over the centuries.

The pastry is light, parve (dairy-free) and easy to make, just make sure you roll it very thin – 2mm (¹/₁₆in). You can use ready-rolled pastry such as puff pastry or flaky pâte brisée if you don't want to make your own – and roll it thinner – but frankly it takes hardly any time to make, and tastes delicate and quite different from shop bought pastries, so do give it a go.

The quantities of each filling are enough for one batch of pastry, plus a little extra.

FOR THE PASTRY

Put the oil, tepid water and salt in a bowl and stir. Gradually add the flour while continuing to stir. Eventually start kneading the dough by hand (on the worktop or in the bowl) – it should feel soft but not sticky. Work the dough for a couple of minutes, then wrap in clingfilm and leave to rest at room temperature while you move on to the filling of your choice.

FOR THE MEAT FILLING

Heat the oil in a frying pan over a medium heat, add the onion and cook, covered, for 5 minutes, then add the cinnamon, nutmeg, and a pinch each of salt and pepper. Stir well and cook for a minute, then add the minced meat, increase the heat to medium and cook, uncovered, for 10–12 minutes, breaking up the mince with a wooden spoon and adding the wine halfway through. Transfer to a shallow heatproof bowl or plate and leave to cool for a few minutes, then spoon in the moistened soft breadcrumbs and mix well with your hands or a fork.

FOR THE TUNA FILLING

Flake the tuna and put it into a shallow bowl with all of its oil. Add the anchovies, olives, capers, egg (if using) and the lemon zest and juice; mix well.

FOR THE AUBERGINE AND TOMATO FILLING

Heat the oil in a saucepan or frying pan over a low to medium heat, add the onion and cook, covered, for 5 minutes until soft but not browned, then add the chilli powder (if using), stir, and add the aubergine. Sauté over a medium to high heat for 10–15 minutes, then add the passata, 2–3 tablespoons of water, a good pinch of salt, and a pinch of pepper. Stir, cover, and cook over a low heat for about 30–40 minutes, stirring occasionally, until the aubergine is soft and easy to mash. Transfer to a bowl, mash with a fork and leave to cool to room temperature.

ASSEMBLING AND BAKING

1 Preheat the oven to 200°C (180°C fan/400°F/gas mark 6) and line a baking tray with baking parchment.

2 Unwrap the pastry, divide it in two and roll each piece out to a circle about 2mm (1/16in) thick. It is important to make it very thin or the parcels will be too pastry-heavy and dry.

3 Cut out 8–9cm (3¼–3½in) circles using a large glass or a biscuit cutter. I usually twist the trimmings into miniature pastry bites, but you can roll them out again to make more parcels if you prefer.

4 Put a teaspoon of the filling of your choice in the centre of each pastry circle and fold the pastry over into a half-moon shape. The surfaces should stick together easily, but if the pastry is a touch dry, simply wet the edges with a little water. Gently press the edges with a fork or pinch them with your fingertips to seal.

5 Brush each parcel with beaten egg for a glazed finish and sprinkle sesame or poppy seeds over the top if you like (the original recipe doesn't have seeds but I think they look and taste lovely!). Place on the lined tray and bake for 20–25 minutes until golden. Eat hot or warm.

Haraimi

LIBYAN FISH IN SPICY TOMATO SAUCE

Preparation:
10 minutes
Cooking:
45 minutes–1¼ hours

SERVES 4

Ingredients
100ml (3½fl oz/scant ½ cup)
    extra virgin olive oil
½ onion, finely chopped
felfel u ciuma (below)
140g (5oz/⅔ cup)
    tomato paste or purée
150ml (5fl oz/⅔ cup) water
1 teaspoon ground caraway,
    plus extra to serve
4 fresh fish steaks or fillets
    of snapper, grey mullet,
    tuna, sea bream or sea bass

FELFEL U CIUMA
6 garlic cloves, crushed
½ teaspoon chilli powder
1 tablespoon paprika
½ teaspoon sea salt
juice of ½ lemon
½ teaspoon ground
    caraway (optional)
2 tablespoons water

TIP: *Prepare larger quantities of* felfel u ciuma, *then keep leftovers in a glass jar in the fridge, covered with a thin layer of olive oil, and use it when you feel like adding a spicy kick to your dishes.*

*T*his is probably the most famous Tripolitanian Jewish dish and much loved by the wider Libyan community and beyond. The recipe was kindly given to me by Hamos Guetta, who arrived in Rome as a child with his family after fleeing Tripoli in 1967. Hamos has a passion for cooking and keeping traditions alive and does a magnificent job of sharing stories and preserving recipes on his YouTube channel, Hamos Guetta.

The key to a great haraimi is to make a good felfel u ciuma, which is a paprika (felfel) and garlic (ciuma) paste and forms the base of many Libyan dishes. All the Libyan Jews I know have a jar in the fridge and their own secret recipe, with different proportions of chilli, garlic and paprika.

The tomato sauce here is very spicy. The quantities given are therefore suggestions (Hamos' recipe calls for twice as much chilli powder, but my taste buds couldn't take that!) and you may have to play around a bit to get it right for you. The fish can be cut into steaks, halved or kept as large pieces on the bone (heads removed), which helps give the dish depth of flavour. If you don't like fish bones, you can use fillets instead. Haraimi is usually eaten with bread on a weekday or with couscous on Shabbat and Jewish festivals. It is often served as a starter at room temperature, although I also like it hot. Cumin can be used as a substitute to caraway, and tinned tuna also works well as a fish. This dish keeps well in the fridge for a few days.

1 Heat the oil in a large, deep, non-stick frying pan over a low heat, add the onion and shallow-fry, covered, for about 5 minutes, until softened but not browned.

2 Meanwhile, prepare the *felfel u ciuma* by combining all the ingredients in a small bowl and stirring well to create a paste.

3 Add all the *felfel u ciuma* to the pan with the onions, stir well and cook gently for about 5 minutes, then add the tomato paste or purée, stir and cook for another couple of minutes. Add the water, stir well, cover and cook for about 30–45 minutes over a low heat. The longer you cook it, the deeper the flavour. The sauce should be dense but not dry so, if necessary, add more water.

4 When the sauce is ready, add the caraway and stir, then add the fish. Spoon the sauce over each fish steak or fillet and cook, partially covered, for about 10 minutes for steaks and 5 minutes for fillets. Serve, sprinkled with more caraway if desired, with bread or couscous, and enjoy the spiciness!

CHAPTER 3

Vegetable dishes

Vegetables are at the heart of all my cooking. Everything that my family in Italy and London cooks day in, day out, revolves around flavoursome, uncomplicated vegetable recipes. My parents' Friday night dinner table regularly boasts ten different vegetable dishes, and mid-week meals are not far off that number.

If you see *verdure* or *contorni* on an Italian restaurant menu, it refers to vegetable side dishes that are intended to be eaten alongside or following a main course. Almost all the dishes in this chapter are side dishes, with the exception of a handful that can be served either as a first or main course, and they all have a Jewish soul, due to an ingredient, a combination of ingredients, or the cooking method. Sometimes, I've simply included a dish because it's a special family recipe.

The chapter features a wide variety of uncomplicated sautéed, roasted and grilled vegetable dishes, and plenty of dishes made with aubergines, which I particularly love. These include *melanzane alla parmigiana* (both the classic hot version and a special cold version made by my late grandmother, Nonna Bianca, that's ideal for Shabbat), *peperoni ripieni di melanzane e mozzarella*, and *caponata di melanzane alla giudia*, which not only uses aubergines but also combines deep-frying with sweet and sour flavours, both of which are key characteristics of Italian Jewish cuisine. Deep-frying has, in fact, been an extremely popular cooking method in Italy for centuries, particularly in Roman Jewish cuisine, with dishes such as the renowned *carciofi alla giudia, concia di zucchine* and, of course, *fiori di zucca*, wonderful fried courgette flowers, a

version of which I have included here, stuffed with mozzarella and anchovies.

The combination of pine nuts and raisins is also a staple of Italian Jewish cuisine, shown here by the inclusion of the Roman *spinaci con pinoli e passerine* or the Venetian *carote sofegae*, a slow-cooked carrot dish which also has the sweet and sour flavour combination, as does the deliciously addictive *cipolline in agrodolce*.

The use of vinegar in food, with or without sugar, was common, pre-refrigeration, to help dishes keep for longer, making them ideal to eat at room temperature for Shabbat when no cooking or reheating is allowed. *Concia di zucchine*, as well as the *zucchine marinate*, are good examples of this, the latter with the addition of quintessential Italian herbs such as rosemary, sage and bay leaves.

There are then two Passover frittatas, one from my great-grandmother, Silvia, and the slightly sweet Venetian *frittata dolce di spinaci*. I also could not leave out a couple of my favourite Libyan Jewish recipes – I chose the famous *shakshuka* as well as a spicy dip: *merduma*.

Other recipes in this chapter are unpretentious but nonetheless still exquisite. They have earned their place because of their popularity in my home, and include griddled and roasted *antipasti di verdure* and a variety of sautéed vegetables, such as broccoli, peppers, courgettes and carrots.

Any of the vegetable dishes will go wonderfully with any of the meat, chicken or fish dishes in this book. Their versatility comes from being equally good served hot or at room temperature, making them ideal for a Shabbat meal.

ARTICHOKES

There are very few vegetables whose availability is strictly seasonal. Come February or March, I often find myself longing for Romanesco artichokes. These are rare and expensive in London, so every year, if I can, I travel home to satisfy my appetite for them. In the all-too-short artichoke season, I head straight for Mercato Trionfale or one of Rome's other large food markets, where they are abundant and beautiful. My mum prepares them almost every day of my visit, knowing I adore them alla Giudia (see page 192), or al Tegame (see page 196). Together, we also serve them exquisitely simply – thinly sliced and raw, with a squeeze of lemon juice and Parmesan shavings. When returning to London, I usually stuff half my suitcase with artichokes, then freeze them at home, waiting then for what feels like an eternity until the season comes round again: my supplies never seem to last long enough, as my husband and daughters have always fallen madly on whatever I bring back from Italy. It seems I have passed artichoke fever on to them!

I must admit that I love everything about artichokes, starting from the idea that they are actually flowers or, more precisely, thistles, that you can eat. They look fabulous when still young and closed, and I marvel at how they blossom with a gorgeous purple flower in the middle. Though tough and sometimes spiky on the outside, their insides are soft and they manage to be both sweet and savoury. Artichokes come in all sizes and alluring colours, from green through purple to brown outside, and yellow or white inside. Only the bottom (or heart) of some varieties is edible, but there are others that can be eaten whole after just a little 'magic' trim of the hard bits.

Reflecting the inventiveness of much Italian Jewish cuisine, artichokes reign supreme in an almost endless choice of dishes: they can be eaten raw in salads, boiled, roasted, stewed, braised and, of course, fried as in *carciofi alla Giudia*, the quintessential Roman Jewish dish, indeed one that is perhaps emblematic of all Italian Jewish cooking. They also come bottled and preserved, can be mashed into a pâté,

stuffed with meat, rice, or breadcrumbs and herbs, are often a key ingredient in pasta sauces or in risottos, and are excellent cooked with meat, chicken or fish. There is even a bitter liqueur called Cynar (from the Latin name *Cynara scolymus*) that's made with artichokes and drunk throughout Italy as an aperitif or digestif. Artichokes are renowned for their digestive and diuretic properties and are said to lower cholesterol while providing plenty of mineral salts, vitamins and folic acid. With very few calories, they really do seem to be a dream food!

The artichokes we use in Italian Jewish cooking are not the big, green, tough globe artichokes you may be familiar with. Italy is the largest producer of many varieties of smaller artichokes which have been grown around the Mediterranean since the times of the ancient Greeks and Romans. In winter, small spiky ones come from Sardinia, Liguria and Sicily, followed by purple varieties from Tuscany, Veneto and Lazio. These include the Violetto di Sant'Erasmo, popular in Venetian Jewish cuisine, as well as the Romanesco, also

called Mammole, grown in the region surrounding Rome. This is the variety I describe here, and which is used for *carciofi alla Giudia*; the 'Jewish style' in the recipe's name refers to the skilful way Jews found to clean and trim the vegetables so that everything that remains is edible and the artichoke can be eaten whole. It avoids what is referred to in Roman slang as *ciancica e sputa* – literally to 'chew with difficulty and spit out'. This may not sound very charming but is the best description of what happens when you eat artichokes that have not been properly trimmed! Knowledge of the trimming technique still survives today among the Jews of Rome and in a few market stalls in the area around the city's former ghetto.

If you can get hold of Romanesco artichokes, then the best ones to use are the *cimaroli*, i.e. the *cima* or 'top of the bush' in Italian – these are the first flowers to appear at the centre of the plant, which are plentiful at the start of the season. The stem of a *cimarolo* is chunky and visibly larger than the 'arms' that spring from the plant's sides.

The *bracci* artichokes that grow on these 'arms' are more easily available and are also good even if smaller in size and more fibrous inside.

Romanesco artichokes are in season in Italy from January until May, with the best ones at their peak in February to March. By late April or early May, my mother will stop buying them, saying their leaves are too tough to trim and their heart is too hairy. If you can't get hold of Romanesco artichokes, seek advice from your greengrocer and perhaps ask for small French, Spanish or Egyptian purple artichokes instead; they will work fine in these recipes if they are tender with closed leaves and have as little hair inside as possible. Unfortunately, the variety you are most likely to find in northern Europe and the US is the globe artichoke, which is the one I would avoid for the purposes of the artichoke recipes in this book. However, if that's all you can get hold of, then boil it whole and dip each leaf in a *pinzimonio* dressing – extra virgin olive oil with salt, pepper and lemon juice – delicious.

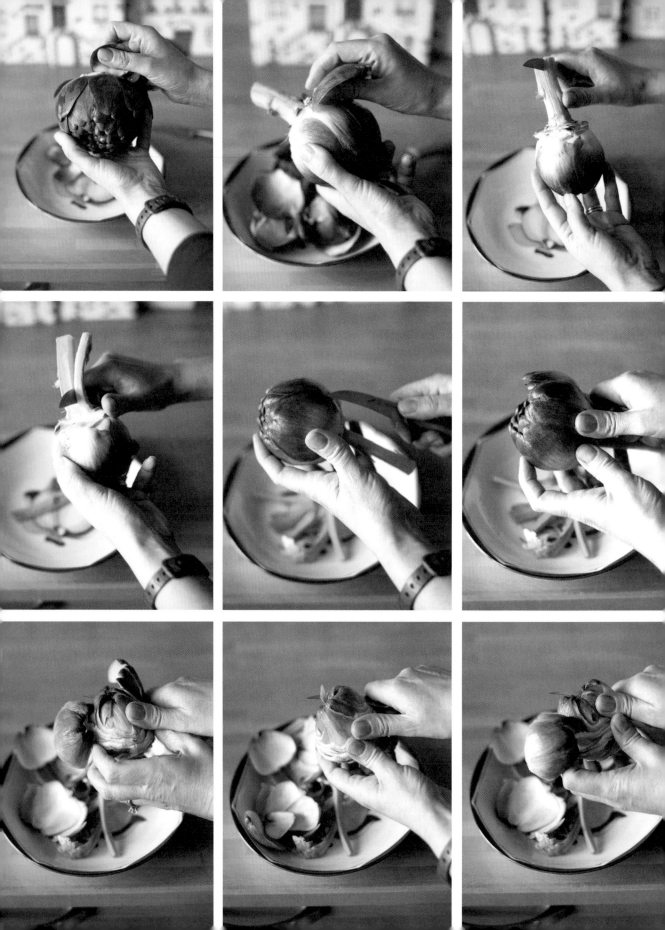

This is the Roman Jewish way to trim and clean Romanesco artichokes. It requires practise but you won't forget it once you have mastered it – and a whole world of delicious artichoke dishes will open up to you. Good luck!

METHOD

1. Start by pulling the small outer leaves off each artichoke, as well as the bigger ones that are still green at the bottom, until you reach the leaves with a lighter-coloured base, which are tender and edible.

2. If the stem is long, trim it to 2–3cm (¾–1¼in). Don't throw away the trimmings as they're delicious – just cut off the hard, green, stringy, outer layer to reveal the soft lighter-coloured centre. Smear the trimmings with lemon and place in the acidulated water. Do the same with the stem still attached to the leaves; smear that with lemon, too.

3. Next, with one hand, hold the artichoke with the stem downwards, and with the other hand insert the top of the knife vertically behind one of the bottom leaves, at the point where the leaf colour changes from dark to lighter. Turn the artichoke slowly while you cut off the purple-green tip of the leaf. Keep turning and trimming off the tough darker bit of each leaf, moving upwards in a spiral. The hard parts of the leaves will fall away, revealing the soft and edible parts. Smear the whole trimmed artichoke with lemon and place it in the water.

4. If you find it too difficult to work with a knife, then try using scissors to cut off the hard purple-green part of each leaf, still working around the artichoke in a spiral fashion. You should end up with a 'closed rose', where you can see only the paler parts of the leaves.

5. Repeat with the rest of the artichokes.

STEP-BY STEP GUIDE TO CLEANING ARTICHOKES

You will need:

A sharp paring knife or *spelucchino* (a curved knife with the sharp edge on the inside) or a small sharp knife or pair of scissors.

A bowl filled with cold water and lemon juice to prevent discoloration: squeeze the juice of ½ lemon into the water and cut the other half into quarters for smearing over the artichoke's trimmed sides as you prepare it.

Thin disposable gloves to avoid staining your hands (optional).

Carciofi alla Giudia

JEWISH-STYLE FRIED ARTICHOKES

*T*his recipe is emblematic of Roman, if not all, Italian Jewish cuisine. If I had to name my
favourite artichoke dish, it would be this. Its sunflower looks, crispy leaves, tender heart and
savoury-sweet taste make it unique.

As the artichokes are eaten whole, it is important to choose a variety which has little hair
inside, such as the tender Cimarolo – the best of the bunch of the Romanesco or Mammole varieties,
available mostly in the area around Rome in winter and early spring. To read more about how to
choose and trim artichokes, see pages 188–191.

In Rome, my family cooks artichokes almost non-stop in peak season. Our Passover Seder night
would just not be the same without them, as my mum fries more than fifty. Traditionally, extra
virgin olive oil is used to deep-fry them, but light olive or sunflower oil can be used instead, for a
lighter version.

You might think these are a labour of love – and you'd be right. For all the effort that goes into
them, it's worth cooking a big batch. They also freeze very well.

Preparation:
20 minutes
Cooking:
20–30 minutes

**MAKES 4
ARTICHOKES**

Ingredients
4 fresh artichokes, ideally
Cimarolo, Romanesco
or Mammole
2 lemons, quartered
(for acidulating
the water)
olive oil or sunflower oil,
for deep-frying
sea salt and black pepper,
to taste

1 Clean and trim the artichokes as described on page 191, acidulating the
water with the lemon quarters.

2 When they are all ready to cook, drain the artichokes from the water,
shake off as much liquid as possible, and pat dry. Gently tap each
flower, stem up, to loosely open the centre where the petals meet.
Smear a little salt and pepper wherever you can reach inside, and all
around the outside.

3 There are two stages to cooking the artichokes. First, you cook them as
they are with the flower closed, to soften the heart, and let them cool a
little, then open up the petals for a second round of fast frying to finish
them off. This fixes the artichokes perfectly open, with most petals intact.

4 For the first stage, ideally heat the oil in a deep-fat fryer to 150°C/300°F.
Alternatively, fill a large, deep, heavy-based saucepan or casserole with oil
to a depth of 4–5cm (1½–2in) and warm over a medium heat until hot.
(If you don't have a thermometer, test the oil is hot enough by dropping
in a cube of bread: it should float rather than sink, and sizzle immediately
on contact with the oil.)

5 Deep-fry the artichokes for 15–20 minutes, stem down, in the deep oil. They should fit comfortably, but if not, cook in batches. They should sit on the bottom of the fryer or pan, three quarters covered with oil, and not float around. Gently rotate them every 2–3 minutes, always with the stem facing downwards, until the heart is tender. If a fork inserted into the heart comes out easily when you test them, they're done. If you are cooking them on the hob and they start to brown too fast, reduce the heat as they shouldn't cook too quickly.

6 Place the cooked – but still partially closed – artichokes in a sieve to drain the oil and leave to cool down slightly. At this stage, you can set them aside to finish off later. If you plan to serve them within a few hours, keep them at room temperature; if they are to be eaten the next day, cover and transfer them to the fridge. The artichokes can also be frozen

at this stage and thawed completely before being fried again.

7 Ten minutes before serving, gently open up the leaves of the artichokes where the petals meet, using your hands or two forks. Heat the same oil, this time to about 170°C/340°F. Place the opened artichokes back in the hot oil, stem down, and fry for 1–2 minutes, then carefully turn them so that the open leaves point downwards this time and the stems stick up out of the pan – you'll hear a lovely sizzling noise. Fry for a further minute or so, until the leaves turn golden and crispy. A few leaves may become separated, but don't worry – they make delicious artichoke 'chips'. Remove from the oil with a slotted spoon and place in a sieve to drain the oil. After a minute, transfer them to a plate lined with kitchen paper to absorb any excess oil.

8 Serve immediately... and enjoy!

Carciofi al Tegame

BRAISED ARTICHOKES WITH GARLIC AND PARSLEY

T his is another wonderful way to cook and eat artichokes, and it's such a classic in my family. Easy to serve as a side dish, it also works brilliantly as a pasta sauce or in a risotto – cooked with it or added to the riso giallo del sabato *(see page 124).*

It is preferable to use young peak-season artichokes (available in February and March when they are at their most tender and have very little hair inside and can be cooked whole). Otherwise, cut them in half first, so that the hairy inner choke and any spiky inner petals can be removed, revealing the softest parts for eating. This is a sister dish to the better-known carciofi alla Romana, *which has the addition of* mentuccia, *an aromatic small-leaf wild mint. To try this, you can mix the parsley with a few leaves of fresh mint and cook it in the same way. Either version will keep in the fridge for a few days, and also freeze well.*

Preparation:
30 minutes
Cooking:
50 minutes–1 hour

SERVES 4–5

Ingredients
4 or 5 artichokes,
   ideally Romanesco
   or Mammole
2 lemons, quartered
**4 tablespoons extra virgin
   olive oil**
3 garlic cloves, crushed
**1 tablespoon finely chopped
   fresh flat-leaf parsley**, plus
   extra to garnish
**about 100ml (3½fl oz/scant
   ½ cup) white wine**
**about 150ml (5fl oz/
   ⅔ cup) water**
sea salt and black pepper,
   to taste

1   Clean and trim the artichokes as described on page 191. If cooking the artichokes whole, skip the next step.

2   If you are cooking the artichokes in halves, cut each artichoke in half lengthways through the stem and leaves to reveal the heart. Remove any hair with the tip of a small paring knife, then trim away any purple spiky petals (if there are any), until only tender pale ones remain. Smear lemon quarters all over each half and return them to the acidulated water used in the preparation stage. Repeat with the rest of the artichokes.

3   Put the oil, garlic, parsley and a pinch each of salt and pepper in a large, heavy-based saucepan or casserole and place over a low to medium heat. Cook for a couple of minutes, keeping an eye on it so the garlic doesn't burn, then add half the wine and cook for a further minute or so.

4   Place the artichokes in the pan and stir gently so they all get coated with the cooking oil, then arrange them in a single layer – whole ones stem up, or halves flat-side down – together with any stem trimmings. Add the water and a pinch of salt and simmer, covered, for 40–45 minutes, gently turning them halfway through if cooking them in halves, or basting the stems with the cooking juices from time to time if cooking them whole. You can set a heat diffuser under the pan to help the artichokes cook evenly, if you have one. If you don't have a heat diffuser, and they start to dry out, just add a little warm water.

5   Pierce the hearts with a fork to check they are soft. When they are, remove the lid, add the last splash of wine, increase the heat a little and cook for a final 5–7 minutes until they turn light golden. Serve warm or at room temperature.

TIP: *Cooking times can vary depending on the age of the artichokes and the pan you are using. Artichokes with hardly any hair cook more quickly; tougher, older artichokes may need more time. The key is to cook them long enough for both the heart and leaves to be tender.*

Zucchine e Carote Trifolate

SAUTÉED COURGETTES AND CARROTS

*O*ur Shabbat dinner table often features this side dish, and it's one that both children and adults usually enjoy. Anchovies are not essential, but they give it a little kick. Sometimes I just cook courgettes on their own, but pairing them with carrots as I do here gives the dish a lovely mix of textures and colours; my mum also likes to add a couple of potatoes, cut into sticks. This keeps well in the fridge for a few days.

Preparation:
15 minutes
Cooking:
45 minutes

SERVES 4–6

Ingredients
3–4 tablespoons extra virgin olive oil
2 garlic cloves, crushed
2 anchovy fillets in oil (optional)
splash of white wine
4 carrots, peeled and cut in half crossways, then into 1cm (½in)-thick sticks
3 courgettes, cut in half crossways, then into 1cm (½in)-thick sticks
sea salt and black pepper, to taste

1 Put the oil, garlic, anchovies (if using) and a pinch each of salt and pepper in a large, non-stick frying pan and place over a low to medium heat. Cook for a couple of minutes, then stir, add the wine and cook for another minute.

2 Trim off the ends of the carrots and courgettes, then cut each in half crossways to create two cylinders. Then cut into sticks 1cm (1/2in) thick.

3 Add the carrots to the pan and stir, cover and cook over a low to medium heat for about 10 minutes.

4 Finally, add the courgettes with a good pinch of salt and a pinch of pepper and stir well. Cook, uncovered, over a medium heat for 25–30 minutes until softened and golden, stirring occasionally.

5 Serve warm or at room temperature.

Zucchine Marinate

COURGETTES MARINATED IN FRESH HERBS, VINEGAR AND WINE

*I*f you like bold flavours, do try this recipe. The courgettes are sautéed in oil, then left to marinate in a delightful rich mixture of onion and fresh herbs slowly cooked with vinegar and wine. Ideally, it's best to leave the dish for a day or two, to allow the flavours to blend, but sometimes I can't wait and I eat them straight away, as they are also lovely eaten when the flavour is more delicate.

Marinated courgettes are ideal for serving at room temperature for a Shabbat meal. They keep for several days in the fridge.

Preparation:
15 minutes, plus
4 hours (or overnight)
marinating (optional)
Cooking:
45–50 minutes

SERVES 4

Ingredients
5 tablespoons extra virgin olive oil
1kg (2lb 4oz) courgettes, cut in half crossways, then into 1cm (½in)-thick sticks
1 onion, finely chopped
1 garlic clove, crushed
4 or 5 fresh sage leaves, plus extra to garnish
2 sprigs of fresh rosemary, plus extra to garnish
1 bay leaf
4 tablespoons red wine vinegar or cider vinegar
2 tablespoons white wine
sea salt and black pepper, to taste

You will also need a non-reactive glass or ceramic dish.

1 Heat 3 tablespoons of the oil in a large, non-stick frying pan over a medium heat. Add the courgettes with a good pinch of salt and a pinch of pepper, then sauté, uncovered, for 25–30 minutes, stirring occasionally, until cooked and lightly golden. Remove from the heat. Lift out the courgettes with a slotted spoon, leaving any extra oil in the pan, and transfer them to the non-reactive dish.

2 Add the onion to the pan with the remaining 2 tablespoons of oil and cook, covered, over a low to medium heat for 5 minutes, then add the garlic, sage, rosemary and bay leaf, stir and sauté for a couple of minutes, then add the vinegar, wine and a pinch of salt and pepper. Reduce the heat to low and cook, still covered, for about 15 minutes, then remove the lid and cook for five more minutes.

3 Transfer the onion and herb mixture to the dish of courgettes and stir.

4 Marinate, covered, at room temperature for 4 hours, or overnight in the fridge. Stir well before serving. Alternatively, stir and serve at once, removing the cooked herbs and scattering a few fresh sage and rosemary leaves on top just before serving.

Concia di Zucchine

FRIED AND MARINATED COURGETTES

*T*he aroma of fried courgettes combined with fragrant vinegar and garlic immediately
transports me home, where my mum makes the best concia. This is a staple of Roman
Jewish cuisine and one of my family's absolute favourites.

The courgettes need to marinate in the fridge for at least a day, ideally two, and can be left
for up to a week, with the vinegar acting as a preservative. Don't be put off by their rather dull
appearance once they are marinated, as these courgettes are bursting with flavour!

We usually serve concia very simply on bread as bruschetta, or in little panini sandwiches
for parties or kiddush for Bar/Bat Mitzvah or weddings. It also works well as a cold or room-
temperature side dish – never eat it warm or hot.

Preparation:
15 minutes
Cooking:
20 minutes, plus
1–2 days marinating

SERVES 4

Ingredients
1kg (2lb 4oz) courgettes, trimmed
light olive oil or sunflower oil, for deep-frying
2 garlic cloves, quartered
3–4 fresh basil leaves, torn, plus extra to garnish
8–10 tablespoons white wine vinegar or cider vinegar
sea salt, to taste

You will also need a non-reactive glass or ceramic dish, about 20 x 15cm (8 x 6in), preferably with a lid.

1 Cut each courgette crossways, then cut each half again into long strips about 5mm (¼in)-thick.

TIP: *If you have time, it's worth allowing the courgette strips to dry a little before frying them. Spread them out on kitchen paper or clean tea towels laid on a tray and leave for a couple of hours, even overnight. The courgettes will release liquid, which reduces the frying time and means less oil is absorbed. However, you can skip this step if you are short of time.*

2 Ideally, heat the oil in a deep-fat fryer to 180°C/350°F. Alternatively, fill a large, deep, heavy-based saucepan with oil to a depth of 4–5cm (1½–2in) and warm over a medium heat until hot. You can test the oil is hot enough by dropping in a bread cube: it should float and sizzle when it hits the oil. Lower about a third or a quarter of the courgette strips into the hot oil until you have a crowded single layer with no overlaps. Stir carefully.

3 Deep-fry over a medium to high heat for 3–4 minutes, turning the strips once or twice, until they are golden on both sides. Lift out with a slotted spoon and place them in a sieve over a plate or bowl to drain for a few minutes while the next batch cooks, then, just before draining the next lot, transfer them to the non-reactive dish – there's no need to drain them on paper.

4 Scatter two pieces of the garlic, a sprinkle of salt, a torn basil leaf, and 2 tablespoons of vinegar over the slices (making sure the vinegar is sprinkled over each slice). Do not mix. Fry the remaining courgettes, a batch at a time, placing them on top of each dressed layer. Repeat the seasoning process for each layer until you have three or four layers in total.

5 Leave to cool to room temperature, then cover the dish and put it in the fridge for 24 hours. After that time, uncover it and stir gently. Taste and add a little more salt or vinegar if it is a little bland. Cover and return to the fridge for at least another hour before serving (ideally 1 or 2 days' marinating time is best – stirring and tasting it again each day).

6 Serve at room temperature, or cold from the fridge. The dish keeps well in the fridge for up to a week – the longer you leave it, the richer the flavour.

COURGETTE FLOWERS AND ROMAN FRITTO MISTO

Rome and its Jewish inhabitants have a long history of street-frying vegetables. In the hundreds of years between the formation of the ghetto in the mid-16th century and the time its gates were finally opened in 1870, *friggitori* stands on street corners in the cramped ghetto quarters sold fried vegetables and fish, as also described by Claudia Roden in her gorgeous *The Book of Jewish Food*. People would flock from all over the city in search of them – the ghetto dwellers may have had restricted freedom, but their fritto misto spread beyond the ghetto's walls to find great popularity as a signature food of all Roman cuisine.

To Romans, the 'mother' of fried vegetables in batter is the yellow or orange courgette flower, possibly as beloved as bruschetta. The flowers are available only in summer and early autumn, when they bloom abundantly. Served in many casual trattorias or pizzerias as a quick starter, *fiori di zucca* are usually filled with mozzarella and anchovies – to my mind the classic and best filling. They are served on their own or as part of a broad *fritto misto* of mixed vegetable morsels (also called *pezzetti fritti*), small fresh anchovies, and the delicious *filetti di baccalá* (fried battered salt cod), another signature dish of Roman cuisine.

Courgette flowers have also recently been elevated to fine dining status, with the inclusion of other cheese fillings, such as the delicate ricotta or the smoked *scamorza*, and they remain a popular topping for pizzas as well. In my family, we love to eat them stuffed and fried in a light batter (see page 206) and they are also quite delicious roasted. My mother makes a wonderful bake of layers of courgette flowers with mozzarella and anchovies, and we also sauté them for a delicate pasta dish or risotto.

The term *fiori di zucca* encompasses both courgette and pumpkin flowers. The 'male' flowers, which first sprout in profusion from the stem, and the 'female' flowers, which burst later from the courgette or pumpkin fruit itself, are both perfect for frying. My parents grow both pumpkins and courgettes in the vegetable garden of our seaside house outside Rome. It is a pleasure to go out first thing in the morning to pick the flowers when they are in full bloom. That's the time to pluck out the yellow pistils from inside the flowers, as the flowers stay open for just a few hours. The petals close up during the day, then reopen again at night. In high season, we can easily harvest 30 to 40 flowers a day (yes!); that is the time for a courgette-flower feast, when visitors 'happen' to drop by and the delicious *fiori di zucca* disappear in no time!

Sadly, as is so often the case with some beautiful things in life, the flowers only last a few days at most and that's why you will rarely find them beyond the Mediterranean, unless they are grown locally or exported quickly. My heart lifts when I spot them in shops or farmers' markets in the UK – it's the female flowers attached to small courgettes that are sold most commonly here, and they have a slightly longer life span. You can, of course, grow your own, and if you can do this or find them anywhere on sale, don't miss the opportunity to try this traditional Roman delicacy!

Fiori di Zucca Fritti con Mozzarella e Alici

FRIED COURGETTE FLOWERS WITH MOZZARELLA AND ANCHOVY

*T*hese gorgeous yellow blossoms are very popular in Rome, and I absolutely love them *(see page 204 for more on courgette flowers). Restaurants often serve them coated in a thick batter made with yeast or beer, but I prefer a much lighter one made with just flour and water, which lets you taste all the flavours inside: the flower itself and the mozzarella and anchovy filling. The key to a crispy batter is using ice-cold sparkling water, the colder and fizzier the better.*

'Male' flowers from the courgette stem or 'female' flowers sprouting from the fruit can be used, with female flowers needing a little more frying time. You may find it hard to source courgette flowers in the UK, but if you come across them at a market, or grow your own, this recipe is definitely worth a try. It makes a great starter.

Preparation:
20 minutes
Cooking:
10 minutes

SERVES 4

Ingredients
12 courgette flowers
about 230g (8oz) mozzarella,
cut into 24 strips
6 anchovy fillets in oil, halved
sunflower oil, for frying
about 100g (3½oz/⅔ cup)
plain white flour
about 200ml (7fl oz/
scant 1 cup) chilled
sparkling water
sea salt and black pepper,
to taste

1 Very gently open each flower and pull out the yellow pistils, or cut them out with scissors – sometimes they are sold with the pistils already removed. Be careful not to break the petals. If any flowers do split, you can coat them twice with batter to help seal them.

2 Fill each flower with two strips of mozzarella and half an anchovy fillet, then gently close the petals around its filling.

3 Fill a large, deep, heavy-based saucepan with oil to a depth of 4–5cm (1½–2in) and start to warm it over a low heat. While the oil is warming up, mix the flour with a good pinch of salt in a wide, shallow bowl. Add the chilled water and stir until the mixture has a loose gluey consistency. If it's too runny, add another tablespoon of flour. Dip each courgette flower in the batter to coat.

4 Increase the heat under the oil until it reaches about 170°C/335°F on a thermometer. You can test the oil is hot enough by dropping in a bread cube: it should float and sizzle when it hits the oil. When the oil is hot, gently slip in the batter-coated courgette flowers, one by one, until a single layer covers the pan – you may need to batter and cook them in two batches. Fry for 2–3 minutes on each side, until golden.

5 Remove each one with a slotted spoon and place in a sieve over a bowl to drain the oil. Serve as soon as they are all ready.

Carote Sofegae

SWEET AND SOUR CARROTS WITH PINE NUTS AND RAISINS

Preparation: 15 minutes
Cooking: 1–1¼ hours

SERVES 4

Ingredients

1kg (2lb 4oz) carrots, peeled and cut into 5mm (¼in)-thick rounds, or thinner

3–4 tablespoons extra virgin olive oil
1 onion, finely chopped
2 tablespoons raisins or sultanas, soaked in lukewarm water for 5 minutes
2 tablespoons pine nuts
2 tablespoons white wine vinegar or cider vinegar
sea salt and black pepper, to taste

*C*arote sofegae *takes its name from the Venetian dialect word for 'suffocated', indicating a vegetable that's submerged in oil and water and cooked slowly until softened and ever so sweet. The cooking method may be similar to other Ashkenazi or Sephardi slightly sweet carrot dishes, but the addition of pine nuts, raisins and a splash of vinegar make all the difference here. The key is to let the carrots cook low and slow, and to let them become deep golden in the process.*

I soak the sliced carrots in water for 5 minutes before they go in the pan, rather than following the traditional method of adding water during the cooking process. This way the carrots cook steadily until they are tender and thoroughly golden. Embodying the versatility of the best Italian Jewish cuisine, this can be eaten either warm or at room temperature. It is one of my signature dishes and it keeps well in the fridge for up to five days – if you have any left!

1 Submerge the carrot slices in a bowl of cold water while you prepare the *soffritto*. They will cook better, without burning, if they are wet when added to the pan.

> **TIP:** *Use the wide slice setting of a food processor or a mandoline to cut large quantities of carrots quickly and evenly.*

2 Heat the oil in a large, non-stick frying pan over a low heat, then add the onion, together with a pinch each of salt and pepper. Cook for 10 minutes, stirring occasionally.

3 Drain the carrots and add them to the pan, increasing the heat to medium. Stir thoroughly and cook, uncovered, for 5 minutes, then add a good pinch of salt and a pinch of pepper, stir, reduce the heat and cover with a lid.

4 Cook over a low heat for about 30–40 minutes, stirring occasionally, until the carrots soften and start to turn golden, then remove the lid, add the raisins or sultanas (drained of their soaking water) and the pine nuts, stir and increase the heat to medium. Remove the lid and cook for a further 10–15 minutes.

5 Once the carrots are a deep golden colour and have shrunk a little in size, add the vinegar, toss and sauté, uncovered, over a medium to high heat for a final couple of minutes. Stir and remove from the heat.

6 Serve warm or at room temperature.

Cipolline in Agrodolce

SWEET AND SOUR SHALLOTS

S weet and sour is a classic combination of flavours in Italian Jewish cuisine and one that we love in my family, in particular in these shallots. My daughter Bianca can eat the whole lot in one go! In Italy, we make it with fresh, ready-peeled small white onions which are easily found in bags in markets – so wonderful! – and cuts the prep time to nothing. In the UK, a good version can be made with small, round brown shallots. They taste great but they do take a little time to peel.

The key to maximising the flavour here is slow cooking. The longer you let them simmer, the more caramelised the shallots become. If you like a little extra sweetness, do add the raisins or sultanas.

This cipolline works well as a warm accompaniment to roast beef, or fish, and when cold or at room temperature, they make a yummy chutney for bread and cheese. They keep well in the fridge for several days, and also freeze well.

Preparation:
20 minutes
Cooking:
2 hours

SERVES 4–6

Ingredients

1.2kg (2lb 12oz) round shallots or small fresh white onions

3–4 tablespoons extra virgin olive oil

2 tablespoons granulated sugar

3 tablespoons white wine vinegar or cider vinegar

1 tablespoon raisins or sultanas (optional), soaked in lukewarm water for 5 minutes

3 tablespoons Marsala or sweet wine

sea salt and black pepper, to taste

1 Soak the shallots in a bowl of lukewarm water for at least 5 minutes to help loosen the skin (if using skin-on shallots), then peel them, leaving most of the root intact so the layers stay together.

2 Heat the oil in a large, heavy-based saucepan or casserole over a high heat, then add the shallots or onions with a pinch each of salt and pepper. Cook for 5–8 minutes until golden.

3 Add the sugar, vinegar and 3 tablespoons of warm water. Stir, reduce the heat to the lowest setting, cover with a lid and simmer, stirring occasionally, for 1¼–1½ hours, until the shallots/onions are mostly softened. If at any stage the contents of the pan look dry, add a tablespoon or two of water.

> **TIP:** *A heat diffuser under the pan is handy for cooking the shallots/ onions gently without them sticking or burning. You want a slow, even heat for the best caramelisation.*

4 Add the raisins or sultanas (if using), drained of their soaking water, together with the Marsala wine, stir well, partially cover and cook for a further 25–30 minutes, or until the shallots/onions are fully cooked and golden and the sauce is dense and caramelised.

5 Serve either warm or at room temperature.

Polpettine di Spinaci

SPINACH CROQUETTES

This Venetian Jewish dish makes a great starter or finger food. The recipe calls for both fresh and dried breadcrumbs. For soft crumbs, challah works well but, failing that, sourdough is also good. If you prefer your croquettes bright green, just fry them without a coating. A squeeze of lemon juice before serving is a tasty touch, and I sometimes serve them with crème fraîche (although this is not very Italian!).

Preparation:
15 minutes
Cooking:
20 minutes

SERVES 4–6

Ingredients

**450g (1lb) fresh
spinach**, washed
**1 teaspoon coarse
or kosher salt**
**100ml (3½fl oz/scant ½ cup)
extra virgin olive oil**
1 garlic clove, crushed
**40g (1½oz/generous ½ cup)
soft bread crumbs**, from
challah or sourdough
3 tablespoons milk (any type)
1 large egg and 1 yolk
pinch of ground nutmeg
**2 tablespoons freshly
grated Parmesan cheese**
**2 tablespoons dried
breadcrumbs** for the mix,
plus 50g (1¾oz/1 cup)
for the coating (optional –
see Tip opposite)
1 lemon, cut in segments,
to serve
crème fraîche (optional)
sea salt and black pepper,
to taste

1 Put the spinach in a deep saucepan (with the water from washing still clinging to its leaves), add the coarse or kosher salt, cover and cook over a high heat for 4–5 minutes, stirring once or twice.

2 Once the spinach has wilted and is tender, drain it, rinse under cold water and, using your hands, squeeze out as much of the water as you can. Roughly chop.

3 Heat a non-stick frying pan over a low heat, add 2 tablespoons of the oil and the garlic, and cook for a minute or two until lightly golden. Add the chopped spinach and a pinch each of salt and pepper, then stir and sauté, uncovered, over a low to medium heat for 8–10 minutes. Remove from the heat and leave to cool.

4 Meanwhile, in a bowl, soak the soft bread crumbs in the milk, then break them into a pulp until all the liquid is mopped up. Gently beat the egg and extra yolk in a medium bowl and add it to the bread and milk mixture, then add the nutmeg, Parmesan, the 2 tablespoons of dried breadcrumbs and a pinch of salt. Add the spinach and mix well.

5 Use your hands to mould the mixture into round or oblong shapes, about 3cm (1¼in) long and 1cm (½in) thick.

6 Heat the remaining oil in a non-stick frying pan over a medium heat. Once hot, add the croquettes and shallow-fry for a couple of minutes on each side until golden.

7 Once cooked, gently lift out the croquettes and place them in a sieve over a plate or bowl to drain the oil. After a minute, transfer them to a plate lined with kitchen paper to absorb any excess oil.

8 Serve with a squeeze of lemon juice and a spoonful of crème fraîche on the side (if desired).

TIP: *If you like them crunchier, roll the shaped croquettes in the 50g (1¾oz/1 cup) dried panko breadcrumbs before frying.*

Spinaci con Pinoli e Passerine

SAUTÉED SPINACH WITH PINE NUTS AND RAISINS

*T*his gem of a dish is popular across the Sephardi culinary world, from Catalonia in Spain, to Greece, Turkey and, of course, Italy, where both Roman and Venetian Jews claim it as theirs. I grew up thinking it was classic Italian, unaware of its Jewish origin. I still make it regularly in London and it often graces dinner tables for Shabbat and festivals of Italian Jews.

The combination of pine nuts with raisins – in Roman slang passerine (from uva passa, meaning 'raisins') – gives the spinach a sweet twist. It is usually served as a side dish for fish or meat, but you can also turn it into a bruschetta topping for a starter. It keeps well for a few days in the fridge.

Preparation:
10 minutes
Cooking:
30 minutes

SERVES 4–6

Ingredients

1kg (2lb 4oz) fresh
  spinach, washed
1 teaspoon coarse
  or kosher salt
3–4 tablespoons extra
  virgin olive oil
1 onion, finely chopped
1½ tablespoons raisins
  or sultanas, soaked in
  lukewarm water for
  5 minutes
1½ tablespoons pine nuts
sea salt and black pepper,
  to taste

1 Put the spinach in a large, deep saucepan (with the water from washing still clinging to its leaves), add the coarse or kosher salt, cover and cook over a high heat for 4–5 minutes, stirring once or twice. You may need to do this in two batches, depending on the size of your pan.

2 Once the spinach has wilted and is tender, drain it, rinse under cold water and, using your hands, squeeze out most of the water – it's fine to leave a little moisture in the spinach for this recipe.

3 Meanwhile, heat the oil in a medium, non-stick frying pan over a low to medium heat, then add the onion with a pinch each of salt and pepper. Cook, stirring occasionally, for 5–7 minutes until softened and starting to turn golden.

4 Add the spinach and stir to blend it with the onion. Sauté, uncovered (with the heat still low to medium) for about 10 minutes, stirring occasionally.

5 Add the raisins or sultanas (drained of their soaking water), pine nuts and a pinch each of salt and pepper. Stir well and sauté over a medium heat for a final 5–7 minutes.

6 Remove from the heat and serve warm or at room temperature.

Crespelle al Forno con Ricotta e Spinaci

OVEN-BAKED RICOTTA AND SPINACH PANCAKES

Preparation: 20 minutes
Cooking: 45 minutes

MAKES 4–6 CRESPELLE

Ingredients
CRESPELLE BATTER
20g (¾oz/1½ tablespoons)
    butter, plus a little extra
    for cooking the crespelle
1 large egg
180ml (6fl oz/¾ cup) full-fat
    or semi-skimmed milk
100g (3½oz/⅔ cup)
    plain white flour

FILLING
200g (7oz) fresh
    spinach, washed
250g (9oz/1 cup plus 2
    tablespoons) ricotta cheese
4 tablespoons freshly grated
    Parmesan cheese
¼ teaspoon ground nutmeg
sea salt and black pepper,
    to taste

TO ASSEMBLE AND SERVE
50ml (1¾fl oz/3½ tablespoons)
    double cream
half quantity of Onion-based
    Tomato Sauce (see page 92)
a couple of fresh basil sprigs

You will also need a rectangular
oven dish, about 30 x 25cm
(12 x 10in).

C respelle *is the lovely Italian word for crêpes, or thin pancakes. They can be
savoury or sweet and the filling options are endless. Here, I propose a classic
ricotta and spinach filling, topped with tomato and a touch of cream. What's
not to like?! I make these for Shavuot, when it is the tradition to eat dairy food,
however, my family in London loves them so much that I end up making them
regularly. I like to play with different filling ingredients to go with ricotta, such as
mushrooms and thyme, butternut squash and sage, and roasted peppers – feel free
to experiment once you're familiar with the method.*

*This mixture will make four to six crespelle, depending on the size of your
frying pan and how thin you spread the mixture. The first crespella is rarely
perfect, so don't be hard on yourself – they will taste delicious no matter how
they look. A great bonus is that the recipe is easy to prepare in advance, either the
entire assembled dish ready to bake, or the individual components (the ricotta and
spinach mixture, the crespelle, the tomato sauce).*

1   First, make the crespelle batter. Melt the butter in a small saucepan or microwave,
    then set it aside to cool slightly. In a bowl, lightly beat the egg with a hand whisk,
    then add the milk and a pinch of salt and gradually mix in the flour, ensuring there
    are no lumps. Add the melted butter, mix again and cover with clingfilm. Put the
    crespelle batter in the fridge while you prepare the tomato sauce and the filling.

2　Make the onion-based tomato sauce (see page 92). For the filling, wilt the spinach (with the water from washing still clinging to its leaves) in a medium saucepan over a medium heat for 4–5 minutes, covered and stirring once or twice, then drain, cool it under cold running water and squeeze the water out. Roughly chop the spinach, then mix it in a bowl with the ricotta, 3 tablespoons of the grated cheese, the nutmeg, and a generous pinch of salt and a pinch of pepper. Set aside.

3　Cook the crespelle in a flat, non-stick crêpe pan or frying pan about 25cm (10in) in diameter. Melt a small knob of butter and add half a ladle of the chilled batter. Spread it thinly over the pan, cook it over a low to medium heat for about a minute until the base is firm, then flip it over and cook the other side until both sides are light golden. Remove and set aside on a plate. Continue with the rest of the mixture and make as

4　many crespelle as the mixture allows. Preheat the oven to 220°C (200°C fan/425°F/ gas mark 7).

5　Spread each crespella with 2 generous tablespoons of the ricotta and spinach mixture to create a thin layer – not too much filling or they will be too rich! – then fold it in half, and half again, to make a triangle shape. Keep any leftover spinach and ricotta mixture to garnish the top before baking it.

6　Mix half of the double cream with a couple of tablespoons of the tomato sauce, then spread it into the oven dish. Arrange the crespelle triangles on top as one layer – they may overlap slightly, that's fine. Top each crespella with the remaining tomato sauce, the remaining double cream and dollops of any leftover ricotta and spinach mixture. Sprinkle the remaining tablespoon of grated cheese on top and bake in the oven for 15–18 minutes. Remove from the oven, scatter the basil sprigs on top and serve hot or warm.

Frittata Dolce di Patate di Bisnonna Silvia

GREAT-GRANDMA SILVIA'S PASSOVER FRITTATA

*I*t is a tradition in my family to eat this frittata for lunch before Passover, in the hours before it starts, when neither bread nor the festival's unleavened bread (matzah) are permitted. Potatoes are a good substitute for both.

The recipe comes from my namesake, my maternal great-grandmother Silvia, whom I never had the pleasure to meet but my mother adored. My mum still makes this frittata every year, and until recently she used the same iron pan her Nonna used, until it proved too sticky to turn the frittata and she switched to a non-stick one! This dish is usually eaten warm or at room temperature.

Preparation:
15 minutes
Cooking:
45 minutes

SERVES 4–6

Ingredients
500g (1lb 2oz) King Edward, Maris Piper or Desirée potatoes, peeled and cut into large chunks
2 large eggs
3½ tablespoons granulated sugar
1½ teaspoons ground cinnamon
½ teaspoon sea salt
3 tablespoons extra virgin olive oil

TIP: *You can also bake the frittata in an oven-safe frying pan or oven dish in a preheated oven (about 220°C (200°C fan/425°F/ gas mark 7) for 15–20 minutes.*

1 Bring a large saucepan of salted water to the boil. When it starts boiling, add the potatoes. Cook over a low to medium heat, partially covered, for 15–20 minutes, until soft when pierced with a fork. Drain and leave to cool for 5 minutes before pressing the potatoes through a potato ricer or mashing them.

2 Beat the eggs with the sugar, cinnamon and sea salt in a bowl. Add the mashed potatoes and mix well. I enjoy doing this with my hands, but a large spoon or hand whisk would also work.

3 Heat the oil in a non-stick frying pan (about 30cm/12in) over a low heat and add the potato mixture in an even layer. Cover and cook for 12–15 minutes until the bottom is set. The frittata is ready for turning when the edges are firm and cooked. Check by gently shaking the pan. If the frittata slips away from the base, it is ready; if it is still wet, it needs to cook a little longer. Ease the sides up with a spatula to make sure it is fully free of the base.

4 To flip the frittata, remove the pan from the heat and, using a tea towel or oven gloves, take a flat lid or plate (large enough to cover the pan) and place it on top of the frying pan. Pressing the lid or plate firmly against the pan, quickly turn over the pan and let the frittata tip onto the plate or lid. Gently slide the frittata back into the pan, uncooked-side down. Cook for another 5–7 minutes until the bottom is set and just golden. Transfer to a serving platter and serve warm or at room temperature.

Frittata Dolce di Spinaci

SWEET SPINACH FRITTATA

Preparation:
15 minutes
Cooking:
40 minutes

SERVES 4–6

Ingredients

500g (1lb 2oz) fresh spinach, washed
1 teaspoon coarse or kosher salt
5 tablespoons extra virgin olive oil
1 red onion, finely chopped
3 large eggs
3 tablespoons raisins or sultanas, soaked in lukewarm water for 5 minutes
2 tablespoons pine nuts
1 tablespoon granulated sugar
2 tablespoons medium matzah meal or dried breadcrumbs (not for Passover)
icing sugar, for dusting (optional)
sea salt and black pepper, to taste

TIP: *You can also bake the frittata in an oven-safe frying pan or oven dish in a preheated oven (about 220°C (200°C fan/425°F/ gas mark 7) for 15–20 minutes.*

*T*his Venetian Jewish recipe is traditional for Passover. A savoury frittata with a sweet twist of sugar, it features pine nuts and raisins – the trademark marriage of Sephardi influence with Italian cooking.

I get a lot of satisfaction when I flip a frittata and it lands back in the pan correctly! You will need a non-stick frying pan to lift and turn it; one with a flat lid will make quick work of this. If you'd rather not risk flipping it, use an oven dish or oven-safe frying pan instead and bake it in the oven.

The frittata is usually served as a side dish or starter and is a great idea for brunch or a Passover picnic as it's good at room temperature. It keeps well in the fridge for a couple of days.

1 Put the spinach in a deep saucepan (with the water from washing still clinging to its leaves), add the coarse or kosher salt, cover and cook over a high heat for 4–5 minutes, stirring once or twice. Once the spinach has wilted and is tender, drain it, rinse under cold water and, using your hands, squeeze out most of the water – it's fine to leave a little moisture in the spinach for this recipe.

2 Heat 3 tablespoons of the oil in a medium, non-stick frying pan over a low heat, then add the onion, with a pinch each of salt and pepper. Cook, stirring occasionally, for 10 minutes until softened and starting to turn golden, then add the squeezed spinach, stir well and sauté for 8–10 minutes. Remove from the heat and leave to cool slightly.

3 Meanwhile, in a bowl, mix the eggs, raisins or sultanas (drained of their soaking water), pine nuts, sugar and a pinch each of salt and pepper. Add the matzah meal or breadcrumbs (if not Passover), along with the spinach mixture, and mix well.

4 Heat the remaining 2 tablespoons of oil in the same frying pan you used earlier, over a low heat. Add the egg and spinach mixture, cover and cook for about 10 minutes until the bottom is cooked and set. The frittata is ready for turning when the edges are firm and cooked. Check by

gently shaking the pan. If the frittata slips away from the base, it is ready; if it is still wet, it needs to cook a little longer. Ease the sides up with a spatula to make sure it is fully free of the base.

5 To flip the frittata, remove the pan from the heat and, using a tea towel or oven gloves, take a flat lid or plate (large enough to cover the pan) and place it on top of the frying pan. Pressing the lid or plate firmly against the pan, quickly turn over the pan and let the frittata tip onto the plate or lid. Gently slide the frittata back into the pan, uncooked-side down. Cook for another few minutes until the bottom is set and just golden.

6 Transfer to a serving platter and serve warm, or at room temperature, with a dusting of icing sugar on top, if you wish.

Peperoni Ripieni di Melanzane e Mozzarella

PEPPERS STUFFED WITH AUBERGINES AND MOZZARELLA

*T*his great versatile dish works equally well as a starter or main course. I like to mix the aubergines with a basil pesto and sometimes I mix a little crumbled feta with the mozzarella – even if that's breaking Italian culinary rules! The stuffed peppers keep well in the fridge for a few days, and also freeze well.

Preparation:
15 minutes
Cooking:
1 hour 20 minutes

SERVES 4–6

Ingredients

5 tablespoons extra virgin olive oil, plus 1–2 tablespoons for the pesto and extra for greasing
2–3 aubergines, about 700g (1lb 9oz), cut into 1cm (½in) cubes
20g (¾oz) fresh basil, leaves and stems
2 tablespoons freshly grated Parmesan cheese
4–5 peppers of any colour
about 150g (5½oz) mozzarella, sliced
sea salt and black pepper, to taste

TIP: *Be patient. Even if the aubergines seem dry, don't add more oil! When cooked, they will release most of the oil they have absorbed.*

1 Heat the 5 tablespoons of oil in a large, non-stick frying pan over a medium heat, add the cubed aubergines with a pinch each of salt and pepper and stir well.

2 Cook the aubergines for 10 minutes, partially covered and stirring occasionally, until tender, then remove the lid and cook for a further 10 minutes until lightly golden. Remove from the heat.

3 Meanwhile, using a stick blender, a food processor, or a mortar and pestle, mix the basil, Parmesan, a pinch of salt and just enough oil to bind the mixture (1–2 tablespoons). Add this to the cooked aubergines and stir well.

4 Preheat the oven to 200°C (180°C fan/400°F/gas mark 6). Cut the peppers in half or thirds lengthways, removing the seeds and white membranes, and rinse. Put them, hollow-side up, in a single layer in an oiled oven dish.

5 Fill each pepper piece with some of the aubergine and basil mixture, distributing it evenly among them. Bake in the oven for about 50 minutes, or until the peppers are tender and golden. Remove from the oven. You can prepare the dish up to this stage ahead of time and set it aside, then warm it through again before serving.

6 If serving immediately, place a mozzarella slice on top of each segment and then put the dish under a medium grill for a couple of minutes until the cheese melts. If you've prepared the dish ahead of time, put it back in a hot oven for about 10 minutes, then add the cheese and place under the grill for a final 2–3 minutes. Serve hot, ideally with bread.

AUBERGINES
'VILE' FOOD OF ITALIAN JEWS

Aubergines (*melanzana*) have a special place in Italian Jewish cooking. And yet, for hundreds of years, they were regarded with suspicion by a large part of the general Italian population. In northern and central regions particularly, many Italians looked down on them as food for the poor and associated them negatively with Jews.

The aubergine has its origins in India, and quickly became popular throughout Asia and what is now the Middle East. Known as *al-badingian*, it was widely used in North Africa, from where the Moors took it to Sicily, the busy Mediterranean trade hub, in the Middle Ages. Jews had lived in Sicily since Roman times and, like their fellow inhabitants on the cosmopolitan island, they learned to cook and appreciate aubergines throughout the centuries, as a much-loved staple food.

Further north, however, aubergines didn't become customary for another few centuries. It was mostly the Jews, expelled from Sicily and the south during the Spanish Inquisition which started in 1492, who took aubergines with them when they settled in the centre-north of Italy in the 16th and 17th centuries. Throughout the centuries that followed, aubergines remained on the culinary sidelines, in part due to their association with Jewish cooking, which was often looked down upon. Even the name *melanzana* conveys negative connotations, as it apparently derives from the words mela *insana* ('unhealthy apple' or 'apple of madness') and so reflects a host of pretexts for shunning them; unlike other fruit and vegetables, aubergines cannot be eaten raw, and they are part of the solanum/nightshade family which includes potatoes and tomatoes and the poisonous deadly nightshade.

The link between Jews and aubergines can be found in Italian food literature as early as the 1600s. 'Aubergines should be eaten only by people of lowly station or by Jews,' wrote Antonio Frugoli in *Pratica e Scalcaria* (*Practice and Banquet Organising*) in 1638. Another gastronome, Vincenzo Tanara, echoes the same association in *L'Economia del Cittadino in Villa* (*The Finances of a City Dweller*), in 1644: 'Aubergines are for the consumption of people from the countryside ... and especially for families, since they are a customary food of the Jews.' The twin negative connotations of Jews and this strange vegetable persisted, even into the 20th century. In *La Scienza in Cucina e l'Arte di Mangiar Bene* (*Science in the Kitchen and The Art of Eating Well*), which was initially self-published in 1891 but has endured as a classic and is still in print today, the famous Italian author Pellegrino Artusi noted that aubergines (he called them *petonciani*, as they were known in Tuscany at the time) had only recently become acceptable: 'Forty years ago [so the mid 1800s], one could hardly see aubergines and fennel in the Florentine markets; they were considered vile foods of the Jews.' He went on: '[this shows evidence] as in more important issues, of [Jews] having a better flair than Christians for discovering good things.'

Curiously, that last comment, about Jews having more refined taste than others, was removed from editions of the Artusi cookbook published during the Fascist period. It has only recently been reinstated in the text, and not yet in all editions.

Today, aubergines are sold widely across Italy and *melanzane alla parmigiana* can be found not only in the South but also on menus in restaurants from Florence to Milan. Neither the Italian in the street, nor most Italian Jews, would have any idea that aubergines were once particularly associated with Jews. I had no awareness of this historical context until I started my own research many years ago.

I only knew that at home we cooked and ate lots of aubergines prepared in every possible way. It was fascinating to discover that this was perhaps more than a simple love of the 'apple of madness', more likely a long and deep-rooted tradition.

There is possibly only one aubergine dish whose name reveals its connection to Jewish food: the Sicilian *caponata di melanzane alla Giudia* (Jewish-style aubergine caponata), a delicious sweet and sour dish of aubergines, tomatoes, olives, sugar and vinegar – I've included a recipe for it, along with *melanzane alla parmigiana*, *melanzane alla parmigiana di Nonna Bianca*, *pasta alla Norma* and *antipasti di verdure*... Yes, I love aubergines! For me it is the fact that aubergines have been cooked in so many different ways by Jews in Italy, century after century, that gives this vegetable its special place in Italian Jewish cuisine.

In central and northern Europe, however, aubergines have long remained somewhat of an anomaly.Only a few years ago, I went to buy vegetables for a cookery lesson from a greengrocer not far from my home in London. I often chatted with the English owner about his produce and on this occasion, I asked him if he salted aubergines before cooking them as sometimes it is done to remove their bitter taste. He looked at me somewhat suspiciously and said: 'I've never cooked an aubergine. Is it any good?' – as if it was a strange food with unknown powers. I was amused that he sold aubergines every day but had never tasted them, and immediately recalled the passage in Artusi's book; aubergines could still be considered a threatening food! When I told my London friends about this, they explained that aubergines had not been part of English food culture when they were growing up 30–40 years ago, but today they are available and widely appreciated throughout the UK. So, we have seen how, in our lifetime, the aubergine, like many other ingredients, has entered a country's culinary culture and is slowly becoming familiar, even if not everyone yet dares to cook or eat it!

HOW TO CHOOSE AUBERGINES

The most widely available variety of aubergine in Europe and North America is dark purple and shaped like a bell; all my recipes call for this type. In Sicily, large, round pale-purple and white aubergines are also common. These, too, are delicious and can be used for any of the recipes in this book.

When buying aubergines, make sure they are firm, their skin is shiny, and that the dark green stem is still green, not grey or drying. An aubergine that feels soft and spongy and whose surface is not glossy is no longer fresh. Aubergines are at their best in summer, their natural season.

SALTING OR DEGORGING

It used to be common to salt aubergines before cooking them to get rid of their bitter taste. This is not widely practised anymore, mostly because aubergines are not as bitter as they used to be, however, it is a useful and interesting method to learn if you are not familiar with it. The process is properly called 'degorging' and in this book I only suggest doing it for *melanzane alla parmigiana di Nonna Bianca*, mainly to pay respect to my late grandmother and her cooking – but also because she told me it was 'very important' to do so!

It's worth noting that after salting to remove any bitterness, aubergines also absorb less oil. The process results in aubergines that are less greasy and more crispy, particularly when deep-fried, and it gives them an intense and intriguingly smoky flavour. So, if you want to have a go, just follow these steps.

Slice the aubergines according to the recipe instructions and place them in a large colander in layers, with a tablespoon of coarse or kosher salt sprinkled over each layer. Weigh them down with something heavy (a bowl or saucepan full of cold water is ideal) and leave them for 30–40 minutes. When a dark liquid appears, rinse off the salt under cold running water – don't worry,

they won't reabsorb the liquid they've just lost. Pat the slices dry with kitchen paper and they're ready to cook.

COOKING

Aubergines can be griddled, roasted, steamed and shallow- or deep-fried. In fact, you can cook them using almost any method. They should never be eaten raw. Deep-frying is probably the oldest, and often thought to be the tastiest, way of cooking aubergines.

Whatever approach you choose, aubergines must always be thoroughly cooked to do them justice; undercooked, they will be hard and spongy, and also bitter and not easy to digest. They are, interestingly, the opposite nutritionally to most vegetables, as they retain most of their vitamins and nutrients regardless of the cooking method. When cooking aubergines, I always leave the skin on and love the way it changes colour in the pan as it is a great indicator of the aubergine's cooking stages: halfway through, the skin turns pale, then it goes dark again when the aubergine is cooked. I also always suggest cooking aubergines until their flesh turns golden, a final step which makes them look beautiful and adds an extra depth of flavour.

Contrary to common belief, aubergines don't need to be cooked in loads of oil, unless you are deep-frying them. Having such a porous texture, they take in oil very quickly and this might lead you to think you need to add more. Do resist the temptation to do so as they will release much of the oil they initially absorbed once they are cooked; if you wish, you can then discard this released oil, or use kitchen paper to absorb some of the excess.

Caponata di Melanzane alla Giudia

JEWISH-STYLE AUBERGINE CAPONATA

I so love this dish – it is always appreciated by family, friends and clients. Caponata is a traditional aubergine dish from Sicily which the Jews took north with them after their expulsion from the island following the arrival of the Spanish Inquisition there in 1492. It is a brilliant blend of aubergines, tomatoes and olives cooked with sugar and vinegar, which gives the dish a sweet and sour twist. There are many versions, some including pine nuts and raisins, others peppers; here, I share my favourite version. Deep-frying the aubergines gives them a real depth of flavour, but if you prefer a lighter version, go for shallow-frying. There are many ways to serve caponata: on its own, as a great accompaniment for meat, chicken or fish, as a tasty antipasto with buffalo mozzarella or burrata, or even spooned on top of toasted bread for bruschetta. It keeps well in the fridge for up to 5 days, and also freezes well.

Preparation: 15 minutes
Cooking: 1 hour

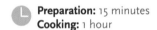

SERVES 4–6

Ingredients

3–4 tablespoons extra virgin olive oil
1 onion, finely chopped
1 carrot, peeled and finely chopped
1 celery stick, finely chopped
400g (14½oz) tin peeled plum tomatoes
40g (1½oz) pitted green olives
40g (1½oz) good-quality pitted black olives, such as Taggiasca or Kalamata
3 tablespoons capers
1 tablespoon granulated sugar
1 tablespoon white wine vinegar or cider vinegar
light olive oil or sunflower oil, for frying
2–3 aubergines, about 700–800g (1lb 9oz–1lb 12oz), cut into 1.5cm (5/8in) cubes
5–6 fresh basil sprigs
sea salt and black pepper, to taste

1 Heat the extra virgin olive oil in a shallow saucepan over a medium heat, then add the onion, carrot and celery and cook for 1 minute. Add 2–3 tablespoons of water (to help the *soffritto* soften) and cook for about 5 minutes, then, once the water has evaporated, cook for a further 5–7 minutes until the vegetables turn light golden.

2 Add the tomatoes (crushed by hand or with a fork as you add them), olives, capers, sugar, vinegar, a good pinch of salt and a pinch of pepper. Rinse out the tomato tin with a little water and add the liquid to the pan. Stir well and cook, partially covered, over a medium heat for about 30 minutes, stirring occasionally.

3 Meanwhile, fill a large, shallow, heavy-based saucepan with the light olive or sunflower oil to a depth of 4–5cm (1½–2in) and warm over a medium heat until sizzling hot, ideally to 180°C/ 350°F, then carefully add the cubed aubergines. You may need to fry the aubergine in batches. Fry over a high heat, turning the pieces occasionally, until golden. This may take 4–5 minutes per batch. Remove the aubergine pieces carefully with a slotted spoon and place in a sieve over a bowl or plate to drain the oil. Just before the next batch is ready, transfer them to a plate lined with kitchen paper to absorb any excess oil.

4 Add the fried aubergine pieces to the tomato sauce and cook, uncovered, for a final 10 minutes over a medium heat. Remove from the heat, season to taste, and tear in the basil sprigs. Serve warm or at room temperature and enjoy the tangy flavour!

TIP: *For speed, I usually pulse the onion, carrot and celery in a food processor until finely chopped, but this can also be done by hand.*

TIP: *As it cools down, quite a lot of oil may be released. I usually tilt the pan so the oil pools to one side, then suck it away with a baster, or remove it patiently with a spoon.*

Melanzane alla Parmigiana di Nonna Bianca

NONNA BIANCA'S AUBERGINE PARMIGIANA

Preparation:
1 hour if salting the aubergines,
15 minutes if not
Cooking:
30 minutes

SERVES 4–6

Ingredients

3–4 aubergines, about
1.2kg (2lb 12oz),
cut into round 5mm
(¼in)-thick slices
4–5 tablespoons coarse
or kosher salt, to salt
the aubergines
4 tablespoons extra virgin
olive oil
2 garlic cloves, crushed
600–700g (1lb 5oz–
1lb 9oz/2½–scant
3 cups) passata
5–6 fresh basil leaves
light olive oil or sunflower
oil, for deep-frying
100–120g (3½–4¼oz)
Parmesan cheese,
freshly grated
sea salt and black pepper,
to taste

You will also need a non-
reactive glass or ceramic
dish, about 15 x 20cm
(6 x 8in).

F or a large part of my childhood, I thought that Nonna Bianca's parmigiana, which is served cold, was the real recipe and the hot baked version (see page 230) was but a variation of it. Of course, it is the other way around, and I feel lucky that I had a grandma who was so creative in the kitchen that she could invent this marvellous dish. It was a cornerstone of her Roman Thursday lunches, and ideal for summer.

This dish may seem similar to its sister recipe melanzane alla parmigiana, but it results in quite a different eating experience. It is eaten cold, has no mozzarella, needs no baking and you salt the aubergines. It's another example of the amazing versatility of Italian Jewish cooking that creates its own classics by making just a few small adjustments.

Nonna Bianca always said it was important to salt (degorge) the aubergines so their bitter liquid would run off and they would absorb less oil. I follow her advice, not only out of respect for her, but also because I can see how a dish that is eaten cold would otherwise feel laden with oil. Degorging also makes the aubergines taste interestingly smoky. This recipe would be quicker without salting, but if you take your time and go through all the steps, you will probably never look back.

The finished dish keeps well for several days in the fridge.

1 Salt the aubergine slices according to the method on page 227.

2 For the tomato sauce, put the oil and garlic in a medium frying pan and cook over a low heat for a couple of minutes, then add the passata, a good pinch of salt and a pinch of pepper. Cook for 25–30 minutes, partially covered, stirring occasionally. Once cooked, tear in a couple of the basil, stir and set aside to cool. Keep the remaining basil leaves to garnish.

3 Before using the salted aubergines, rinse them gently under fresh running water and pat them dry with kitchen paper. Don't worry if the slices now look a little wrinkly, that's normal!

4   Ideally, heat the oil in a deep-fat fryer set to 180°C/350°F. Alternatively, fill a large, heavy-based, shallow saucepan with oil to a depth of 4–5cm (1½–2in) and warm over a medium heat until hot. (If you don't have a thermometer, test the oil is hot enough by dropping in a cube of bread: it should float rather than sink, and sizzle immediately on contact with the oil.)

5   Lower a few aubergine slices into the hot oil until you have a thick single layer with no overlaps. Deep-fry the aubergine slices for a couple of minutes on each side until golden. Remove the slices carefully with a slotted spoon and place in a sieve over a bowl or plate to drain the oil. Just before the next batch is ready, transfer them to a plate lined with kitchen paper to absorb any excess oil. Repeat the frying process with the remaining aubergine slices.

6   To assemble, spread a thin layer of the tomato sauce on the base of the glass/ceramic dish, then add a layer of aubergine slices, 4 tablespoons of tomato sauce divided into small portions over each slice and 2–3 tablespoons of grated Parmesan. Add another layer of aubergine slices and repeat until all the ingredients have been used. There should be enough for four layers, the final one being tomato sauce and Parmesan, with more basil leaves as garnish.

7   Leave to stand, covered with clingfilm, for a few hours, and serve at room temperature. It is even better refrigerated and eaten the following day. Simply remove from the fridge about 30 minutes beforehand, and serve it, ideally with bread.

8   My family likes to pass the dish around the table for everyone to take a portion from the layers, one by one. We don't cut right through – as you would do with a baked dish – perhaps because this way we can savour every delicious juicy bite…

Melanzane alla Parmigiana

AUBERGINE PARMIGIANA

*I*f I were marooned on a desert island with just one luxury, this would be it (oh – and carciofi alla Giudia!). It's a classic that never fails to win hearts. You may hesitate to deep fry anything these days, but I promise you this dish tastes far better and is really easy to prepare this way. Perhaps don't make it so often, but when you do, follow the time-honoured approach. If you must roast the aubergines instead, then brush the aubergine slices with oil and roast them at 240°C (220°C fan/475°F/gas mark 9) for 30 minutes until golden – the rest of the recipe is the same.

I don't usually salt the aubergines for this recipe, but degorging them does result in a less oily dish, so if you have the time and patience, give it a go (see page 227). I usually make large batches of this as it is an ideal dish to freeze. It also keeps well in the fridge for a few days. Enjoy!

Preparation:
15 minutes
Cooking: 1 hour

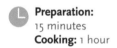

SERVES 4–6

Ingredients

3 tablespoons extra virgin olive oil
2 garlic cloves, thinly sliced
600–700g (1lb 5oz–1lb 9z /2½–scant 3 cups) passata
small bunch fresh basil leaves
light olive oil or sunflower oil, for deep-frying
3–4 aubergines, about 1.2kg (2lb 12oz), cut into round 5mm (¼in) slices
300g (10½oz) mozzarella, ideally the semi-hard cooking type, finely diced
80g (2¾oz) Parmesan cheese, freshly grated
sea salt and black pepper, to taste

You will also need a rectangular oven dish, about 30 x 25cm (12 x 10in).

1. First, prepare the tomato sauce. Put the oil and garlic in a medium frying pan and cook over a low heat for a couple of minutes, then add the passata and a pinch each of salt and pepper. Cook for 25–30 minutes, partially covered, stirring occasionally. Once cooked, tear in most of the basil leaves and stir. Once cooked, tear in a couple of basil leaves and stir.

2. While the tomato sauce is cooking, wash and slice the aubergines.

3. Ideally, heat the oil in a deep-fat fryer set to 180°C/350°F. Alternatively, fill a large, shallow, heavy-based saucepan with light olive or sunflower oil to a depth of 4–5cm (1½–2in) and warm over a medium heat until hot. (If you don't have a thermometer, test the oil is hot enough by dropping in a cube of bread: it should float rather than sink, and sizzle immediately on contact with the oil.) Lower a few aubergine slices into the hot oil until you have a thick single layer with no overlaps.

4. Deep-fry the aubergine slices for a couple of minutes on each side until golden. Lift out the slices carefully with a slotted spoon and place in a sieve over a plate lined with kitchen paper to drain the oil. Just before the next batch is ready, transfer them to a plate lined with kitchen paper to absorb any excess oil. Repeat the frying process with the remaining aubergine slices.

5. Preheat the oven to 200°C (180°C fan/400°F/gas mark 6).

6 To assemble, spread a thin layer of the tomato sauce on the base of the oven dish, then add a layer of aubergine slices. Top each slice with a teaspoon of the tomato sauce, and sprinkle almost half the mozzarella, Parmesan and basil over this layer and scatter with fresh basil.

7 Add a second layer of aubergine slices and repeat the toppings until you have built three layers of aubergine, tomato sauce and cheeses. You will use most of the cheeses on the first two layers – you only need a little for the top layer, which should have more tomato sauce and less cheese. Scatter more fresh basil on top.

8 Bake for 20–25 minutes, until just golden on top. Remove from the oven and let it rest for 5 minutes before serving. If it is too greasy, tilt the dish slightly and scoop up some of the excess oil – a baster will be handy for this.

9 Serve hot, ideally with bread.

Finocchi e Cipolle Gratinati

ROASTED FENNEL AND ONION

*D*id you know that there is a 'male' and 'female' fennel? The male is rounder, more tender and ideal for eating raw, and the female is more slender and a bit tougher, so is usually cooked. The smaller the fennel, the more tender, especially the female. For this recipe, look for long and ideally smallish female fennel, or round male ones cut into slices or quarters.

This is a great side dish to a fish meal, and also works well as part of mixed antipasti. I like to use sweet, colourful red onions, but white or brown onions work, too. You can cook a variety of vegetables in the same way: try raw courgettes, peppers or aubergines, arranged in a single layer on the oven tray and with the same ingredients as here.

This dish keeps well in the fridge for a few days.

Preparation:
15 minutes
Cooking:
1 hour

SERVES 4–6

Ingredients

3 fennel bulbs, washed and trimmed
3 large onions
about **½ teaspoon garlic granules or powder**
4–5 tablespoons dry breadcrumbs
small bunch of fresh flat-leaf parsley, finely chopped
extra virgin olive oil, for drizzling
sea salt and black pepper, to taste

You will also need two baking trays, lined with baking parchment.

1   Bring a large pan of salted water to the boil. Cut each fennel bulb lengthways into 2cm (3/4in) slices and boil for 10 minutes, then gently drain and transfer them to a plate lined with kitchen paper.

2   Meanwhile, peel the onions and cut them into round 2cm (¾in)-thick slices.

3   Preheat the oven to 200°C (180°C fan/400°F/gas mark 6).

4   Distribute the onion and fennel slices in a single layer on the lined baking trays – one tray with onions and the other tray with fennel, as their cooking times may vary slightly.

5   Sprinkle a little salt and pepper, and the garlic granules or powder, on top of the slices. Scatter with the breadcrumbs and parsley and, finally, drizzle some oil on top.

6   Roast in the oven for 45–50 minutes, until all the vegetables are softened and a deep golden colour.

7   Serve on a platter while warm, or at room temperature.

Insalata di Finocchio, Arance Rosse e Olive

FENNEL, BLOOD ORANGE AND OLIVE SALAD

*F*ennel, alongside aubergine, was considered a 'vile food of the Jews' in Italy for quite some time, as Pellegrino Artusi tells us in La Scienza in Cucina e l'Arte di Mangiar Bene (Science in the Kitchen and The Art of Eating Well) – read more about this on page 222. Now a popular ingredient across Italy, fennel is often used in salads. My favourite combination of flavours is fennel, oranges and olives and this dish exemplifies simplicity and seasonality at its best. I've always adored blood oranges, and their season is relatively short, from late winter to early spring. Fennel is also at its best in the winter months and the two blend really well together. The olives accentuate the contrast of sweet and savoury, and add texture and colour. I like to use dry black olives for this dish, as they have an intense flavour and vibrant colour, however, you can also use Taggiasche olives or Kalamata, or any other good-quality olives of your choice.

To accentuate the salty flavour contrast, I also sometimes put a couple of anchovy fillets on top – they do that in Sicily and it is delicious! My mum makes this salad regularly with any type of oranges, cut into segments and tossed in a bowl, whereas I like to slice them into rounds to show off the texture of the orange slice – feel free to get creative in your presentation.

Preparation:
10 minutes, plus
30 minutes chilling
(or start with chilled
oranges)

SERVES 4

Ingredients
8 blood oranges (or any
good-quality oranges)
1 small fennel bulb,
washed and trimmed
**handful of pitted dry
black olives**
**3–4 anchovy fillets
in oil** (optional)
**2–3 tablespoons
good-quality extra
virgin olive oil**
sea salt and black pepper,
to taste

1 Peel the oranges with a sharp knife, removing the pith as well as the skin. Cut each orange into 1cm (½in)-thick rounds and arrange them on individual starter plates or on a serving platter.

2 Thinly slice the fennel and scatter it on top of the orange slices.

3 Halve the olives and scatter them on top. If you are using anchovy fillets, scatter those on top as well.

4 Season the salad with a sprinkle each of salt and pepper, and dress with a generous drizzle of extra virgin olive oil.

5 Serve immediately or keep covered, refrigerated, for up to 3 hours before serving.

Antipasti di Verdure

VEGETABLE ANTIPASTI

Preparation:
15 minutes
Cooking:
1 hour

SERVES 4

Ingredients

4 mixed coloured peppers
good-quality extra virgin olive oil, for drizzling
3–4 garlic cloves, peeled then quartered
1 tablespoon capers
2–3 tablespoons finely chopped fresh flat-leaf parsley
balsamic vinegar, to taste (optional)
1 aubergine, cut into round 5mm (¼in)-thick slices
2 courgettes, cut in half crossways, then into 5mm (¼in)-thick strips
sea salt and black pepper, to taste

You will also need a griddle pan or barbecue and three shallow, non-reactive glass or ceramic containers or dishes, ideally with lids.

*I*t is rare that more than a couple of weeks go by without me making antipasti (starters) with peppers, aubergines and courgettes, or maybe just two, or even only one, of these vegetables.

Each variation is tasty and I like to play around, sometimes roasting, sometimes griddling them. In this recipe, I propose a combination of all three – roasted peppers with griddled courgettes and aubergines – but feel free to mix and match as you wish.

The vegetables go straight on the hot griddle and cook with no oil; only when removed from the griddle into a dish is the extra virgin olive oil added, together with some seasoning, bringing out the flavours and colours of the vegetable(s). For this recipe, it's worth using the best extra virgin olive oil you can find.

All three vegetables can easily be prepared ahead of time, and the peppers in particular gain in flavour from being left to marinate. All keep well for a few days in the fridge. These are not only good served as antipasti, but also on bread as bruschetta or as a side dish to a main course. If you have any leftover antipasti, they can be chopped and sautéed with any remaining oil and garlic and turned into a great next-day pasta sauce.

1 Preheat the oven to 240°C (220°C fan/475°F/gas mark 9).

2 Slice the tops off the peppers and remove the stems, seeds and white membranes. Rinse and put the whole peppers onto an oven tray lined with baking parchment. Roast in the oven for 35–40 minutes, without oil or seasoning, turning them once or twice. They are done when most of the skin is charred or deep golden, and the flesh softened. They may need a further 5–10 minutes roasting to reach this point. When cooked, remove from the oven, and place on a colander or sieve, cover it with cling film, and when cooled, remove the skins.

3 Cut the skinned peppers lengthways into 2cm (¾in)-thick strips and return them to the colander or sieve to drain for a further 10–15 minutes, then transfer them to a shallow, non-reactive container or dish and add 3–4 tablespoons of oil, a garlic clove quarter, all the capers, a good pinch of salt, a pinch of pepper and a sprinkle of the chopped parsley. Mix gently, cover and set aside. If you are a fan of balsamic vinegar, you can also add a dash.

4 Heat a griddle pan or barbecue to a high temperature for cooking the aubergines and courgettes. Once it is very hot, lay some of the aubergine slices on it, being careful that they don't overlap. Griddle for a couple of minutes on each side until golden, with black char marks on both sides. Transfer directly to one of the remaining two containers. While the aubergine is still warm, add a couple of garlic clove quarters, a pinch each of salt and pepper, a sprinkle of the parsley and a drizzle of oil. Do not mix them.

5 Griddle the remaining aubergine and place it over the previous layer in the container, adding more garlic, salt, pepper, parsley and oil. Repeat until all the aubergine is cooked.

6 Griddle the courgette strips in exactly the same way. Place these in the third container, layering with the flavourings as before.

7 When ready to serve, gently stir and arrange all the vegetables on a serving platter. I usually put the peppers in the middle of the platter and the aubergine and courgettes on the sides, as the peppers tend to release some natural juices.

TIP: *Any leftover oil from the containers in which the vegetables marinated is delicious used in a dressing or for cooking.*

Pomodori a Mezzo

ROASTED TOMATOES

*T his is a wonderful Roman Jewish dish and a classic of my mum's repertoire. Pomodori a
mezzo literally means 'halved tomatoes', which reflects its utter simplicity. The secret is to
use casalino – gorgeous 'bumpy' tomatoes from the Lazio region – and to let them roast for a long
time, until they are slightly charred, as that's when they reveal their full sweetness. Some people
add a little sugar – in our family we don't, but try both ways and see how you prefer it.*

*We often make this at the seaside, where my parents grow a plethora of casalino tomatoes.
If you can't get casalino, then try it with the best quality tomatoes you can find, be it vine,
plum, beef or cherry tomatoes. You can also change the recipe slightly by adding a handful of
breadcrumbs on top to make it 'au gratin' – just don't call them Pomodori a mezzo if you do, as my
mother would not approve!*

*These are best served at room temperature or cold. They are easy to prepare in advance, keep
well in the fridge and freeze well.*

Preparation:
10 minutes
Cooking:
1 hour, plus
minimum 10 minutes
resting time

SERVES 4

Ingredients

**1kg (2lb 4oz) casalino
tomatoes or other best
quality tomatoes**

**4–5 tablespoons extra
virgin olive oil**

2–3 garlic cloves, crushed
or finely chopped

**¼ teaspoon granulated
sugar** (optional)

**1 tablespoon finely
chopped fresh flat-leaf
parsley or oregano**
(optional)

sea salt and black pepper,
to taste

You will also need a
baking tray lined with
baking parchment.

1   Preheat the oven to 240°C (220°C fan/475°F/gas mark 9).

2   Wash the tomatoes, cut them in half lengthways and use your fingertips
or a teaspoon to gently scoop out most of the seeds, but don't worry if a
few remain.

> **TIP:** *To prevent the tomatoes from becoming soggy while cooking, and if
> you have the time, sprinkle the cut halves with a little salt and put them
> flat-side down in a colander or on a cooling rack for 10–15 minutes to drain
> any liquid.*

3   Lay the tomatoes cut side up on an oiled baking dish. You can pack them
closely together as they will shrink while roasting.

4   Sprinkle a little pepper, garlic, sugar, and parsley or oregano (if using)
over each tomato half. Finally, drizzle with plenty of olive oil.

5   Place the baking dish in the oven and roast at the initial high temperature
for 15 minutes, then reduce the oven temperature to 190°C (170°C
fan/375°F/gas mark 5) and roast for about 45 minutes, until the tomatoes
are tender and a deep red colour with golden edges.

6   Remove from the oven and leave to cool before serving at room
temperature or cold as a side dish, a starter, or on top of bread.

Broccoli Ripassati

SAUTÉED BROCCOLI WITH GARLIC AND CHILLI

*B*roccoli cooked this way is hard to beat and I genuinely make it every week. The secret is two-fold: anchovies and wine give the dish pungency without a fishy aftertaste, and sautéing the broccoli until slightly charred adds richness. It doesn't matter if the pieces break up a little, as these are often the tastiest bits.

I like to use both the head and stems, but this also works well with just the florets. I sometimes mix the broccoli with cauliflower florets, or use the long stemmed broccoli (not as widely available in Italy), which looks and tastes lovely and absorbs less oil.

Preparation:
10 minutes
Cooking:
25–30 minutes

SERVES 4

Ingredients
1 teaspoon coarse or kosher salt
800g (1lb 12oz) broccoli
5–6 tablespoons extra virgin olive oil
3–4 garlic cloves, crushed or sliced
2 anchovy fillets in oil (optional)
1 fresh mild red chilli, partially deseeded and thinly sliced, **or a pinch of dried red chilli flakes or chilli powder**
splash of white wine
sea salt and black pepper, to taste

1   Bring a large saucepan of water to the boil, then add the coarse or kosher salt. If you are using the whole broccoli, peel the tough outer part of the stem and cut the tender inner part into finger-size sticks. Divide the head into florets, and if they are big, half them.

2   When the water boils, add the broccoli. Bring it back to the boil, covered, then remove the lid and boil for 5–7 minutes. Drain and rinse the broccoli under cold running water. If you are using long-stem broccoli, 2–3 minutes boiling time is enough.

3   Put the oil, garlic, anchovy fillets (if using) and chilli in a large, non-stick frying pan and warm over a low heat for a couple of minutes until the anchovy fillets melt. Increase the heat to medium, add the wine and cook for a further minute.

4   Stir the broccoli into the pan, add a good pinch of salt and a pinch of pepper and sauté, uncovered, for 10–15 minutes over a medium heat until deep golden, stirring occasionally.

5   Serve warm or at room temperature.

Peperoni in Padella

SAUTÉED PEPPERS

Preparation: 10 minutes
Cooking: 1 hour

SERVES 4

Ingredients
3 tablespoons extra virgin olive oil
2–3 garlic cloves, crushed

2 anchovy fillets in oil
splash of white wine
5–6 peppers of different colours, stems, seeds and white membranes removed, and flesh cut into long 1cm (½in)-wide strips
sea salt and black pepper, to taste

T his is the most uncomplicated, delightful dish: peppers simply cooked in padella (in a frying pan). The longer you cook them, the more intense and sweet the flavour, so if you have the time, do go for the long, low and slow simmer. The anchovies are almost undetectable yet add a welcome depth to the dish. A similar lip-smacking version can also be made by roasting the peppers in the oven instead – at 200°C (425°F/gas Mark 7) fan for 45-50 minutes until deep golden.

For all their simplicity, these peppers, besides being a wonderful starter over bread or side dish, are incredibly useful – spread them on puff pastry for a tart, or cut them into smaller pieces and add them to hot pasta with a drizzle of extra virgin olive oil, or double cream for a decadent version. They keep in the fridge for a few days, and also freeze well.

1 Put the oil, garlic, anchovy fillets (if using) and a pinch each of salt and pepper in a large, non-stick frying pan and cook over a medium heat for a minute, then add the wine.

2 Once the wine has evaporated (this will take about a minute), add the peppers and a pinch each of salt and pepper, stir well and cook, covered, over a low heat for about 30 minutes, stirring occasionally. Once the peppers have softened, remove the lid, slightly increase the heat and cook for a further 15–20 minutes, stirring occasionally, until the peppers turn golden.

3 Serve warm or at room temperature, for a side dish, or as bruschetta on toasted bread.

Shakshuka

POACHED EGGS IN SPICY TOMATO AND PEPPER SAUCE

Preparation:
15 minutes
Cooking:
50–55 minutes

SERVES 2–4

Ingredients

3–4 tablespoons extra
  virgin olive oil
3–4 garlic cloves, crushed
2 teaspoons ground cumin
  or caraway (I prefer
  caraway but cumin is
  more commonly used),
  plus a little optional extra
  to serve
1 teaspoon paprika
1 teaspoon *felfel u ciuma*
  (see recipe on
  page 185) **or harissa**
3 red, yellow or orange
  peppers, stems, seeds
  and white membranes
  removed, and flesh
  cut into 5mm
  (¼in)-thick strips
2 ripe vine tomatoes,
  diced, **or 10 cherry
  tomatoes**, halved
  (optional)
500g (1lb 2oz/generous
  2 cups) passata
1 tablespoon finely
  chopped fresh
  flat-leaf parsley
4 eggs
sea salt and black pepper,
  to taste
bread, to serve

Many Middle Eastern cuisines claim this dish as their own. Libyan Jews are no exception, and those who migrated to Italy took it with them. Shakshuka has become popular all around the world and today, many of Rome's kosher restaurants have it on their menus, reflecting not just the city's large Libyan Jewish population but also the food of Israel, where shakshuka is very well known. The dish has definitely been part of my cooking repertoire since my student years living in Jerusalem.

There are endless ways of making this bold and flavoursome dish. This is my favourie. I like the egg yolks runny and the sauce quite dense. It takes a little practise to get the eggs just right, with the whites set and the yolks still liquid. You can make the dish more or less spicy, to taste. The sauce can easily be made in advance, making it ideal for brunch, when all you have to do is warm up the sauce and cook the eggs in it.

1. Put the oil, garlic, 1 teaspoon of cumin or caraway, paprika and *felfel u ciuma* or harissa in a large, non-stick frying pan, stir and cook over a low heat for 5 minutes.

2. Add the peppers to the pan, stir, add a pinch each of salt and pepper and cook, covered, over a low to medium heat for about 15 minutes until the peppers start to soften.

3. Add the tomatoes (if using) and toss for 5 minutes, then add the passata with a pinch each of salt and pepper and cook for another 20–25 minutes, covered, and stirring occasionally. Remove the lid, add half the parsley, and the second teaspoon of cumin or caraway, stir and taste for seasoning. You can cook the eggs in the mixture straight away, or make the recipe up to this point and keep the sauce ready in the fridge for up to 3 days.

4. When you're ready to cook the eggs, make four dips in the sauce (reheating the sauce if you've made it ahead of time) with the back of a spoon and gently break an egg into each one. Cover and simmer over a low to medium heat for 6–8 minutes until the egg whites are just set but the yolks are still runny.

5. Sprinkle with the remaining parsley and, if you like, a little more cumin or caraway. Serve hot, ideally with bread.

Merduma

SPICY GARLICKY TOMATO DIP

*T*his was the first Libyan Jewish dish I came across and I have enjoyed it in so many different Tripolitanian friends' homes, from Italy to Israel. I absolutely love it. Merduma is spicy and garlicky and is traditionally served at room temperature as a starter with crostini or bread, as a spread in sandwiches, or as a side dish. I also like it with couscous, and although it's unorthodox, as a good Italian I sometimes turn leftovers into a pasta sauce, like a rich arrabbiata. You can make it more or less spicy to your liking and use a green or red chilli – green chillies are usually hotter and sharper, but heat levels largely depend on the variety you use.

I barely stir it and I like to add the oil only at the end, as Liliana Jaffe, the mother of my dear friend Patty from Milan, once showed me. The dip keeps well in the fridge for up to a week, and it also freezes well.

Preparation:
10 minutes
Cooking:
2 hours

SERVES 4-6

Ingredients

2 yellow peppers,
stems, seeds and white membranes removed, and flesh cut into 5mm (¼in)-thick strips
6 whole garlic cloves, peeled
1 fresh green or red chilli,
roughly chopped, with seeds included (or removed if prefer less spicy)
2 x 400g (14½oz) tins peeled plum tomatoes
80ml (2¾fl oz/⅓ cup) extra virgin olive oil
½ teaspoon white wine or cider vinegar
sea salt and black pepper,
to taste

1 Put the peppers, garlic, chilli, tomatoes (crushed by hand or with a fork as you add them) and a pinch of sea salt into a medium casserole or non-stick saucepan over a medium heat. Rinse out the tomato tins with a little water and add the liquid to the pan. Stir well, cover and bring to the boil, then reduce the heat to low and simmer (still covered) for almost 2 hours – yes, that long!

2 Stir only once or twice during the cooking time. The consistency should be quite dense when it is done, and the garlic cloves will melt into the sauce. Stir in the oil and cook, uncovered, over a medium heat for a final 5 minutes. Taste and season with a pinch of salt and pepper if needed and, finally, add the vinegar, stir and remove from the heat. Serve at room temperature.

3 Serve at room temperature with bread, or warm with couscous.

Zucca Barucca Disfatta

'BLESSED' PUMPKIN MASH

*P*umpkin has played a big part in Italian Jewish cooking since it was brought into Italy from the New World by successive waves of migrant Jews. In Veneto today there is a funny bumpy-looking variety called Zucca Barucca (ideal for this recipe), whose name is worth explaining. In Venetian dialect this sounds like the Italian word for verruca, a bumpy and annoying wart on the skin. The same word is baruca in Latin. But another, more kindly explanation comes from the popularity of pumpkin among Jews in Venice and the north of Italy, for whom it was and still is a classic High Holy Day ingredient. Its elevated status for these festivals was inspired by the Hebrew word baruch, meaning 'blessed', and changed to sound Italian. I like to think both explanations carry some truth, reflecting the continuous interchange between Jews and Italians over the centuries.

The most famous recipes for mashed pumpkin are zucca disfatta, or zucca sfranta which both mean 'mashed' or 'crushed'. They are particularly popular in Ferrara and Venice for the meal that breaks the Yom Kippur fast. This version is sweetened with sugar and cinnamon. There is also a lovely version which uses cedro lemon instead (known as etrog in Hebrew), a tart citrus fruit which appears at the time of the autumn Sukkot festival. If you can find it, I recommend it, or you can use candied citrus peel or lemon zest instead.

Preparation:
10 minutes
Cooking:
30 minutes

SERVES 4–6

Ingredients

3–4 tablespoons extra virgin olive oil
1 onion, finely chopped
700g (1lb 9oz) peeled and deseeded pumpkin or butternut squash, thinly sliced (no need to be precise – it will be mashed)
1 teaspoon granulated sugar (optional)
½ teaspoon ground cinnamon
1 tablespoon chopped fresh flat-leaf parsley
sea salt and black pepper, to taste

1 Heat the oil in a large, non-stick frying pan over a low heat, then add the onion, a pinch of salt and a couple of tablespoons of water. Leave to cook, uncovered, for 5 minutes, until the onion is softened and the water has evaporated.

2 Rinse and drain the slices of pumpkin or squash, as they cook better when slightly wet. Add it to the onion with a good pinch of salt and a pinch of pepper. Cover and cook for 20–30 minutes, stirring occasionally until completely soft and easy to crush with a fork.

3 I love this dish just as it is, naturally sweet, but to make it sweeter, as the Ferrarese do, add the sugar to the crushed pumpkin/squash and cook for a further couple of minutes.

4 Transfer into a small, heatproof serving bowl, sprinkle the cinnamon and parsley on top and serve warm or at room temperature.

5 For the version using cedro lemon, finely chop the peel of the fresh fruit, or a mix of candied citrus peel or grated lemon zest, and add to the pumpkin/squash halfway through cooking (step 2). There is no need for further sweetening with sugar or cinnamon in this version.

CHAPTER 4

Desserts, Sweets and Bakes

This section could easily be a book in itself. All the Jewish festivals – and there are many! – are, of course, celebrated by eating something sweet and often symbolic, for instance, apples and honey for Rosh Hashanah, fried food for Hanukkah, fruit and food from the new harvest for Sukkot and Tu BiShvat, *orecchie di Amman* for Purim, and cheesy desserts for Shavuot. There is also a wide variety of unleavened and flourless desserts made for Passover, which has by far the widest portfolio of desserts, mainly because the festival lasts for eight days. There are then weekly desserts for Shabbat, which are often *parve* (dairy-free), made to accompany a meat meal usually eaten on the Friday night, or Saturday Shabbat meals.

With so many desserts to choose from I found it difficult to select only a few. Eventually, I decided to order them by Jewish holiday and include only those recipes which hold special significance for me and my family. This might be because they have been made for years in my family – desserts like *pizzarelle col miele*, *torta di carote e mandorle*, *torta Susanna*, *orecchie di Amman*, *cassola*, *ginetti* and *pizza ebraica* – or because they are part of my more recent repertoire of recipes I've created that have an Italian flavour to them, such as *cheesecake di Amaretti*, *mascarpone e lamponi*, *sufganiot con la Nutella* o *crema di marroni*, and *torta d'uva*. Or, they might just be recipes that I find fascinating and unusual, like *sfratti di Pitigliano*, the Libyan Jewish *sefra* or a green *torta di spinaci e mandorle*. Then there are the sweets and bakes – not strictly desserts, but recipes like *charoset*, a sweet symbolic paste made to form part of the Seder plate at Passover. There are also two wonderful challah recipes (as this could not be a book on Jewish food without at least one challah in it!)

Finally, there are other recipes with a soul, Jewish or not, which have a story and a raison d'être. These include my late Nonna Bianca's lemon sponge, *Teresa's pangiallo*, *salame di cioccolata*, the unmissable *tiramisù*, and my sister Simona's *mousse al cioccolato*.

You don't need a special occasion to eat something sweet! A last note about sugar: old and classic Italian recipes were and often still are made using white granulated sugar (I know, not the healthiest!) and to stay loyal to this, all the recipes in this chapter suggest granulated or caster sugar. If you want to use a brown sugar, however, please do so. I often use demerara or golden sugar instead of white sugar, in the same quantities.

Challah di Loredana

LOREDANA'S CHALLAH BREAD

*T*his great challah bread is my sister-in-law's recipe. Loredana keeps alive the Roman Jewish tradition of baking a simple unsweetened loaf for Shabbat, rather than the more widely known brioche-type braided challah. She often brings it to my parents' house for Friday night dinner and I enjoy baking it in London from time to time. The crust is crispy and the inner crumb soft and white. The barley malt extract gives the bread a subtle kick.

If you can plan ahead, let the challah dough rise slowly for at least 12 hours (and up to 24 hours), covered, in the fridge. The slow proving will give you a tastier bread with a more complex flavour.

Loredana usually uses only fresh yeast and makes twice the quantities below to make two very large loaves of bread. I make it using half her quantities, which is enough for our family (the quantities below make one large or two medium loaves), but feel free to increase quantities to your needs. I enjoy the leftovers as regular bread, or toasted and made into bruschetta with garlic lightly brushed over, salt and good-quality extra virgin olive oil. It also freezes well.

Preparation:
3½–4 hours, including rising and proving time
Baking:
30–45 minutes

MAKES 2 MEDIUM LOAVES OR 1 LARGE LOAF

Ingredients
280ml (9½fl oz/scant 1¼ cups) warm water
1 heaped teaspoon barley malt extract
12g (⅖oz) fresh yeast or 1 x 7g (¼oz) sachet of fast-action dried yeast
500g (1lb 2oz/4 cups) strong or very strong white bread flour, plus extra for dusting
3 tablespoons extra virgin olive oil, plus extra for greasing
1 teaspoon fine sea salt coarse or kosher salt, to sprinkle on top (optional)

1 **If using fresh yeast:** Pour the warm water into a large bowl and add the malt extract, then crumble in the fresh yeast and add 2 tablespoons of the flour. Gently stir to combine all the ingredients and to break up any lumps, then cover with a clean tea towel or clingfilm and leave to rest for 20–30 minutes at room temperature, until the mixture becomes foamy. Add the remaining flour, the oil and the salt and work the dough thoroughly until it is smooth and elastic. You can do this by hand or using a stand mixer fitted with a dough hook: by hand (on a lightly floured surface) it will take about 10 minutes, and in the stand mixer about 5–7 minutes at medium speed.

2 **If using fast-action dried yeast:** Mix the flour with all the other ingredients (except the coarse or kosher salt) in the bowl of a stand mixer fitted with the dough hook, then mix at medium speed for 5–7 minutes until the dough is smooth and elastic. Alternatively, mix the ingredients in a large bowl, then knead by hand (on a lightly floured surface) for a good 10 minutes until you achieve the same consistency.

3 Put the smooth dough into a large, lightly oiled bowl, cover with a clean tea towel or clingfilm and leave it to rise in a warm place (I use the oven set at 30°C/86°F) until roughly doubled in size (this will take about 2 hours). Alternatively, to slow-rise your dough in the fridge instead, place it in a lightly oiled bowl, cover tightly with clingfilm, leave at room temperature for about 1 hour, then place in the fridge for 12–24 hours. Then remove it and leave it at room temperature for another 30–40 minutes.

sticking. Put on a large baking tray lined with baking parchment or a silicone mat – leaving plenty of space between the loaves if making two – cover the loaf/loaves again and leave to proof for another hour at room temperature or in a warm place (such as the oven set at 30°C/85°F) until about doubled in size. If proving the challah in the oven, remove it before preheating the oven to 200°C (180°C fan/400°F/gas mark 6). Close any open windows and avoid draughts at this stage as the dough is a little delicate and can easily deflate.

5 To keep the bread moist while baking, put a small ovenproof saucepan or small oven dish, half-filled with lukewarm water, at the bottom of the oven when you add the bread.

6 Just before baking, score the top of the loaf/loaves by cutting a couple of shallow slashes in the dough with a sharp blade. If you like your bread to have a salty crust (as I do), sprinkle a little water and coarse or kosher salt on top of the dough – the water helps the salt to stick. Otherwise, leave it plain.

7 Bake for 30–35 minutes if making two medium loaves, or 45–50 minutes for a large loaf, until the bread is golden and crispy on the outside and sounds hollow when tapped on the top and bottom.

> **TIP:** *For an extra-crispy crust, transfer the baked bread from the tray to the oven rack and keep it inside the turned-off oven with the door ajar for 5 minutes.*

8 Remove the bread from the oven and transfer immediately onto a cooling rack so the bottom stays crisp.

4 Once you are ready to shape the loaves, remove the dough from the bowl. If you want to make two medium loaves, halve the dough and form into two round or oval loaves, or work the whole amount for a large loaf. To form the loaf/loaves, fold the dough a couple of times, then shape it gently into a loaf/loaves, making sure the folds are at the bottom/base and that the top is smooth – you may need to dust your hands or the surface lightly with flour to prevent them

Challah di Silvia

SILVIA'S CHALLAH BREAD

Preparation:
4 hours,
including rising
and proving time
Baking:
30-40 minutes

**MAKES 2
MEDIUM
LOAVES OR
1 LARGE LOAF**

Ingredients
2 large eggs
180ml (6fl oz/¾ cup)
   warm water
40g (1½oz/generous
   3 tablespoons) caster
   or granulated sugar
12g (⅖oz) fresh yeast or
   1 x 7g (¼oz) sachet of
   fast-action dried yeast
500g (1lb 2oz/4 cups)
   strong or very strong
   white bread flour, plus
   extra for dusting
50ml (1¾fl oz/3½
   tablespoons) sunflower
   or light olive oil, plus
   extra for greasing
8g (½oz/1¼ teaspoon) fine
   sea salt
sesame, poppy, sunflower
   or pumpkin seeds, to
   garnish (or a mixture)

I started making braided challah only a few years ago. I tried many different versions and eventually settled on a recipe of my own, based on various challot that I've tasted over time and those that some of my lovely Ashkenazi students and clients have shared with me (for which I am grateful). It undoubtedly has an Ashkenazi influence as the dough is slightly sweet, and it contains eggs and oil, making it more brioche-like than the bread loaf I grew up with for Shabbat. Perhaps this is what happens to an Italian Jew who left Italy 30 years ago!

Nowadays, I bake challah every Friday – alternating between this and Loredana's challah (see page 254) – and I love making it now more than ever. If you have the time, I invite you to bake your own, as it is highly rewarding and utterly delicious.

What is perhaps unusual about this challah is the number of times it rises. I allow it two rises: after the first rise I pound it down, then I leave it to rise a second time, letting it double in size, then braiding it and leaving it to proof before baking. The resulting bread is fluffy and light. If you prefer your challah denser, cut down the rises to just one. The quantities here make one large or two medium loaves. I make it with fresh or fast-action dried yeast, and both work very well.

1 Lightly beat the eggs in a bowl and keep 2 tablespoonfuls aside to brush over the challah before baking.

2 **If using fresh yeast:** Pour the warm water into the bowl of a stand mixer and add 1 teaspoon of sugar, crumble in the fresh yeast and add 2 tablespoons of the flour. Gently stir to combine all the ingredients and to break up any lumps. Cover with a clean tea towel or clingfilm and leave to rest for 20–30 minutes at room temperature, until the mixture becomes foamy. Add the remaining flour, the eggs, the remaining sugar, the oil and salt and work the dough thoroughly until it is smooth and elastic. You can do this by hand or using a stand mixer fitted with a dough hook: by hand (on a lightly floured surface) it will take about 10 minutes, and in the stand mixer about 5–6 minutes at medium speed.

3 **If using fast-action dried yeast:** Mix the flour with all the other ingredients (except the seeds and the two tablespoonfuls of beaten eggs) in a mixer fitted with the dough hook, then mix at medium speed for 5–6 minutes

until the dough is smooth and elastic (this method is so easy!). Alternatively, mix the ingredients in a large bowl, then knead by hand (on a lightly floured surface) for a good 10 minutes until you achieve the same consistency.

4 Put the smooth dough into a large, lightly oiled bowl, cover with clingfilm and leave it to rise in a warm place (I use the oven set at 30°C/86°F) for 1½ hours, or until roughly one-and-a-half times its size.

5 When it has risen, pound down the dough with a few punches – inside the bowl – then fold it and shape it into a round loaf/ball. Cover it and leave it in a warm place to rise for the second time, for 1½ hours, until doubled in size (I usually put it back in the oven now switched off).

6 Remove the dough from the bowl. If you want to make two medium loaves, halve the dough, or work the whole amount for a large loaf. On a lightly floured surface, gently braid the dough. At this stage, I tend to work the dough as little and as gently as possible, as I believe that the texture of the baked challah is lighter the less you handle it. I like to opt for a simple three-strand braid: divide the dough (for

one loaf or for each of the two loaves) into three and – gently – fold and roll it into three long strands. Braid each loaf and fold the ends under to form a neat round edge. If you like a denser challah, or prefer more strands, work your dough and roll away! You can make braids using four or six strands, or as many strands as you want.

7 Put the challah onto a baking tray lined with baking parchment or a silicone mat – leaving plenty of space between the loaves if making two, or using two trays – cover gently with clingfilm and leave to proof at room temperature or in a warm place for another 30–40 minutes.

8 If proving the challah in the oven, remove it before preheating the oven to 220°C (200°C fan/425°F/gas mark 7). Just before baking, brush the challah with the reserved beaten egg. Finally, add the seed topping of your choice, e.g. sesame, poppy, sunflower or pumpkin seeds, or a mixture.

9 Bake for 10 minutes, then reduce the temperature to 200°C (180°C fan/400°F/gas mark 6) and bake for a further 15–20 minutes for two medium loaves, or 25–30 minutes if baking one large one, until the bread is deep golden and sounds hollow when tapped on the top and bottom. If you are baking two loaves on separate trays, check them three-quarters of the way through the baking time to make sure they're baking evenly, swapping the trays around if necessary.

10 Remove the baked challah bread from the oven and transfer immediately onto a cooling rack so the bottom does not become soggy.

CHALLAH

A lthough my mother is the most wonderful cook, she is no bread baker, and neither were my two grandmothers. Our Friday night *hamotzi* (blessing on bread) has always been made with shop-bought bread, either over two *rosette* or *ciriole*, or *pane casareccio*, a type of sourdough. Times have changed, but this is not unusual among Italian Jews. Most of my friends across Italy grew up in the same way, be it in Milan, Venice, Florence, Bologna or Livorno, all making *hamotzi* on Shabbat and High Holidays over ordinary shop-bought bread. And the few friends and family who baked their own challah made it as a regular unsweetened round loaf – a particular long-lasting tradition of Rome.

This is because the challah we often refer to nowadays, i.e. a soft, sweet, braided brioche-type bread, is Ashkenazi in origin. It first appeared in the Middle Ages in the south of Germany, and soon spread to the Jewish communities of eastern Europe and around the world, wherever Ashkenazi Jews settled. As Rome had little or no Ashkenazi influence, and the rest of Italy had only some in the north, the braided challah took a good few hundred years to arrive, but it is now firmly established, even in Roman culinary culture, thanks to globalisation.

The name challah comes from the Biblical Hebrew for a 'portion', relating to the piece of risen bread dough that Jews used as an offering to the priests (the Cohanim) of the Temple in Jerusalem. Making challah is a mitzvah, or divine commandment, that is specifically reserved for women (although it isn't exclusive, so both men and women can make challah).

Two challah are used to say the *hamotzi* on Shabbat and High Holidays, representing the double portion of manna sent from God on a Friday or before the Festivals (so they would rest on Shabbat and High Holidays) to feed the Israelites in the desert during their 40 years' exodus from Egypt. To this day, the manna is symbolised by the addition of various seeds that can be sprinkled on top.

The two challah loaves are kept covered by a cloth during the kiddush (blessing on the wine), then uncovered and lifted to recite the *hamotzi*. After this, they are divided, dipped in salt (to remember the salt that was scattered on the Temple for sacrifices – salt is an essential element in Judaism, representing the eternal covenant with

God) and distributed around the table. Some people cut the bread, some tear it, some pass it around and others throw it to each person, the customs vary! The blessings are traditionally said by a man, usually the head of the family. In my household, we all sing the kiddush together to the Roman Jewish tune, and my young daughters, filled with pride, recite the *hamotzi* before a grown-up. After the *hamotzi* over the challah, the family meal of Shabbat or High Holiday is served.

After the destruction of the Second Temple in 70CE, it became the custom to 'take challah', meaning to tear off a small piece of bread dough and burn it while reciting a blessing, in order to remember the destruction of the Temple. If you wish to say this blessing, first look up the one you need to say, as there are slightly different endings according to Ashkenazi and Sephardi customs. If you want to 'take challa' and say the blessing, you need a minimum amount of flour and that specific amount may vary slightly according to different rabbi's opinions or among different Halachic communities. As I use a relatively small amount of flour in both recipes in this book, the blessing is not needed.

Italian Jews are not the only ones who have been buying and baking other kinds of bread for Shabbat – not just braided challah bread. Throughout the Middle East, Sephardi and Mizrahi (Oriental) Jews, and further afield, Yemenite and Ethiopian Jews, made their festive bread in many different ways, and in various shapes: flat, round or braided, or even in the shape of a hand, bird and many more. When communal ovens were part of everyday life, each housewife would make her own bread for Shabbat in a slightly different shape so she would recognise it when it came out of the oven. Spices and other ingredients in or on top of the bread

(such as caraway, saffron, sesame and dried fruit) were, and still are, popular.

It is traditional among Italian and Sephardi-Mizrachi Jews (but not Ashkenazi Jews) to make 'water challa' – a loaf made without any egg or sugar. They consider this the only bread with which you can say the *hamotzi* blessing. For them, anything containing egg and sugar would require the sweet-bake blessing, which is different. Although the dough remains unsweetend, many Italian and Sephardi-Mizrachi Jews have now adopted the traditional braided shape for its symbolism: the braid symbolises the 'bridal wreath' which represents Shabbat, unity and love. Braids can be made with three, four or six strands, each with its own meaning, and the symbolism carries on in the number of 'humps', with 12 humps representing the 12 tribes of Israel.

For Rosh Hashanah, it is a widespread tradition to make challah in a round, spiral shape, to symbolise the continuity of life, and it is dipped in honey, instead of salt, wishing for a sweet year ahead.

Nowadays, beautiful braided and round challot can be bought worldwide, and across Jewish communities in Italy they are available both in bakeries and in some kosher butchers. Whatever the shape, with or without eggs and sugar, it seems to be playing a more central role in Jewish lives than ever before, and more people are baking their own.

For me, so long as we remember our roots, we are aware and respectful of the different customs, and continue old traditions as well as introducing new ones, deliciously soft challah is welcome. It is, in my view, the single most successful food from the Ashkenazi repertoire that the wider world welcomed, appreciated and adopted – me included!

Torta di Nonna Bianca

NONNA BIANCA'S LEMON SPONGE

⏱ **Preparation:**
15 minutes
Baking:
40–45 minutes

🍴 **SERVES 8–10**

Ingredients

unsalted butter or dairy-free spread, for greasing
plain white flour or fine dry breadcrumbs, for coating
3 large eggs
300g (10½oz/1½ cups) granulated or caster sugar
200ml (7fl oz/scant 1 cup) sunflower or light olive oil
grated zest and juice of 2 unwaxed lemons (you need 100ml/3½fl oz/scant ½ cup juice)
100ml (3½fl oz/scant ½ cup) full-fat or semi-skimmed milk or dry white wine
pinch of sea salt
300g (10½oz/scant 2½ cups) plain white flour (ideally 'oo' type)
1 x 16g (½oz) sachet of *lievito per dolci* (or 1½ tablespoons baking powder, plus 1 teaspoon vanilla extract)
icing sugar, to decorate

You will also need a 23cm (9in) round springform baking tin, the base lined with baking parchment (with the parchment held in place using the springform seal).

*T*his lemon sponge is such a classic in our family and is probably the cake I bake most frequently. My late paternal grandmother, Nonna Bianca, used to bake it weekly, either for her fabulous Thursday lunches at her home or for Friday night Shabbat dinner when she came over to ours. We ate it as dessert after a meal and loved any leftovers for breakfast, but if you are in the UK, then it is perfect for tea! Everyone in my family still makes this cake, and all slightly differently, as its beauty is its versatility. In fact, it can be made parve (dairy-free), too, using white wine instead of milk.

The rule of thumb, whatever adaptations you might like to try, is to use equal proportions of oil and liquid. For the liquid, I use lemon juice and milk (for the dairy one) or white wine (for the parve version), however, this can be replaced by all milk, all wine or even brewed coffee, drinking chocolate or freshly squeezed orange juice. Try different versions and see which one you prefer. Happy baking!

This is perfect served with Nonna Bianca's strawberries (see page 264).

1   Preheat the oven to 200°C (180°C fan/400°F/gas mark 6).

2   Spread a thin coating of butter or dairy-free spread all over the lined base and around the sides of the tin. Sprinkle flour or breadcrumbs into the tin and tilt the tin, moving it around to create a thin, even coating (it will stick to the fat), then tip the tin upside down to remove any excess. Set aside.

3   Beat the eggs with the caster or granulated sugar for a couple of minutes until pale and creamy, either in a bowl with an electric hand mixer or in the bowl of a stand mixer fitted with the paddle attachment.

4   Add the oil, lemon zest and juice, the milk or wine and salt to the bowl or mixer and mix well (adding the vanilla extract too, if using baking powder, not *lievito per dolci*), then sift in the flour and *lievito per dolci* (or baking powder) and mix again on low speed until just combined.

> **TIP:** *It's important not to overwork the mixture at this point, as you want the sponge to remain light and airy. Just mix it enough to blend in the flour.*

5 Transfer the cake mixture into the prepared baking tin and bake in the oven for 40–45 minutes, or until a skewer or cake tester inserted into the centre of the cake comes out clean and dry. If it comes out wet, put the cake back in the oven and bake for another 5 minutes, then check again.

6 Remove the cake from the oven and leave it to cool in the tin on a cooling rack for at least 30 minutes, then remove it from the tin. Serve the cake warm or at room temperature, sifting icing sugar on top before serving. It keeps well, in an airtight container, at room temperature for 3–4 days.

Fragole al Limone

NONNA BIANCA'S STRAWBERRIES
WITH LEMON AND SUGAR

*N*onna Bianca used to make these strawberries as soon as they were in season in spring. Instead of rinsing them in water, she used white wine, to give extra flavour; I do the same today. She served them alongside her lemon sponge (see page 262) – a perfect combination.

Strawberries with lemon and sugar is a popular dessert throughout Italy, and such a simple and refreshing way to end a meal.

Preparation:
10 minutes, plus
1–5 hours marinating
in the fridge

SERVES 4–6

Ingredients
800g (1lb 12oz) fresh
   strawberries
200ml (7fl oz/scant 1 cup)
   dry white wine (optional)
2–3 tablespoons
   granulated sugar,
   to taste
juice of 2 lemons

TIP: *Feel free to add other types of fresh berries to the strawberries, such as blueberries and blackberries (raspberries are a little too fragile for this dish). Sometimes, although it's not very Italian, I also like to add a few fresh mint leaves, either whole (for a delicate flavour) or finely chopped (for a more intense hit of mint).*

1 Hull the strawberries and remove any white tips. If rinsing them with wine, pour the wine into a shallow bowl and rinse the strawberries in batches. Throw the wine away afterwards. If you'd rather not use wine, simply rinse the strawberries under cold running water.

2 Cut the strawberries into roughly 1cm (½in) pieces and place them in a non-reactive bowl with the sugar and lemon juice.

3 Stir well, taste and add more lemon juice or sugar to taste, bearing in mind that the flavour will deepen as the strawberries marinate. Place in the fridge, covered, for 1 hour, or up to 5 hours, stirring a couple of times.

4 Remove from the fridge 10 minutes before serving. Serve the strawberries on their own or with Nonna Bianca's Lemon Sponge (see page 262).

Torta di Miele, Caffè e Noci

HONEY, COFFEE AND WALNUT CAKE

Preparation:
15 minutes
Baking:
50 minutes–1 hour

SERVES 8–10

Ingredients
2 large eggs
200g (7oz/1 cup) caster
  or granulated sugar
200ml (7fl oz/scant 1 cup)
  runny honey
120ml (4fl oz/½ cup)
  sunflower oil
120ml (4fl oz/½ cup)
  brewed espresso or
  strong coffee (warm or
  cold – just not hot)
2 tablespoons rum,
  Cognac or Cointreau
grated zest of 2 oranges
½ teaspoon ground
  cinnamon
pinch of sea salt
300g (10½oz/scant
  2½ cups) plain white
  flour (ideally '00' type)
1 x 16g (½oz) sachet of
  lievito per dolci
  (or 1½ tablespoons
  baking powder, plus 1
  teaspoon vanilla extract)
300g (10½oz/3 cups)
  walnuts, roughly chopped

You will also need a 23cm
(9in) round springform
baking tin, the base lined
with baking parchment
(with the parchment
held in place using the
springform seal).

*H*oney cake is traditional for Rosh Hashanah, the Jewish New Year, as honey is a symbol of a sweet start to the new year. It is traditionally an Ashkenazi cake, though variations also have their place in Italian Jewish cooking. This recipe is inspired by various honey cakes that I've tasted over the years, with my personal twist of added coffee and orange zest which lift and lighten it, as I often find honey cakes too heavy! I roughly chop the walnuts as I prefer them chunky, but you can finely chop them or use ground walnuts, if you prefer.

1 Preheat the oven to 200°C (180°C fan/400°F/gas mark 6). Beat the eggs with the sugar for a couple of minutes until pale and creamy, either in a bowl with an electric hand mixer or in the bowl of a stand mixer fitted with the paddle attachment, then add the honey, oil, coffee, alcohol of your choice, orange zest, cinnamon and salt. Beat well again for another minute, adding the vanilla extract, too (if using baking powder, not *lievito per dolci*).

2 Sift in the flour and *lievito per dolci* (or baking powder) and mix again on low speed until just combined. Finally, add the walnuts and fold them in gently with a large metal spoon or spatula.

> **TIP:** *If you like, you can reserve a few walnuts, whole or chopped, to scatter on top of the cake mixture for decoration just before putting it in the oven.*

3 Transfer the cake mixture into the prepared baking tin and scatter any remaining walnuts evenly on top (if using). Bake in the oven for 50 minutes–1 hour, or until a skewer or cake tester inserted into the centre of the cake comes out dry. If it comes out wet, put the cake back in the oven and bake for another 5 minutes, then check again.

4 Remove the cake from the oven and leave it to cool in the tin on a cooling rack for at least 30 minutes, then remove it from the tin. Serve the cake warm or at room temperature. It keeps well, in an airtight container, at room temperature for 3–4 days.

Torta di Mele

APPLE CAKE

*P*erfect for celebrating Rosh Hashanah with plenty of apples, as tradition demands, this cake is moist and uncomplicated. You can make it parve using dairy-free spread instead of butter, however, the dairy version wins on the taste stakes in my opinion! I like to use sweet red apples, but you can substitute your favourite kind. When you pour the cake mixture into the baking tin, you may think there isn't enough, and that it's quite thin. Don't worry: once you add both layers of apples and bake it, it will rise to just the right height. If you like deeper cakes, then use a smaller 20cm (8in) cake tin instead and bake it for 10–15 minutes longer.

Preparation:
20 minutes
Baking:
45–50 minutes

SERVES 8–10

Ingredients
100g (3½oz) unsalted butter or dairy-free spread, plus extra for greasing
4 red eating apples (about 450g/1lb), such as Pink Lady, Royal Gala or Braeburn, washed
2 large eggs
200g (7oz/1 cup) caster or granulated sugar
1 teaspoon ground cinnamon
pinch of sea salt
200g (7oz/1¼ cups) plain white flour (ideally '00' type)
1 tablespoon *lievito per dolci* (or 1 tablespoon baking powder, plus ½ teaspoon vanilla extract)
1 tablespoon brown sugar (any kind), for the glaze

You will also need a 23cm (9in) round springform baking tin, the base lined with baking parchment (with the parchment held in place using the springform seal).

1 Preheat the oven to 200°C (180°C fan/400°F/gas mark 6).

2 Grease the base and sides of the tin with a little butter or dairy-free spread.

3 Core the apples, then cut them into moon-shaped slices (about 5mm/¼in thick), leaving the peel on.

4 Gently whisk the eggs with the sugar in a large bowl using a hand whisk until just combined.

5 Melt the butter or dairy-free spread in a small saucepan or in the microwave, then stir it into the eggs and sugar mixture (adding the vanilla extract, too, if using baking powder, not *lievito per dolci*). Add the cinnamon and salt, then sift in the flour and *lievito per dolci* (or baking powder). Mix gently with a hand whisk or large metal spoon until just combined, being careful not to overwork the mixture.

6 Pour the cake mixture into the prepared tin, then place half of the apple slices on top in a single layer. Push the slices down into the cake mixture so they are entirely covered, then place a second layer of apple slices on top, pushing them just very slightly into the mixture – they should be clearly visible on the surface. You may want to create a nice design or pattern of your choice with the second layer of apples – I like circles – as they will be visible once the cake is baked.

> **TIP:** If you are in a hurry, you can mix the apple slices into the cake mixture and pour it all into the tin at once, keeping back a handful of apple slices to scatter on the top before baking, as they do look nice and golden once baked.

7 Sprinkle the brown sugar evenly on top to give a caramelised glaze, then bake in the oven for 45–50 minutes, or until a skewer or cake tester inserted into the centre of the cake comes out dry. If it comes out wet, put the cake back in the oven and bake for another 5 minutes, then check again.

8 Remove the cake from the oven and leave it to cool in the tin on a cooling rack for at least 30 minutes, then remove it from the tin. Serve the cake warm or at room temperature. It keeps well, covered, at room temperature for a couple of days, or for 3–4 days in the fridge.

Sfratti di Pitigliano

WALNUT AND HONEY PASTRY CIGARS

Preparation:
40 minutes, plus
minimum 20
minutes resting time
for the pastry
Baking:
12–15 minutes

MAKES
30–35 CIGARS

Ingredients
PASTRY
250–300g (9–10½oz/
scant 1⅔–scant 2½
cups) plain white flour
(ideally '00' type), plus
extra for dusting
¼ teaspoon *lievito per
dolci* or baking powder
pinch of sea salt
100g (3½oz/½ cup)
caster sugar
grated zest of
1 unwaxed lemon
100g (3½oz) unsalted butter
or dairy-free spread, chilled
1 large egg

FILLING
150g (5½oz/generous
⅓ cup) runny honey
½ teaspoon ground
cinnamon
pinch of ground cloves
pinch of ground black
pepper
grated zest of 1 orange
150g (5½oz/1½ cups)
walnuts, finely chopped
sunflower oil, for greasing
your hands

You will also need a large
baking tray, lined with
baking parchment.

*T*hese sweets originate from the charming Tuscan town of
Pitigliano, once home of a thriving Jewish community. Edda Servi
Machlin, author of the wonderful collection of books The Classic
Cuisine of the Italian Jews grew up there. The name Sfratti comes from
the Italian sfratto, meaning eviction, as they are made in the shape
of the sticks used to bang on Jewish homes in the 17th century, when
the Grand Duke Cosimo II de' Medici issued an eviction decree to force
Jews to leave their homes in the small towns of Sorano, Sovana and
Pitigliano and move to the ghetto of Pitigliano. The sweets, with their
honey, spice and nut filling, are traditional for Rosh Hashanah. Non-
Jewish residents of Pitigliano have also adopted them over time, often
unaware of their Jewish origin, and they have become a classic and
popular local Christmas dessert now that Jews no longer live there.

For these sfratti, I have tried numerous types of pastry (which is
traditionally parve (dairy-free) over the years and settled in the end
with a type of shortcrust that works well and can be made parve or
with butter. I make my sfratti cigar-sized, although the classic sfratti
are larger and longer, like a stick. They require time and patience, but
are fun to make and delicious to eat, so are definitely worth a try.
They will make a unique addition to your Rosh Hashanah dessert
table and are perfect with a cup of tea.

1 First, prepare the pastry, either by hand in a mixing bowl or using a
food processor. Combine 250g (9oz/scant 1⅔ cups) of the flour with
the *lievieto per dolci* or baking powder, the salt, sugar and lemon
zest, then add the butter or dairy-free spread and egg and mix until
it becomes malleable but is not sticky; if necessary, add a little more
flour. Wrap the pastry in clingfilm and put it in the fridge to firm up
for at least 20 minutes.

2 Meanwhile, prepare the filling. Place the honey in a small (ideally non-
stick) saucepan. Bring to the boil, then reduce the heat and simmer,
stirring occasionally, for 10–15 minutes, until it slightly darkens and
forms a ribbon when it falls from a lifted wooden spoon. Add the
cinnamon, cloves, pepper and orange zest and stir, then add the
walnuts and simmer for a further 5 minutes, stirring occasionally.

3 Remove from the heat and pour the honey mixture onto the lined baking

Pitigliano, Tuscany

parchment dusted with flour so it doesn't stick, then removing the top sheet of parchment.

7 Cut one of the rolled-out sheets of pastry in half lengthways to create two rectangles approximately 10 x 30cm (4 x 12in) – the edges may be roundish rather than straight lines but that's fine – you don't need to cut or discard any pastry. Place the honey-nut ropes lengthways onto each rectangle (2 or 3 ropes for each rectangle, laid end to end).

tray. Leave to cool for about 10 minutes until lukewarm. Don't leave it to cool down too much or it will become difficult to work with.

4 Now the fun starts! You're going to create long, thin ropes from the filling. As it is sticky, oil your hands with a little sunflower oil. Take a tablespoon at a time of the lukewarm honey-nut filling and gently but swiftly roll it between the palms of your hands to create a rope approximately 1cm (½in) thick and 10cm (4in) long. Place each rope back on the baking tray until ready to use. You'll make 10–12 ropes.

5 Preheat the oven to 190°C (170°C fan/375°F/gas mark 5).

6 Remove the pastry from the fridge, unwrap it, cut it in half and dust each portion with flour. On a clean work surface, roll out each portion into a thin rectangular shape, about 20 x 60cm (8 x 24in) and about 3mm (1/8in) thick. You can make this easier by rolling out each portion of the pastry between two sheets of baking

8 Gently brush the edges of each rectangle with water, roll up the pastry to enclose the filling and press to seal. Cut into 5–6cm (2–2½in)-long cigars, or longer if you prefer to make sticks. Repeat the same process with the remaining pastry and filling, to make a total of 30–35 cigars, using any leftover pastry to make small shortcrust biscuits.

9 Place the cigars back on the baking tray, leaving 1–2cm (½–¾in) between them (spread across two trays if needed). Bake in the oven for 12–15 minutes until just golden. Some of the filling may melt and leak out of the cigars. Simply discard it once it has cooled down (or save it as a treat – I usually collect it in a little bowl and nibble on it later!).

10 Remove from the oven, leave to cool a little on the baking tray before moving them to a cooling rack, and enjoy them warm or at room temperature. Once completely cool, store any remaining cigars in an airtight cookie jar or container. They will last for several days.

Sefra

AROMATIC SEMOLINA BAKE WITH A HONEY GLAZE

Preparation:
10 minutes
Baking:
40 minutes

**MAKES 25–30
DIAMONDS**

Ingredients
300g (10½oz/generous
    1½ cups) fine or
    medium semolina
1 large egg
100g (3½oz/½ cup) caster
    or granulated sugar
100g (3½oz/⅔ cup) raisins
    or sultanas
100ml (3½fl oz/scant
    ½ cup) water
100ml (3½fl oz/scant
    ½ cup) sunflower oil
1 tablespoon baking powder
pinch of sea salt
25–30 whole almonds
    (blanched or skin-on,
    or a mix of both)
1 tablespoon
    sesame seeds

HONEY GLAZE
150ml (5fl oz/⅔ cup) water
150g (5½oz/generous
    ⅔ cup) caster or
    granulated sugar
3 tablespoons runny honey
grated zest of 1 orange
    or 1 tablespoon orange
    blossom water (optional)

You will also need a
30 x 25cm (12 x 10in)
rectangular oven dish,
base and sides lined with
baking parchment.

*T*his wonderful dessert is another 'gift' from the Libyan Jewish community. It is a rich and aromatic semolina bake containing raisins and almonds, with a scrumptious honey glaze. Most people also add orange blossom water and a few prefer rose water – my favourite version is the orange blossom water one (suggested here). It is traditionally cut into squares or diamond-shape portions and served with tea, mostly for Rosh Hashana and Yom Kippur, but I make it all year round!

This recipe was inspired by Rossella Tammam Vaturi, the aunt of my dear friend Sharon Tammam, who was born in Rome to Libyan parents who arrived in 1967. Rossella wrote a fantastic book, La Cucina Ebraica Tripolina, and this recipe is from there; I've just added raisins and a handful of sesame seeds and almonds on top, a variation which I found in other versions of sefra and which, in my opinion, works very well, adding interest to both the flavour and appearance.

1. Preheat the oven to 180°C (160°C fan/350°F/gas mark 4).

2. Scatter the semolina onto a baking tray and toast it in the oven for 10 minutes, shaking the tray halfway through.

3. Meanwhile, mix the egg, sugar, raisins or sultanas, water, oil, baking powder and salt in a large bowl. Once the semolina is toasted, add it to the mixture while it's still warm.

4. Transfer the mixture to the lined oven dish, spread it out evenly, and score shallow 2.5cm (1in) squares or diamond shapes in the mixture with a knife. Put an almond in the middle of each segment and scatter over the sesame seeds.

TIP: *As the mixture is soft, the square/diamond shapes won't hold firm at this stage, but don't worry, the scoring of the shapes is to help you create an initial design/pattern and arrange the almonds. You will mark out the squares or diamonds again halfway through baking, giving them a firmer shape, and then cut them again at the end, once the dessert has cooled down.*

5 Bake in the oven for 10 minutes, then remove it from the oven and mark out the shapes again with a knife. This time, the lines should stay. Put it back in the oven and bake for another 15–20 minutes.

6 Meanwhile, prepare the honey glaze. Heat the water and sugar gently, ideally in a non-stick saucepan, and simmer for 8–10 minutes, stirring occasionally. Add the honey and the orange zest or orange blossom water (or both!), if using, to the sugar syrup and bring to a gentle boil for 1 minute.

7 As soon as the bake comes out of the oven, gently pour the glaze evenly all over the top, so the almonds and sesame seeds shine. Place it back in the oven for a couple of minutes (the oven should still be on). Take it out again and ideally leave it to cool completely in the dish for at least 1 hour to avoid crumbling, before cutting out the squares or diamonds.

8 Arrange the squares or diamonds piled up on a serving dish and enjoy with tea! They keep for up to 3–4 days, covered, in an airtight container at room temperature or longer in the fridge.

Torta d'Uva

GRAPE CAKE

 Preparation:
15 minutes
Baking:
1 hour

 **SERVES 8–10**

Ingredients

unsalted butter or dairy-free spread,
  for greasing
**190g (6¾oz/scant 1¼ cups) plain
  white flour** (ideally 'oo' type), plus
  extra for dusting the tin and grapes
3 large eggs
**190g (6¾oz/scant 1 cup) caster
  or granulated sugar**
190ml (7fl oz/scant 1 cup) sunflower oil
grated zest of 1 unwaxed lemon
pinch of sea salt
1 x 16g (½oz) sachet of *lievito per dolci*
  (or 1½ tablespoons baking powder,
  plus 1 teaspoon vanilla extract)
**600g (1lb 5oz) white, black or red
  seedless grapes**, rinsed and halved

You will also need a 23cm (9in)
round springform baking tin, the
base lined with baking parchment
(with the parchment held in place
using the springform seal).

*T*his cake is moist, light and parve (dairy-free). It is perfect
for celebrating both the Festivals of Sukkot and Tu
BiShvat, when we give thanks for the harvest, and grapes are
a popular symbolic fruit.

I like to use large grapes and to mix white, red or black, but
you can stick to one type, if you prefer, and don't worry, fresh
grapes won't make the cake mixture too wet; it will taste and
look beautiful. The same recipe also works with many other
types of fruit, so feel free to replace the grapes with plums,
peaches or eating apples, depending on the season. Just bear
in mind that the cooking time with the different fruits may
vary as some are wetter than others.

This cake will become a great asset in your repertoire of
parve desserts.

1 Preheat the oven to 190°C (170°C fan/375°F/gas mark 5).

2 Spread a thin coating of butter or dairy-free spread all over the
lined base and around the sides of the tin. Sprinkle flour into
the tin and tilt the tin, moving it around to create a thin, even
coating (it will stick to the fat), then tip the tin upside down to
remove any excess. Set aside.

3 Beat the eggs with the sugar for a couple of minutes until pale
and creamy, either in a bowl with an electric hand mixer or in
the bowl of a stand mixer fitted with the paddle attachment.

4 Add the oil, lemon zest and salt and mix well for 2 minutes
(adding the vanilla extract, too, if using baking powder, not
lievito per dolci), then sift in the flour and *lievito per dolci*
(or baking powder) and mix again on low speed for another
2 minutes.

> **TIP:** It is important to work the mixture a lot for this cake, so
> keep on beating even after you think it's enough!

5 Lightly toss two thirds of the halved grapes in a little flour and gently fold them into the cake mix. The flour will stop the grapes from sinking to the bottom of the cake once cooked.

6 Transfer the cake mixture into the prepared baking tin and scatter the remaining grape halves evenly on top, cut-side up. Bake in the oven for about 1 hour, or until a skewer or cake tester inserted into the centre of the cake comes out clean and dry. If it comes out wet, put the cake back in the oven and bake for another 5 minutes, then check again.

7 Remove the cake from the oven and leave it to cool in the tin on a cooling rack for at least 30 minutes, then remove it from the tin.

8 Serve at room temperature. This cake keeps well, covered, at room temperature for a couple of days, or for 3–4 days in the fridge.

Sufganiot con la Nutella o Crema di Marroni

SILVIA'S DOUGHNUTS WITH NUTELLA OR CHESTNUT CREAM

🕐 **Preparation:**
40–45 minutes, plus 2½ hours rising and proving
Frying:
10 minutes

🍴 **MAKES 18–20 SMALL OR 10–12 LARGE DOUGHNUTS**

Ingredients
12g (⅖oz) fresh yeast or 1 x 7g (¼oz) sachet of fast-action dried yeast
150ml (5fl oz/2 ⁄ 3 cup) lukewarm milk
1 tablespoon caster or granulated sugar
30g (1oz) unsalted butter, at room temperature
2 egg yolks
1 teaspoon vanilla extract
300g (10½oz/scant 2½ cups) plain white flour, or strong bread flour, plus extra for dusting
7g (¼oz) sea salt
about 500ml (17fl oz/generous 2 cups) sunflower, groundnut or corn oil, for greasing and frying
about 200g (7oz) Nutella or chestnut spread (crème de marrons), to fill
marron glacé, icing sugar or golden caster sugar, to decorate

You will also need two large baking trays, lined with baking parchment.

*D*uring Hanukkah, the Jewish Festival of Lights, which falls around December every year and lasts for eight days, it is traditional to eat fried food to remember the miracle of oil (see page 52).

Sufganiot (filled doughnuts in Hebrew) are particularly popular in Israel, though they are also enjoyed by Jewish communities all over the world, including Italy. For me, they are the perfect example of how a new food gets introduced into a country – today through globalisation and the internet rather than immigration, as in the past – enriching its local culinary traditions, and how locals then slightly adapt it to suit their taste buds.

In the last few decades, Italian Jews quickly adopted sufganiot, probably because they remind us of bomboloni, or bombe as we call them in Rome, which are Italian fried doughnuts generally filled with jam or custard. They are available alongside cornetti (croissants) in most coffee bars, where Italians have them with a cappuccino as part of their quick breakfast, standing at the counter. Some bakeries also bake them through the night, making them popular venues for midnight feasts. I had many bomboloni in my late teens years!

For my own version, I've adapted the traditional dough, so they are less doughy than the Israeli sufganiot and lighter than the Italian bomboloni, and the filling, too; as a good Italian, I like to replace the typical filling of jam with Nutella or chestnut spread, another one of my favourite flavours from childhood. I also like to make mini ones (this recipe can be adapted to make either mini or large doughnuts).

These sufganiot are best made and eaten straight away, otherwise they harden a little, but their fleeting freshness shouldn't be a problem as they usually disappear pretty fast.

1 First, make the dough. If using fresh yeast, crumble the yeast into the milk and sugar in the bowl of a stand mixer, cover and leave in a warm place for about 20 minutes until there is a layer of foam on top. Add the butter, egg yolks and vanilla extract to the mixer bowl and mix with the dough hook attachment at medium speed for a couple of minutes. Add half the flour and work the dough for a minute, then slowly add the remaining flour, together with the salt. Continue working the dough at medium speed for about 5 minutes until well combined, smooth and elastic. If you wish, you can make the dough by hand after the yeast, milk and sugar have been left to stand for 20 minutes. Knead the dough in a bowl or floured surface for about 10 minutes until smooth and elastic. If using fast-action dried yeast, simply mix all the ingredients at once in the bowl of a stand mixer and work the dough for about 5 minutes.

2 Place the dough in a large, oiled bowl, cover with clingfilm and leave to rise in a warm place (I use the oven set at 30°C/86°F) until roughly doubled in size (this will take about 2 hours).

3 Transfer the dough to a floured surface. You can make the doughnut shapes in two ways. One way is to divide the dough into as many large or small doughnuts that you want to make. Gently roll each portion of dough into a ball and fold any loose ends at the bottom. Alternatively, gently roll out the whole dough to create a round or oval shape about 1.5–2cm (5/8–¾in) thick, then, using a 4–5cm (1½–2in) or 7–8cm (2¾–3¼in) round cookie cutter, or the rim of a glass, cut the dough into discs. A 4–5cm (1½–2in) cutter should make 18–20 discs, or a 7–8cm (2¾–3¼in) cutter should make 10–12 larger discs.

4 Carefully place the balls or discs of dough onto the lined baking trays, leaving some space between them as they will expand and you don't want them to stick together. Cover loosely with clingfilm and leave for about an hour in a warm place (I usually put it back in the oven now switched off) until roughly double in size.

5 Heat the oil in a large, heavy-based frying pan with high sides or a heavy-based, deep, wide saucepan to 170°C/335°F (if you don't have a thermometer, test the oil is hot enough by dropping in a cube of bread: it should float rather than sink, and sizzle immediately on contact with the oil). Once the oil is hot, gently fry a few doughnuts at a time for about 1 minute on each side (they cook quite quickly), turning them over halfway through with a slotted metal spoon, until evenly pale golden. If you are frying larger doughnuts, they may need 10–15 seconds extra frying

time. Remove them from the oil with a slotted spoon and place them in a sieve to drain the oil. After a minute, transfer them to a plate lined with kitchen paper to help absorb any excess oil. Repeat with the remaining doughnuts.

6 If you are using Nutella, slightly warm it in the microwave or a small saucepan over a low heat until lukewarm, so that it is easier to pipe into the doughnuts. There's no need to warm up the chestnut spread.

> **TIP:** *You can fill some doughnuts with Nutella and some with chestnut spread, so you have a variety of flavours, if you wish.*

7 Make a small hole in the top or on the side of each doughnut and fill it with Nutella or chestnut spread, either using a pastry syringe or a piping bag fitted with a medium nozzle (or you can simply snip a 1cm/½in-hole in the corner of a disposable bag after filling it). Alternatively, just make an unorthodox hole in the top and spoon in the filling!

8 Top with marron glacé pieces, or sprinkle with icing sugar or golden caster sugar, and serve warm or at room temperature. Happy Hanukkah!

Precipizi-Struffoli

MINI DOUGHNUT PYRAMID

Preparation:
15 minutes, plus
15–20 minutes
resting time
Cooking:
10 minutes

**MAKES ONE
20 X 15CM
(8 X 6IN)
PYRAMID
WITH ABOUT
70–80 MINI
DOUGHNUTS**

Ingredients

180–200g (6–7oz/scant
1½ cups–scant
1⅔ cups) plain white
flour (ideally '00' type)
2 tablespoons caster sugar
grated zest of 2 unwaxed
lemons
1 large egg, plus 1 yolk
20g (¾oz) unsalted butter,
melted
50g (1¾oz/3 tablespoons)
ricotta
pinch of sea salt
about 300ml (10fl oz/
1¼ cups) sunflower,
groundnut or corn oil,
for frying
80g (2¾oz/6 tablespoons)
runny honey
grated zest of 1 unwaxed
orange
1 teaspoon orange
blossom water
icing sugar, for dusting

You will also need a tray
or large plate, lined with
baking parchment.

Precipizi is an old Jewish dessert made for Hanukkah that hails from Ancona, in Central Italy. The original recipe is parve (dairy-free) and made with lots of mini fried doughnuts arranged in a single layer, glued together in a rectangular shape with honey, left to dry, then cut and served in chunks. After trying to make the dessert this way a few times but never quite succeeding, I created my own version, as I love the idea and the name of this dessert. I make mine with doughnuts that are olive-sized or slightly bigger, and I like to serve them piled up as a pyramid instead, similar to struffoli, a Christmas dessert from Naples (after all, Hanukkah often falls around Christmastime). This dessert is a beautiful marriage of old Jewish traditions presented in a modern way and inspired by traditional Italian cooking.

I add ricotta and lemon to the dough for extra flavour, as well as to combine the tradition of frying on Hanukkah with the one of eating dairy (see page 52). This dessert can be eaten straight away, shortly after coating it with honey, or left to set, for a few hours, for the doughnuts to absorb the honey. Both versions are delicious!

1 First, make the dough. Mix 180g (6oz/scant 1½ cups) of the flour with the sugar, lemon zest, egg, egg yolk, melted butter, ricotta and salt in a bowl with your hands (or in the bowl of a stand mixer fitted with the dough hook) for 4–5 minutes until the dough is soft and malleable but not sticky. If it's too sticky, simply add more of the flour. Wrap the dough in clingfilm and put it in the fridge to rest for 15–20 minutes.

2 Remove the dough from the fridge and divide it into four pieces. Gently roll each piece on a clean surface or on a pastry mat, using your fingers to form a thin rope about 20–25cm (8–10in) long and 1.5–2cm (½–¾in) thick, then cut each rope into small 1cm (½in) pieces about the size of a hazelnut and put them on the lined tray or plate. You should have a total of 70–80 pieces.

3 Heat the oil in a large, heavy-based saucepan or frying pan to 170°C/335°F (if you don't have a thermometer, test the oil is hot enough by dropping in a cube of bread: it should float rather than sink, and sizzle immediately on contact with the oil). Once it's hot, add a batch of the dough balls – you need to cook them in two or three batches. They should sit in one layer in the oil. Fry for 1½–2 minutes, turning them

often with a metal spoon so they fry evenly, until they turn lightly golden. Remove them from the oil with a slotted spoon and place them in a sieve to drain the oil. Repeat with the remaining batches of dough and transfer each drained batch to a plate or tray lined with kitchen paper to help absorb any excess oil.

4 Warm up the honey, orange zest and orange blossom water in a large pan and add the fried dough pieces. Stir until all the dough is coated, then remove from the heat. Transfer with tongs or a spatula to a cake plate and create the shape of a pyramid. Leave to set (or serve straight away), dusting the mini doughnuts with icing sugar before serving.

Orecchie di Amman

HAMAN'S EARS TWO WAYS

Preparation:
15 minutes, plus
15–20 minutes
resting time
Cooking:
10 minutes

**MAKES 20–25
STRIPS OR
TRIANGLES**

Ingredients
1 large egg
50g (1¾oz/¼ cup) caster
    or granulated sugar
grated zest of
    1 orange
pinch of ground
    cinnamon (optional)
40ml (1¼fl oz/
    2½ tablespoons)
    sunflower oil
pinch of sea salt
170g (5¾oz/scant 1¼
    cups) plain white flour,
    plus extra for dusting
about 500ml (17fl oz/
    generous 2 cups)
    groundnut or sunflower
    oil, for frying
icing sugar, for dusting

OPTIONAL FILLINGS
A choice of any (or a mix)
of the following:
jam of your choice
Nutella
peanut butter

*T*hese pastry treats are crispy and tasty. They are traditionally made in Italy for the festival of Purim, and this is my family's recipe. My mother likes to pinch the pastry to create a bow or butterfly shape, without any filling, as this is the way her grandmother, Silvia, used to make them. I like to alternate this simple version with filled ones. The dough is the same, just shaped differently, and both versions are fried. For the filled version, the filling is added to the cooked pastries before serving. You can also use the same dough recipe and bake the pastry instead of frying. Just add 1/4 teaspoon of baking powder to the flour and fill them before baking them at 190°C (170°C fan/375°F/gas mark 5) for 15 minutes.

Haman (Amman in Italian) is the villain in the Purim story, as told in the Book of Esther (see page 55), and various pastries are called after him. Ashkenazi Jews around the world bake Hamantaschen (Haman's pockets), filled with poppy seeds or jam, and Israelis bake ozney Haman (Haman's ears), which have the same English name as the Italian version but are more similar to the Ashkenazi pockets!

The reason why the Italian orecchie di Amman are made into strips and fried may be because Purim falls around the time of the Italian Carnevale, when frappe, chiacchere and other similar fried pastry strips are made.

1 First, make the dough. In a bowl, gently whisk the egg with the sugar, orange zest, cinnamon (if using), oil and a pinch of salt. Add the flour and mix again, working the dough by hand. You can work the dough in the bowl or on a work surface for 4–5 minutes. Alternatively, mix the ingredients using a stand mixer fitted with the dough hook attachment. The consistency should be soft and malleable but not sticky. If it's sticky, add a little more flour. Wrap the dough in clingfilm and let it rest at room temperature for 15–20 minutes.

2 When you are ready to make the pastries, remove the clingfilm and cut the dough in half. Take one piece and keep the other wrapped in clingfilm. Dust the work surface with a little flour and roll out the dough to a thickness of 2–3mm (¹⁄₁₆–⅛in). The thinner you roll the dough, the crispier the pastry once fried.

TO MAKE STRIP EARS

Cut the dough, ideally with a crimped pastry wheel to give it pretty edges, or with a knife, into roughly 10 x 2cm (4 x ¾in) strips, then pinch them in the middle to create a bow or butterfly shape. Repeat the same process with the rest of the dough, putting the pieces on a tray dusted with flour. You should have 20–25 strip ears.

TO MAKE TRIANGLE EARS

Using a 7–8cm (3in) round cookie cutter, or the rim of a glass, cut as many circles as you can from the dough. Fold three edges of each circle towards the centre to create a triangle, but do not fill them yet – you will do that once they are cooked. Folding it will create the triangle shape, and they will puff up when frying and open to create a cradle for the filling, while still keeping a triangle cup shape. Repeat the same process with the rest of the dough. You can re-roll the offcuts, and cut out more circles, or leave them as random-shaped strips, or cut out letters and shapes. Put the pieces on a tray dusted with flour. You should have 20–25 triangle ears.

3   Heat the groundnut or sunflower oil for frying in a deep heavy-based saucepan to 170°C/335°F (if you don't have a thermometer, test the oil is hot enough by dropping in a cube of bread: it should float rather than sink, and sizzle immediately on contact with the oil). Once the oil is hot, add some of the pastry strips or triangles (enough to create one layer) and fry for about 1 minute, turning them halfway through with a metal spoon, until they turn pale golden – do not let them brown. They cook very quickly! Remove them from the oil with a slotted spoon and place them in a sieve to drain the oil. Once drained, transfer them to a plate lined with kitchen paper to help absorb any excess oil. Repeat

with the remaining strips or triangles.

4   Leave to cool for 5 minutes, then sprinkle icing sugar on top of the strip ears, or pipe a dollop of your favourite filling into the centre of each triangle (using a piping bag fitted with a medium nozzle, or simply snip a 1cm/½in hole in the corner of a disposable bag after filling it). Ideally serve them straight away, or keep them in an airtight container at room temperature for up to 5 days. If you are keeping them to serve later, sprinkle them with more icing sugar or pipe the filling just before serving.

Charoset

SILVIA'S CHAROSET

Preparation: 15 minutes

MAKES A GENEROUS BOWLFUL – ENOUGH FOR 12–15 PEOPLE

Ingredients
2 red eating apples, such as Royal Gala or Braeburn, washed and cored, skin on

100g (3½oz) stoned dates or dried figs, or a mix of both
100g (3½oz/⅔ cup) almonds
100g (3½oz/⅔ cup) hazelnuts
100ml (3½fl oz/scant ½ cup) Marsala wine or sweet wine
100ml (3½fl oz/scant ½ cup) freshly squeezed orange juice
½ teaspoon ground cinnamon
2 tablespoons red wine
pinch of sea salt

Charoset *is one of the symbolic elements of the Passover Seder plate and I have never met two people who make it the same way. This is part of its beauty: there are endless recipes for it, often linked to the country, city or even* shtetl *(small town or village) of origin in the Ashkenazi case. They all, however, have roughly the same consistency, that of mortar, as that is what this dish is meant to remind us of. In fact, its meaning – from the Hebrew* cheres *which means 'clay'– symbolises the mortar used with bricks by the enslaved Israelites in Ancient Egypt. It is eaten together with matzah and* maror *(a bitter herb) with a blessing as part of the Seder.*

Charoset is a sweet paste made of apples, nuts, and frequently wine, but many other ingredients are often added to it, especially in the Sephardi and Middle Eastern traditions. Italian ones are no exception; dates, pomegranate, pine nuts, walnuts, banana and raisins are all possible additions, just to mention a few. The important thing is to keep the right balance between the fruit, nuts and liquid, which are mashed together to create the paste.

If you have your own family recipe, I encourage you to keep making it, as that's how we keep traditions alive. However, if you are on the lookout for a new recipe, then do try this one. I created it many years ago and it is now a classic in our family, along with my cousin's and sister-in-law's. In fact, at our Seder table in Rome, where there are about 40 of us, there are at least three different charosets, and every year we all comment and compare them while devouring them very quickly!

The charoset is best made on the day it is served, but you can make it the day before. The quantity of ingredients used here serves 12–15 people, but the recipe can easily be halved to serve fewer.

1 Dice the apples and dates or figs, then place them together with all the other ingredients in a food processor or blender.

> **TIP:** *The blender will make a smooth paste, while the food processor produces a coarser mixture, so choose which to use depending on the consistency you prefer.*

2 Pulse a few times first to combine everything, then blend for about a minute. If the paste is too dense, add a little more red wine or orange juice, depending on your taste, or if it's too runny, add more nuts or dates/figs. Pulse again until well combined.

3 Divide the *charoset* into small bowls to add to each of your Seder plates (up to 2 hours before Seder starts), covering them with clingfilm until ready to serve.

4 The *charoset* will keep for up to 3 days in the fridge. Just bear in mind that in the fridge it goes a little denser over time, so if you prepare it a day or so before you need it, take it out of the fridge 2–3 hours before the Seder so it has a chance to soften a little.

Pizzarelle col Miele

MATZAH FRITTERS DIPPED IN HONEY

Ingredients

150g (5½oz) matzah (about 5 matzah), the thin, square Israeli-type made of flour and water

2 large eggs

120g (4¼oz/generous ½ cup) granulated or caster sugar

150g (5½oz/1 cup) raisins or sultanas

50g (1¾oz/scant ½ cup) pine nuts

pared and finely chopped peel of 1 unwaxed orange

pinch of sea salt

about 500ml (17fl oz/ generous 2 cups) sunflower oil, for frying

200g (7oz/scant 1 cup) runny honey, for dipping

For the festival of Passover, Roman Jews created pizzarelle col miele, which are delicious matzah fritters filled with orange peel, pine nuts and raisins and eaten dipped in honey. A real treat! Every family has their own pizzarelle recipe, using more or fewer eggs, raisins or no raisins, adding cocoa, nuts and so on. Conversations around the table can go on for quite a while about the best way to make these little jewels!

These fritters are a living tradition in my family and my mum in particular is well known for her spectacular pizzarelle. Every year during Passover, more than 50 relatives and friends are invited to my parents' house for an after-dinner party, where the menu is 'pizzarelle and wine' and it proves extremely popular.

Here is my mum's recipe, which in real terms is more approximate than mine as she doesn't weigh her ingredients. This is as accurate as it gets, as one year I managed to follow her around the kitchen and weigh all the bits and pieces, and I've tested it many times since. She always lets the final mixture rest, covered, in the fridge for a few hours before frying it. If you have the time, then I recommend this step, but the fritters are still delicious if you use the mixture straight away. Enjoy!

1 Soak the matzah for 30 minutes in a bowl filled with cold water. To stop them floating, put another bowl or saucepan filled with cold water on top.

2 In the meantime, beat the eggs with the sugar in a large, shallow bowl to combine – we use a Pyrex dish – then add the raisins or sultanas, pine nuts, orange peel and salt.

3 Once the matzah are soaked and soft, drain the water away and use your hands to squeeze out as much of the water as possible, then shred them into the bowl containing the egg mixture.

> **TIP:** *If you have a vegetable mill, you can use that to shred the matzah (this is what my mum uses), or just use a potato masher or your hands.*

4 Mix all the ingredients thoroughly. If you have time, let the mixture rest in the fridge for a few hours, or just go straight onto the next stage.

5 Heat the oil in a deep-fat fryer, deep, heavy-based saucepan or deep, heavy-based frying pan to 170°C/335°F (if you don't have a thermometer, test the oil is hot enough by dropping in a cube of bread: it should float rather than sink, and sizzle immediately on contact with the oil). The oil should not be too hot or the *pizzarelle* will burn on the outside but remain uncooked inside. If you are using a frying pan, slightly reduce the heat once the oil is piping hot.

6 Fill a glass or cup with water. Dip a dessertspoon into the water, then take a flat spoonful of the matzah mixture and slide it carefully into the hot oil. The water helps to detach the mixture from the spoon more easily (as with ice cream). Repeat the process so that you have a single layer of fritters in the deep-fat fryer, saucepan or frying pan – you will need to fry them in batches.

7 Deep-fry the fritters for 3–4 minutes, turning them halfway through with a metal spoon, until golden. Remove them from the oil with a slotted spoon and place them in a sieve to drain the oil. Just before the next batch is ready, transfer them to a plate lined with kitchen paper to absorb any excess oil. Repeat with the remaining matzah mixture. The fritters should be deep golden and crunchy on the outside and pale, soft and sweet inside.

8 Serve the fritters while they are still warm, with the traditional accompaniment of honey for dipping – or without the honey, if you prefer. If you use honey, heat it gently in a small saucepan over a low heat. Place the warm honey in a small heatproof bowl and serve it next to the fritters for people to serve themselves.

9 *Pizzarelle* are also good eaten cold the following day – if they get there! They are no longer crunchy, but the flavour is still addictive.

Torta di Carote e Mandorle

CARROT AND ALMOND CAKE

Preparation:
15 minutes
Cooking:
40 minutes

SERVES 8–10

Ingredients

unsalted butter or dairy-free spread, for greasing
1 tablespoon matzah meal, for coating
4 large eggs, separated
200g (7oz/1 cup) caster or granulated sugar
200g (7oz) carrots, peeled and finely grated
200g (7oz/1⁄3 cups) whole unblanched almonds, finely ground
pinch of sea salt
2 tablespoons flaked almonds, to decorate (optional)
icing sugar, for dusting

You will also need a 23cm (9in) round springform baking tin, the base lined with baking parchment (with the parchment held in place using the springform seal).

This is a wonderful Passover cake which I enjoy baking, not only every year for Seder night but throughout the year. It is quite different from a classic English carrot cake, both because of the lack of thick buttercream icing – Italian cakes don't usually have any icing on top, just a thin layer of icing sugar, if anything at all – and because of the filling, which is subtle in flavour and moist. It is so light that it slightly crumbles: to minimise this, I add a couple of tablespoons of sugar while whisking the egg whites, which makes them more 'gluey' and helps bind the mixture.

I like to use unblanched (skin-on) almonds, for their flavour and colour, but you can also use blanched almonds instead, if you prefer. Either way, I really recommend using whole almonds and grinding them in a food processor instead of buying them already ground, as they stay a little crunchier and have a nuttier flavour. Of course, if you don't have a way to grind your own, then ready-ground almonds work just as well.

1 Preheat the oven to 200°C (180°C fan/400°F/gas mark 6).

2 Spread a thin coating of butter or dairy-free spread all over the lined base and around the sides of the tin. Sprinkle the matzah meal into the tin and tilt the tin, moving it around to create a thin, even coating (it will stick to the fat), then tip the tin upside down to remove any excess. Set aside.

3 Beat the egg yolks with most of the sugar (keeping 2 tablespoons aside to whisk with the egg whites later) for a couple of minutes until pale and creamy, either in a bowl with an electric hand mixer or in the bowl of a stand mixer fitted with the paddle attachment. Add the carrots, ground almonds and salt and mix again on medium speed for about a minute.

> **TIP:** *Alternatively, if you have a food processor, use it to combine the ingredients. Start with the egg yolks and sugar and mix for a couple of minutes, then add chunks of carrots and mix for another minute, then finally add whole almonds and mix again for a couple of minutes. It's a noisy process but the carrots and nuts will be ground and will blend perfectly with the egg and sugar mix – quick and easy! Transfer to a bowl and carry on with the recipe.*

4 In a separate, clean bowl, whisk the egg whites with an electric hand mixer for about 1 minute until they form soft peaks. Add the 2 tablespoons of sugar you set aside earlier, continuing to whisk for at least 1 minute on high speed until the whites form stiff peaks. Gently fold them into the cake mixture until just combined.

5 Transfer the cake mixture into the prepared baking tin and scatter the flaked almonds (if using) on top. Bake in the oven for about 40 minutes, or until a skewer or cake tester inserted into the centre of the cake comes out dry. If it comes out wet, put the cake back in the oven and bake for another 5 minutes, then check again. Don't worry if it shrinks and sinks a little when ready – that's normal and it still tastes delicious.

6 Remove the cake from the oven and leave it to cool for 30 minutes in the tin on a cooling rack, then remove it from the tin (carefully, otherwise it might break).

7 Sift a thin layer of icing sugar over the top to decorate. Serve warm or at room temperature. The cake will keep in an airtight container for up to 2 days at room temperature, or 3–4 days in the fridge.

Torta di Spinaci e Mandorle

SPINACH AND ALMOND CAKE

Preparation:
20 minutes
Baking:
30 minutes

SERVES 8–10

Ingredients

unsalted butter or dairy-free spread, for greasing
1 tablespoon matzah meal, for coating
500g (1lb 2oz) fresh spinach leaves
4 large eggs, separated
200g (7oz/1½ cup) caster or granulated sugar
200g (7oz/1⅓ cups) blanched almonds, finely ground
pinch of ground nutmeg
pinch of sea salt
2 tablespoons flaked almonds, to decorate
icing sugar, for dusting (optional)

You will also need a 23cm (9in) round springform baking tin, the base lined with baking parchment (with the parchment held in place using the springform seal).

*T*his is my adaptation of a fascinating old recipe from Florence's Jewish community which I first came across in La Cucina nella Tradizione Ebraica by Adei Wizo (Association of Italian Jewish Women). I add more egg whites than in the original recipe to make it a little lighter. The cake is unusual and versatile as it has both sweet and savoury elements. It is deep green inside from the spinach, and while the almonds and sugar have the initial impact on the palate, the spinach eventually kicks in at the end. This green cake always attracts much attention and curiosity! It is great for brunch, or even as a sweet and savoury side dish (without icing sugar on top), or as a dessert. It is also kosher for Passover as there is no flour. Go on, experiment a little...

1 Preheat the oven to 200°C (180°C fan/400°F/gas mark 6).

2 Spread a thin coating of butter or dairy-free spread all over the lined base and around the sides of the tin. Sprinkle the matzah meal into the tin and tilt the tin, moving it around to create a thin, even coating (it will stick to the fat), then tip the tin upside down to remove any excess. Set aside.

3 Wash the spinach and, without draining it, put it in a large, deep saucepan, cover and leave it to cook over a high heat for 4–5 minutes, stirring once or twice. Once the spinach has wilted and is tender, drain it, rinse it under cold running water and, using your hands, squeeze out as much of the water as you can. Roughly chop the leaves.

> **TIP:** You can also put the spinach in a large heatproof bowl and pour boiling water on top. Stir, cover with clingfilm and leave to soak for a few minutes until wilted. Drain and proceed as above.

4 Beat the egg yolks with the sugar for a couple of minutes until pale and creamy, either in a bowl with an electric hand mixer or in the bowl of a stand mixer fitted with the paddle attachment. Add the spinach, the ground almonds, nutmeg and salt and mix thoroughly. You can also combine all the ingredients in a food processor until just combined.

5 In a separate, clean bowl, whisk the egg whites with an electric hand mixer until they form stiff peaks. Gently fold them into the cake mixture until everything is well combined.

6 Transfer the cake mixture into the prepared baking tin and scatter over the flaked almonds. Bake in the oven for about 30 minutes, or until a skewer or cake tester inserted into the centre of the cake comes out dry. If it comes out wet,

put the cake back in the oven and bake for another 5 minutes, then check again.

7 Remove the cake from the oven and leave it to cool for 30 minutes in the tin on a cooling rack, then carefully remove it from the tin.

8 Before serving, sift icing sugar over the top, if you like. The cake will keep, covered, for a day at room temperature or 2–3 days in the fridge.

Torta Caprese

DARK CHOCOLATE AND ALMOND CAKE

I could not leave this out of the collection; it is one of my favourite cakes and one my clients request all the time. There are many versions of 'Caprese' cakes, mostly made with flour. The Italian Jews adopted this flour-free version to make it kosher for Passover and as with most things chocolatey, I owe the recipe to my chocoholic sister, Simona. I use whole almonds for their crunchy texture, but you can use ground ones if you are short of time or don't have a food processor. The butter can be replaced with a dairy-free spread to make it parve, *but the buttery version wins every time!*

Preparation:
15 minutes
Cooking:
40–45 minutes

SERVES 6–8

Ingredients
100g (3½oz) **unsalted butter**, at room temperature, plus extra for greasing
200g (7oz/1 cup) **caster or granulated sugar**
4 **large eggs**
½ teaspoon **vanilla extract**
200g (7oz/1⅓ cups) **whole almonds**, freshly ground
pinch of **sea salt**
150g (5½oz) **dark chocolate (70% cocoa solids)**, finely chopped
2 tablespoons **flaked almonds**, to decorate (optional)

You will also need a 20cm (8in) round springform baking tin, the base lined with baking parchment (with the parchment held in place using the springform seal).

1 Preheat the oven to 200°C (180°C fan/400°F/gas mark 6). Grease the lined base and sides of the tin with butter.

2 Beat the butter with the sugar for a couple of minutes until pale and creamy, ideally in a stand mixer fitted with the paddle attachment, or in a food processor (you can use a bowl and an electric hand mixer, if you prefer).

3 Add 2 whole eggs, one at a time, beating continuously, then separate the other 2 eggs and add the yolks (keeping the 2 whites aside for later) and continue beating until smooth and well incorporated. Add the vanilla extract, ground almonds and salt and beat again. Fold in the chocolate, keeping a tablespoon of it to one side for decorating the cake later.

> **TIP:** *It is easier to cut chocolate when it is cold, so you can put it in the fridge for 30 minutes or in the freezer for 5 minutes before chopping it.*

4 In a separate, clean bowl, whisk the egg whites with an electric hand mixer until they form stiff peaks. Gently fold them into the cake mixture until everything is well combined.

5 Pour the mixture into the prepared baking tin and sprinkle over the reserved chocolate and the flaked almonds, if using. Bake in the oven for 40–45 minutes, or until a skewer or cake tester inserted into the centre of the cake comes out dry. If it comes out wet, put the cake back in the oven and bake for another 5 minutes, then check again.

6 Remove the cake from the oven and leave it to cool for 30 minutes in the tin on a cooling rack, then carefully remove it from the tin.

7 Serve warm or at room temperature. The cake will keep in an airtight container for 3–4 days at room temperature.

Torta di Nocciole e Cioccolato

FLOURLESS AND BUTTERLESS HAZELNUT AND CHOCOLATE CAKE

*H*azelnut and chocolate are a perfect match and one of my favourite flavour combinations. I created this cake many years ago, as I wanted to use nuts other than the classic almonds for Passover, and wanted to keep it dairy-free. In this cake, the flavours shine and the ingredients list keeps things simple. There is no flour, no butter – or any fat, in fact – and only egg whites are used, not yolks. The result is moist and utterly delicious. It's suitable for Passover, but I truly make it all year round!

Preparation:
15 minutes
Cooking:
30 minutes

SERVES 6–8

Ingredients
200g (7oz/2 cups) ground hazelnuts (freshly ground or ready ground)
200g (7oz/1 cup) caster or granulated sugar
pinch of sea salt
120g (4¼oz) dark chocolate (70% cocoa solids), finely chopped
½ teaspoon vanilla extract
6 large egg whites (about 240g/8½oz, if using shop-bought eggs)
handful of chopped or whole hazelnuts, or a mix of both, to decorate

You will also need a 20cm (8in) round springform baking tin, the base lined with baking parchment (with the parchment held in place using the springform seal).

1 Preheat the oven to 200°C (180°C fan/400°F/gas mark 6).

2 Mix the ground hazelnuts with the sugar and salt in a bowl. Keep a handful of the chopped chocolate aside for decoration, and add the rest to the sugar and hazelnuts, together with the vanilla extract.

3 In a separate, clean bowl, beat the egg whites with an electric hand mixer (or in the bowl of a stand mixer fitted with the whisk attachment) until they form stiff peaks. Gradually add the sugar, hazelnut and chocolate mixture to the egg whites, continuing to mix on low speed until you have a thick and homogenous mixture.

4 Pour the mixture into the lined baking tin, sprinkle the chocolate you set aside and the chopped or whole hazelnuts evenly on top and bake in the oven for about 30 minutes, or until a skewer or cake tester inserted into the centre of the cake comes out clean. If it comes out wet, put the cake back in the oven and bake for another 5 minutes, then check again.

5 Remove the cake from the oven and leave it to cool for 30 minutes in the tin on a cooling rack, then carefully remove it from the tin.

6 Serve warm or at room temperature. The cake will keep for up to 2 days at room temperature, or 3–4 days in the fridge.

Bocca di Dama

FLOURLESS LEMON AND ALMOND CAKE

There are quite a few different versions of this cake and the common denominators are eggs, sugar, almonds and lemon. After that, there are lots of variations including with and without flour; the 'with flour' version is usually baked for Rosh Hashanah or Yom Kippur, and the 'without flour' version for Passover. There are also Italian and Libyan takes on this cake, the latter with delicious icing on top. I eventually settled for this simpler recipe as it tastes and feels light and delicate, which I believe works perfectly at the end of a lengthy Seder meal. I like my bocca di dama *('mouth of a lady') lemony, and to top it with plenty of flaked almonds. I also prefer to freshly ground the almonds in the cake with a food processor for extra texture, but you can use ground ones.*

Note that I've suggested either a round or square baking tin as bocca di dama *is often served in squares rather than slices. Either way, it's delicious!*

Preparation:
15 minutes
Baking:
25–30 minutes

SERVES 8-10

Ingredients
unsalted butter or dairy-free spread, for greasing
1 tablespoon matzah meal, for coating
6 large eggs, separated
160g (5½oz/generous ⅔ cup) caster or granulated sugar
220g (7¾oz/1⅓ cups) whole almonds, freshly ground or ready ground
pinch of sea salt
grated zest and juice of 2 unwaxed lemons (about 80–100ml/2¾–3½ fl oz /⅓–scant ½ cup)
2 tablespoons flaked almonds, to decorate
icing sugar, for dusting

You will also need a 23cm (9in) round springform baking tin, or a 22cm (8½in) square baking tin, the base lined with baking parchment.

1 Preheat the oven to 200°C (180°C fan/400°F/gas mark 6).

2 Spread a thin coating of butter or dairy-free spread all over the lined base and around the sides of the tin. Sprinkle the matzah meal into the tin and tilt the tin, moving it around to create a thin, even coating (it will stick to the fat), then tip the tin upside down to remove any excess. Set aside.

3 Beat the egg yolks with the sugar for a couple of minutes until pale and creamy, ideally in a stand mixer fitted with the paddle attachment or in a food processor, but you can also use a bowl and an electric hand mixer. Add the almonds, salt, and lemon zest and juice and beat again for another minute until well combined.

4 In a separate, clean bowl, whisk the egg whites with an electric hand mixer until they form stiff peaks. Gently fold them into the cake mixture until everything is well combined.

5 Transfer the cake mixture into the prepared baking tin and scatter over the flaked almonds. Bake in the oven for 25–30 minutes, or until a skewer or cake tester inserted into the centre of the cake comes out dry. If it comes out wet, put the cake back in the oven and bake for another 5 minutes, then check again.

6 Remove the cake from the oven and leave it to cool for 30 minutes in the tin on a cooling rack, then carefully remove it from the tin. Sift a thin layer of icing sugar over the top to decorate, if you like. Serve warm or at room temperature. The cake will keep in an airtight container for up to 2 days at room temperature, or 3–4 days in the fridge.

Tazzine

EGG AND ALMOND CUPS

*T*his recipe was kindly given to me by Franca Passigli, the mum of my dear friend Deborah Romano Menasci.
She patiently talked me through it, as the prolonged beating technique is unique and unfamiliar to many. These 'small cups' are traditional at their Passover Seder table in Bologna and are served at the end of the meal in an espresso or other small cup, as they are sweet and deliciously intense, with the flavour of almonds, eggs and cinnamon bursting through with each spoonful.

A similar and more well-known dessert, both by name and method, are scodelline (little bowls), from Livorno, Rome and central Italy, where the egg yolks, sugar and almonds are cooked for longer and the whisked whites are added at the very end, so making the mixture somewhat lighter and less intense.

This tazzine is my favourite version, but I have reduced the sugar from the 300g (10oz/scant 10 cups) in Franca's recipe and added the grated zest of a lemon as I think it works very nicely. I hope she will forgive me!

This recipe is simple in terms of ingredients but takes time to make. The key to success is not to rush. Simmer everything very slowly and continuously, and ideally use a heat diffuser to help in the process. Once the mixture is off the hob, it needs 30 minutes' beating time, which sounds like a lot, but when you use a stand mixer, you just need to keep an eye on the process, and it is well worth it!

Preparation:
15 minutes, plus
Booking and beating:
45 minutes

**MAKES 12
ESPRESSO
CUPS OR
SMALL CUPS
OR RAMEKINS**

Ingredients
100ml (3½fl oz/scant ½ cup) water
120g (4¼oz/generous ½ cup) caster or
    granulated sugar
100g (3½oz/⅔ cup) blanched almonds,
    finely ground
10 egg yolks and 4 egg whites,
    at room temperature
grated zest of 1 unwaxed lemon
ground cinnamon, to sprinkle
    (to sprinkle)

1 Put the water, sugar and ground almonds into a medium, heavy-based saucepan over a low heat and slowly bring to the boil, ideally using a heat diffuser so that everything will cook slowly and evenly and not stick or curdle.

2 Reduce the heat to a minimum, add the egg yolks and stir gently.

3 Meanwhile, whisk the egg whites in a clean bowl with an electric hand mixer until they form stiff peaks (not forgetting to frequently stir the egg yolk mixture), then gently fold them into the egg-almond mixture while it's still over the heat. Add the lemon zest and simmer gently on the lowest heat for a further 5–6 minutes, stirring constantly, making sure the mixture doesn't curdle or stick.

4 Remove from the heat and transfer the mixture to the bowl of a stand mixer fitted with the whisk attachment and beat at medium speed for about 30 minutes (yes, 30 minutes!) until smooth and creamy. You might want to stop the machine every 10 minutes – for a minute or two – to allow the engine to cool, if your mixer has a tendency to overheat.

5 Distribute the mixture equally among 12 espresso cups or ramekins, then put these in the fridge, covered with clingfilm, for at least 1 hour before serving. The tazzine can asily be prepared a few hours or even a day ahead.

6 Remove from the fridge 15 minutes before serving and sprinkle a little ground cinnamon on top of each one.

Mousse al Cioccolato

SIMONA'S CHOCOLATE MOUSSE

I enjoy desserts but I don't have a particularly sweet tooth. My sister Simona, on the other hand, is passionate about anything sweet, in particular chocolate. I owe this recipe to her. She likes the pure dark chocolate flavour so uses water for the liquid element, while I prefer to cut the bitter taste of the dark chocolate with freshly squeezed orange juice (don't even think of using the shop-bought stuff)!

When I feel the need for an extra kick, I substitute the orange juice with coffee – being Italian I like espresso, but a strong black coffee or a decaf also works. For an alcoholic version, replace a third of the liquid with Cointreau, Grand Marnier or rum. Whichever flavour you go for, just be sure to maintain the chocolate-to-liquid ratio in the recipe below.

This mousse is parve *(dairy-free), suitable for a meat meal and can easily be prepared a day in advance. It is also kosher for Passover and makes a lighter, fresh alternative to the traditional almond-based desserts served at this time.*

A final piece of advice: the eggs you use should be very fresh, and the egg whites whisked well, or the mousse won't set. Note that this recipe contains raw eggs.

Preparation:
20 minutes, plus minimum 2 hours chilling time

SERVES 6–8

Ingredients

200g (7oz) dark chocolate (70% cocoa solids), broken into pieces

150ml (5fl oz/⅔ cup) water, freshly squeezed orange juice or coffee

grated zest of ½ unwaxed orange (optional)

4 large eggs

2 tablespoons caster or granulated sugar

pinch of sea salt

fresh raspberries and fresh mint leaves, shelled pistachios, roasted hazelnuts or coffee beans, to decorate (optional)

1 Melt the chocolate in a bain-marie: place the chocolate in a heatproof bowl with the water, orange juice or coffee and the orange zest. Sit it over a pan of just-simmering water (making sure the bottom of the bowl isn't touching the water) and stir with a hand whisk until melted. Promptly remove from the heat as soon as it has melted, so the chocolate doesn't split.

> **TIP:** *It is important to use a hand whisk to mix the chocolate as this helps it melt uniformly without any lumps.*

2 Separate the eggs and place 2 of the yolks into a large bowl. You only need 2 yolks for this recipe, so keep the others in the fridge for another day. Put the 4 egg whites in a separate, clean bowl. Add the sugar and the salt to the egg yolks, and beat using a hand whisk, or ideally an electric hand mixer, until pale and creamy. Add the melted chocolate mixture, stir well and leave it to cool for 5–7 minutes, stirring occasionally.

3 Whisk the egg whites with the electric hand mixer (attachments cleaned and dried if you used them for the egg yolks and sugar), or in the bowl of a stand mixer fitted with the whisk attachment, until they form stiff peaks. Adding a large spoonful at a time, gently stir and fold them with a metal spoon or spatula into the cooled chocolate and egg yolk mixture. When all the egg white is fully incorporated, and there are no

lumps, the mousse is ready to go in the fridge. Try not to overmix it – you want lots of air in the mousse to keep it light.

4 Spoon the mousse into a large serving bowl or small individual ramekins or glasses, cover with clingfilm and place in the fridge for at least 2 hours, or until the mousse is set.

5 Before serving, decorate the mousse, if you wish. Among my favourites are raspberries and mint leaves or, for a crunchy texture, use pistachios and/or roasted hazelnuts. If you've used coffee, decorate with whole coffee beans.

6 Serve chilled. The mousse keeps well, covered, in the fridge, for up to 3–4 days.

Amaretti al Limone

ALMOND BISCUITS WITH LEMON ZEST

Preparation:
15 minutes,
plus optional
15–20 minutes
chilling time
Baking:
15–18 minutes

**MAKES ABOUT
25 BISCUITS**

Ingredients
180g (6oz/1¼ cups)
   freshly ground or ready-
   ground almonds
120g (4¼oz/generous
   ½ cup) caster or
   granulated sugar
grated zest of
   3 unwaxed lemons
2 medium egg whites
almonds (whole or flaked),
   shelled pistachios and/
   or pine nuts, to
   decorate (optional)

You will also need a large
baking tray lined with
baking parchment.

A maretti are one of the oldest and most classic Italian biscuits. The best-known are the ones from Lombardy and Piedmont, in the north-west of Italy, where, especially in Piedmont, there was once a thriving web of Jewish communities, today concentrated mostly in Turin.

Jews adopted these biscuits not only because they are delicious and easy to bake, but also because they are both parve (dairy-free) and kosher for Passover. All they are made of is egg whites, sugar and ground almonds, so they are very simple. The original recipe has extract of apricot kernels or a few bitter almonds in it, giving it its distinctive slightly amaro (bitter) flavour. However, they can both be tricky to source and a tasty – though not like-for-like – alternative is to add a few drops of Amaretto liqueur to the dry ingredients. I have left them all out of this recipe and added plenty of lemon zest instead, which I adore. I like to use unblanched nuts and grind them myself, but shop-bought ground almonds also work. You can also substitute almonds for other nuts, such as pistachios or hazelnuts; they all work a treat.

There are soft and dry amaretti and this recipe sits somewhere in between – crispy on the outside and slightly chewy on the inside. Mixed nuts as a final decoration on the top are my favourite personal addition, for the look, texture and flavour. Do try these little addictive jewels of Italian biscuits!

1 Preheat the oven to 190°C (170°C fan/375°F/gas mark 5).

2 Combine the almonds with the sugar and lemon zest in a mixing bowl.

3 Add the egg whites to the almond mixture – there's no need to whisk or beat them first – and stir with a spoon until combined. The mixture will be quite sticky but should still be easy to handle. If it's too sticky, or if you're making the biscuits on a hot summer's day, put the mixture in the fridge for 15–20 minutes to cool and firm up so it will be easier to handle.

4 Take a heaped teaspoonful of the mixture and gently roll it between the palms of your (clean) hands to make a large olive-sized ball. Repeat with the rest of the mixture and place on the lined baking tray, making sure they're approximately 2.5cm (1in) apart. Alternatively, for a rustic look,

simply spoon heaps of mixture directly onto the lined baking tray. I like to decorate each amaretti biscuit with a mix of nuts, such as whole or flaked almonds, pistachios or pine nuts, but you can also keep them classically plain.

5 Bake in the oven for 15–18 minutes until light golden.

6 Remove from the oven and leave to cool on on the baking tray on a cooling rack for at least 15 minutes before removing them from the tray and serving or storing. Eat warm or at room temperature. The biscuits will keep in an airtight container at room temperature for several days.

Ginetti di Miriam

MY MUM'S ROMAN JEWISH COOKIES

Preparation:
25 minutes
Baking:
25 minutes

MAKES ABOUT 30 BISCUITS

Ingredients
300g (10½oz/scant
2½ cups) plain white
flour (ideally 'oo' type)
2 large **eggs**
100g (3½oz/½ cup) caster
or granulated **sugar**
100ml (3½fl oz/scant
½ cup) **sunflower oil**
¼ teaspoon **ground
cinnamon**
grated **zest** of 1
unwaxed **orange**
pinch of **sea salt**
40g (1½oz/generous
¼ cup) **hazelnuts**,
roughly chopped
40g (1½oz/⅓ cup)
walnuts, roughly
chopped
40g (1½oz/generous
¼ cup) **almonds**,
roughly chopped

You will also need a large
baking tray lined with
baking parchment.

G inetti are another delectable traditional sweet bake from the Roman Jewish culinary repertoire. They can be bought at Boccione bakery in the Jewish quarter, however, my mum's recipe (and she is quite renowned among friends and family for making the best ginetti) is a little different from the bakery's. It includes nuts, cinnamon and orange zest. Her version, to me, has a flavour I would recognise among a million others. She used to make them once a year, just before Passover, using kosher-for-Passover flour which was available to buy in kosher shops in Rome until 2009. We used to bake them together late at night, sharing quite special memories as we did so. Nowadays, due to new kosher restrictions, baking ginetti at home before Passover is no longer allowed, however, the tradition is kept alive by making them in kosher communal ovens under rabbinical supervision.

Most Roman Jews make round ciambellette doughnut biscuits, but in our family, we always made ginetti, which are roughly rectangular in shape. I prefer using the traditional hand-whisking method on the worktop, but it can be done in a stand mixer fitted with a paddle attachment.

The use of kosher-for-Passover flour for Pesach baking – and Rome is indeed an orthodox community – is quite a curiosity for the foreign eye, and it may be different from other Jewish customs. If you are considering making Ginetti for Passover, and you keep kosher, I invite you to make these biscuits using plain white flour at any other time of the year instead. They are always a winner!

1 Preheat the oven to 190°C (170°C fan/375°F/gas mark 5).

2 Pour out the flour in a circle (minimum 10–12cm/4–4½in in diameter) on a clean, flat surface, such as a baking mat or worktop, and make a well in the middle. Break the eggs into the well, making sure there is enough flour around the edge to keep them from escaping (the larger the well, the easier it is to mix the eggs). Add the sugar to the eggs inside the well and gently beat the eggs and sugar together with a fork or small whisk, then gradually add the oil. Continue gently whisking while slowly starting to toss the flour into the well. Add the cinnamon, orange zest and salt, and whisk again to incorporate more flour. You may not need all the flour, so keep a little on the side and use only if the dough is sticky at the end.

3   When everything comes together, add all the chopped nuts. The mixture should be malleable and easy to roll. If it's sticky, add a little more flour, an extra tablespoon at a time. The dough does not need to be kneaded much, just combined and uniform.

4   If using a stand mixer, first combine the eggs with the sugar on medium speed for 10–15 seconds, then add the oil, cinnamon, orange zest and salt, mix again and add the flour. Once the flour is fully incorporated, add the nuts and give it a final mix to combine it all together. It does not need much working.

5   Divide the dough in two and roll each half into a long, thick rope, about 50cm (20in) long and 5cm (2in) wide. Cut each rope into 14 or 15 pieces, each about 3–4cm (1 1/4–1½in) long, and gently press each piece with the palm of your hand to flatten it slightly.

6   Place the *ginetti* on the lined baking tray, keeping a little distance between each.

7   Bake in the oven for about 25 minutes until lightly golden. I usually turn the tray halfway through so they bake evenly.

8   Remove from the oven and leave to cool completely on the baking tray. The *ginetti* will keep in an airtight container at room temperature for several days.

Cassola

RICOTTA BAKE

Preparation:
10 minutes
Cooking:
45 minutes

SERVES 6–8

Ingredients
4 large eggs
160g (5½oz/generous ⅔ cup) caster
  or granulated sugar

½ teaspoon ground cinnamon
pinch of sea salt
750g (1lb 10oz/3 cups) ricotta

You will also need a 20–25cm
(7½–9½in) square or rectangular
baking tin, greased with a thin layer
(1 tablespoon) of olive oil over the
base and sides.

*T*his incredibly easy and tasty ricotta dessert is one of the
oldest recipes from the Italian Jewish repertoire and it is
virtually unknown outside of the Roman Jewish community. It
is popular throughout the year and is particularly well suited
for Shavuot, when it is traditional to eat anything cheesy, and
for Pesach with a dairy meal, as it has no flour.

Originally, it would have been cooked in an iron frying pan
in a little olive oil. However, once ovens became commonplace,
people began to bake it and cassola became a more traditional
dessert, slightly reminiscent of a rich cheesecake but without
any base or crusty bits. Interestingly, the legacy of the oil
remained, and today a thin layer of olive oil is still added to
the base of the baking tin, adding a tangy extra flavour.

In Rome and the Lazio region, there is an excellent ewe's-
milk ricotta, which is richer in taste than regular cow's milk
ricotta and it is widely used in cooking, both savoury and
sweet. If you can't get any, then regular cow's milk ricotta
works fine.

This version is the classic baked recipe we make in my
family. It possibly has its roots in the once thriving Jewish
community in Sicily. The recipe contains a touch of cinnamon,
hinting to Sephardic culinary traditions, while ricotta is widely
used in Sicilian desserts. It is already rich in consistency and
flavour, but if you want to make it even more indulgent, you
can throw in some chocolate chips or raisins. It is usually
baked in a square or rectangular baking tin, then served in
small squares.

1 Preheat the oven to 200°C (180°C fan/400°F/gas mark 6).

2 Beat the eggs with the sugar, cinnamon and salt for a couple of minutes until smooth and creamy, ideally in the bowl of a stand mixer fitted with the paddle attachment, but you can also use a bowl and an electric hand mixer or with a hand whisk. Add the ricotta and beat again, this time on a slow setting, so you don't overwork it, but just enough to blend in the ricotta, until creamy and well combined.

3 Pour the ricotta mixture into the oiled baking tin and bake in the oven for about 45 minutes, or until golden.

4 Remove the bake from the oven and leave it to rest in the tin, on a cooling rack, for at least 30 minutes before serving.

> **TIP:** *The bake may rise in the oven and will then sink down a little once it is out; this is normal, so don't panic!*

5 Cut into squares roughly 3 x 3cm (1¼ x 1¼in) and eat warm or at room temperature. It also tastes great straight from the fridge, where it can be kept, covered, for up to 3–4 days.

Torta Susanna

RICH CHOCOLATE CAKE WITH CHOCOLATE SAUCE

Preparation:
20 minutes, plus
ideally 2 hours
chilling time for the
chocolate sauce
Baking:
18–20 minutes

SERVES 6–8

Ingredients
100ml (3½fl oz/scant
  ½ cup) water
50g (1¾oz/½ cup)
  cocoa powder
170g (5¾oz/¾ cup) caster
  or granulated sugar
170g (5¾oz) unsalted
  butter, diced and at
  room temperature
3 large eggs
pinch of sea salt
70g (2½oz/generous
  ½ cup) plain white flour
  (ideally 'oo' type)
½ teaspoon *lievito per
  dolci* or baking powder
grated dark chocolate or
  sprinkles of your choice,
  to decorate (optional)

You will also need a 20cm
(8in) round springform
baking tin, the base lined
with baking parchment
(with the parchment
held in place using the
springform seal).

*I*f you ever get a chocolate urge, then this chocolate cake will satisfy
it. It is known in the Italian Jewish community as torta Susanna;
who Susanna is or was is still a mystery… but she was definitely a great
baker! It has always been a classic in our family in Rome, where we
often serve it cold from the fridge with whipped cream, and it is also a
classic in my family in London, where we are far less patient, so we
often end up eating it shortly after it comes out of the oven, with a
runny chocolate sauce!

The cake contains only a little baking powder so it doesn't rise
much; its consistency is somewhere between a cake and a brownie, and
the chocolate sauce on top is just heaven. This is a moist cake, but it can
dry out easily if overbaked, so you may have to play around with the
timing a little as every oven bakes slightly differently.

My daughters are chocolate-lovers, especially Bianca, and we enjoy
baking this cake together, as well as 'cleaning' all the bowls at the end
and decorating the top with sprinkles. Try both the chilled and the room-
temperature version and see which one you like better. Go on, indulge a little!

Note that the chocolate sauce in this recipe contains raw eggs.

1 Preheat the oven to 190°C (170°C fan/375°F/gas mark 5).

2 Place the water, cocoa powder and sugar in a small saucepan over a
gentle heat, mix with a hand whisk and bring to the boil. As soon as it
reaches boiling point, switch off the heat – but keep it over the hot stove
– and add the butter. Leave the butter to melt, stirring occasionally (this
may take a few minutes).

3 Meanwhile, separate the eggs. Place the yolks in a bowl and, once the
butter has melted, add the chocolate mixture and the salt. Stir with a
hand whisk and leave to cool for 5 minutes, stirring occasionally.

4 Whisk the egg whites in a clean bowl with an electric hand mixer, until
they form soft peaks. Using a metal spoon or spatula, slowly fold the
egg whites into the chocolate mixture until well combined. Put 2 ladles
of this mixture into a separate container and keep it covered in the
fridge for, ideally, at least a couple of hours until chilled; this chocolate
sauce will go on top of the cake once it is baked and has cooled down.

5 Sift the flour and *lievito per dolci* or baking powder into the remaining chocolate mixture and stir gently. Transfer the cake mixture into the prepared tin and bake in the oven for 18–20 minutes, or until a skewer or cake tester inserted into the centre of the cake comes out dry. It cooks quite fast and if overcooked will lose its moisture, so it is worth checking again every couple of minutes if after 18 minutes it isn't quite cooked.

6 Remove the cake from the oven and leave it to cool in the tin on a cooling rack – the cake will shrink a little as it cools, that's normal – then remove it from the tin and transfer to a cake plate with a lip, as the chocolate sauce will run over the sides into the plate. Gently pour over the chilled chocolate cream mixture and serve.

7 You can serve the cake as it is, or grate flakes of dark chocolate on top, or add sprinkles of your choice if you feel like decorating it. Serve the cake with the runny chocolate sauce at room temperature, or put the cake covered with sauce in the fridge to allow the chocolate sauce to firm up. It keeps well in the fridge in an airtight container for 3–4 days, but it's very unlikely that it will last until then!

Cheesecake di Amaretti, Mascarpone e Lamponi

NO-BAKE CHEESECAKE WITH AMARETTI, MASCARPONE AND RASPBERRIES

Preparation:
20–25 minutes, plus minimum 4 hours chilling time

SERVES 6–8

Ingredients
80g (2¾oz) dry Amaretti biscuits
80g (2¾oz) digestive biscuits
80g (2¾oz) unsalted butter, at room temperature
100ml (3½fl oz/scant ½ cup) whipping or double cream
250g (9oz/1 cup) mascarpone cheese
200g (7oz/generous ¾ cup) reduced-fat cream cheese (such as Philadelphia Light)
80g (2¾oz/generous ⅔ cup) icing sugar
grated zest of 1 unwaxed lemon
1 teaspoon vanilla extract
pinch of sea salt
200–250g (7–9oz) fresh raspberries
a few fresh mint leaves and icing sugar, to decorate (optional)

You will also need a 20cm (8in) round springform baking tin, the base lined with baking parchment (with the parchment held in place using the springform seal).

*C*heesecake has only become popular in Italy over the last few decades, so this is a new-generation recipe. As a newcomer, there is no Italian word for it, so the English 'cheesecake' has been adopted.

A few years back, I created this no-bake recipe for Shavuot, when Jews traditionally eat dairy, hence have cheesy desserts of all kinds! I wanted to combine this tradition with the novelty of using Italian ingredients, such as Amaretti biscuits and mascarpone cheese. It quickly became a family favourite, and a classic for Shavuot and the summer months that follow. The flavours are rich and fresh at the same time. I really like the raspberries on top, but you can replace them with mixed fresh berries or conserve, if you prefer, or use both!

1 Blitz the Amaretti and digestive biscuits in a food processor by pulsing a few times until they form fine crumbs. Add the softened butter and blitz again until the mixture clumps together.

2 Press the biscuit and butter mixture evenly over the base of the prepared tin and put it in the fridge while preparing the cheese mixture.

3 In a small bowl, lightly whip the whipping or double cream with an electric hand whisk until it forms soft peaks, then set aside. In a separate large bowl, using the same electric whisk (no need to rinse off the cream), gently whisk together the mascarpone cheese, cream cheese, icing sugar, lemon zest, vanilla extract and salt.

4 Fold the whipped cream into the cheese mixture until combined. Pour the cheese and cream mixture onto the chilled biscuit base and spread it out evenly with a spatula.

5 Cover the tin with clingfilm and place it back in the fridge for a minimum of 4 hours before serving. This can be prepared up to 1 day in advance.

6 Just before serving, cover the top with plenty of raspberries, a few mint leaves, and then sift over a little icing sugar if you like. Serve chilled.

Tiramisù

TIRAMISU

This is such an Italian classic which speaks for itself, and has been one of my signature desserts since my student years. There is no particular Jewish connection to it, besides that Jews in Italy appreciate it as much as any other Italian. It is ideal for Shavuot, when traditionally cheese-based desserts are eaten, but I have to admit I make it whenever I can! There is no alcohol in my recipe, however, should you prefer it with alcohol, then add 2–3 tablespoons of Marsala, rum or sherry (or other alcohol of your choice) to the coffee before dipping the biscuits in (and/or add it to the mascarpone mixture). Good-quality ingredients are key here, so I recommend using Italian savoiardi, mascarpone cheese and espresso coffee, and make sure the eggs are very fresh as otherwise it won't hold firm and the cheese mixture becomes runny.

Ideally prepare this half a day ahead of time. It lasts up to 3 days, covered, in the fridge, and its flavour changes slightly with time, as the savoiardi absorb more of the coffee and cheese cream. Enjoy!

Note that this recipe contains raw eggs.

Preparation:
20 minutes, plus minimum 2 hours chilling time

SERVES 6–8

Ingredients
about 500ml (17fl oz/ generous 2 cups) espresso coffee or strong black coffee
2–3 tablespoons milk
5 large eggs
5 tablespoons caster or granulated sugar
pinch of sea salt
500g (1lb 2oz/2 cups) mascarpone cheese
about 300g (10½oz) *savoiardi* biscuits (ladies' fingers or sponge fingers)
cocoa powder, to dust

You will also need a square, oval or round dish about 30 x 25cm (12 x 10in).

1 First, make the coffee so it has time to cool down a little. Once it's ready, pour it into a shallow bowl and add the milk – the milk softens its flavour and reduces the temperature.

2 Separate the eggs. Beat the yolks with 3 tablespoons of the sugar (keeping 2 tablespoons aside to whisk with the egg whites later) for a couple of minutes until pale and creamy, either in a bowl with an electric hand mixer or in the bowl of a stand mixer fitted with the paddle attachment. Add the salt and stir.

3 Add the mascarpone cheese, a tablespoon at a time, gently whisking it in (either by hand this time, or using the lowest speed setting of the hand or stand mixer) until just combined.

4 In a separate, clean bowl, whisk the egg whites with an electric hand mixer (attachments cleaned and dried if you used them for the egg yolks, sugar and mascarpone) for about 1 minute until they form soft peaks, then add the 2 tablespoons of sugar you set aside earlier, continuing to whisk for at least 1 minute at high speed until the whites form stiff peaks. Slowly fold them into the mascarpone and egg yolk mixture with a metal spoon or spatula – adding the sugar to the whisked egg whites helps hold the mixture together.

5 Spread a thin coat of the mascarpone mixture on the base of your chosen dish. Dip the *savoiardi* on both sides into the coffee, one at a time, and place them close together over the mascarpone mixture until you have a single layer.

....
TIP: *Don't soak the* savoiardi *for too long, as they need to be soft on the outside but still a little dry inside.*
....

6 Spread half of the remaining mascarpone mixture uniformly over the biscuits. Cover it with a second layer of *savoiardi* dipped in coffee, then spread the remaining mascarpone mixture on top. Keep chilled for at least 2 hours until ready to serve. If it's going to be in the fridge for more than 2–3 hours, then cover it with clingfilm.

7 Sift cocoa powder over the top and serve chilled, always.

Semifreddo al Marsala di 'Nonna' Costanza

'NONNA' COSTANZA'S MARSALA SEMIFREDDO

Preparation:
30 minutes, plus minimum 6–8 hours in the freezer

SERVES 6–8

Ingredients
4 large egg yolks
100g (3½oz/½ cup) caster or granulated sugar
200ml (7fl oz/scant 1 cup) Marsala or sweet dessert wine
300ml (10fl oz/1¼ cups) whipping or double cream
chopped nuts or sprinkles, to decorate (optional)

TIP: *You can also freeze the semifreddo in individual portions by pouring it into ramekins, silicone baking moulds or even disposable glasses, which you can then cut off, making it easy to flip the semifreddo onto a plate.*

My dear aunt Isa (Isabella Varsano) made this refreshing dessert many times for our family when I was growing up. She inherited the recipe from her mum, Costanza, who I remember fondly. I always knew her as Nonna Costanza, even if she wasn't my Nonna but rather my cousins' – Gaia and Sara – and this dessert took her name.

This is a brilliant recipe as you don't need an ice-cream maker. The end result is what we call a semifreddo – literally 'semi-cold'– which is not as firm as ice cream but still has a cold, smooth, creamy consistency. It is important to take it out of the freezer about 15 minutes before serving, so that it regains its silky feel.

Semifreddo is generally quite versatile and comes in a wide variety of flavours; you can replace the Marsala with other liquids of your choice, my favourite alternative being coffee – Italian espresso to be precise! – or add texture with nuts, chestnuts or torrone (Italian nougat).

1 Beat the egg yolks with the sugar for a couple of minutes until pale and creamy, either in a bowl with an electric hand mixer or in the bowl of a stand mixer fitted with the paddle attachment. Slowly add the Marsala or dessert wine and gently mix again.

2 Transfer the mixture into a saucepan and place it over a gentle heat. Heat for a few minutes while stirring with a wooden spoon or spatula. Once it starts to gently simmer, keep stirring for another couple of minutes until it thickens in consistency, then remove from the heat and transfer the mixture into a heatproof bowl to cool down for about 10 minutes, stirring occasionally.

3 Whip the whipping or double cream in a separate bowl until stiff, ideally with an electric hand mixer, then gently fold it with a metal spoon or spatula into the cooled egg yolk and Marsala mixture until well combined.

4 Gently transfer the mixture into a freezable container – I like to use a silicone mould as it makes the *semifreddo* easier to remove, though lining other types of freezable containers with clingfilm before filling them also works – and freeze for a minimum of 6 hours and up to 1 month.

5 Remove the *semifreddo* from the freezer about 15 minutes before turning out/scooping and serving. Decorate, if you like, with chopped nuts and/or sprinkles of your choice.

Crostata di Ricotta e Visciole

RICOTTA AND SOUR CHERRY TART

Preparation:
1 hour (including 40 minutes chilling time)
Cooking:
45 minutes

 **SERVES 6-8**

Ingredients
PASTRY
250g (9oz/scant 1⅔ cups) plain white flour (ideally '00' type), plus extra for dusting
150g (5½oz) chilled unsalted butter, diced
100g (3½oz/½ cup) caster or granulated sugar
grated zest of 1 unwaxed lemon
¼ teaspoon vanilla extract
1 medium egg, beaten

FILLING
1 medium egg
50g (1¾oz/¼ cup) caster or granulated sugar
3 tablespoons sherry or sweet dessert wine (optional)
500g (1lb 2oz/2 cups) ricotta
340g (11¾oz/1 cup) sour cherry jam

You will also need a 25cm (10in) round fluted tart tin (about 4cm/1½in deep) with a removable base, lightly greased and dusted with flour.

*T*he little gem that is the kosher bakery Boccione, in the Jewish quarter in Rome, makes a few distinctive desserts, some of which are not much to look at but are delicious. The ricotta and sour cherry tart is one of them, and if you want to buy one, you'd better go in the morning as they usually sell out by lunchtime. Boccione's version is a closed pasty or pie filled with the wonderful ewe's milk ricotta typical of Rome, and visciole, sour cherry (jam), which is a little tart in flavour. Their pastry is quite thick and 'doughy', and I decided not to attempt to recreate their version here, but rather to come up with my own, so if you want the original, you'll have to travel to Rome... I add sherry, as in my opinion, it adds a kick, and I partially close the top with a large pastry lattice, like a traditional crostata, which I love. I opted for my favourite version of shortcrust, which goes well with the filling and there is no need to blind-bake the pastry, otherwise the tart will come out dry.

If you can't find sour cherry jam, or find it too tart, use any other jam instead and reduce the amount of sugar in the filling. I also often replace the jam with a bar of dark chocolate, which I chop and fold in with the ricotta mixture – it is heaven! – so try this version as well; the rest of the ingredients stay the same.

1 First prepare the pastry, either by hand in a mixing bowl or using a food processor (the order of mixing the ingredients is the same). If making it by hand, mix the flour with the butter first, with your fingertips, until the mixture resembles breadcrumbs. Add the sugar, lemon zest and vanilla extract, stir to combine, and finally add the egg. Work the pastry quickly with your hands until it forms a smooth dough. If using a food processor, mix the same ingredients until just combined. Shape the dough into a flat disc, wrap it in clingfilm and put it in the fridge to firm up for about 40 minutes.

2 While the pastry dough is in the fridge, prepare the filling. Gently beat the egg and remove 1 tablespoon into a small bowl and keep aside – this will be used later to brush over the pastry before baking. Mix the remaining egg with the sugar in a bowl, then add the sherry or dessert wine (if using) and the ricotta and gently mix together.

3 Remove the pastry dough from the fridge, unwrap it, cut off two-thirds and wrap the rest back in the clingfilm. Roll out the bigger piece on a floured surface to a thickness of about 3mm (⅛in), or large enough to line the base and sides of the fluted tart tin.

> **TIP:** *You can also roll the pastry out between two sheets of baking parchment, so it doesn't stick.*

4 Preheat the oven to 190°C (170°C fan/375°F/ gas mark 5). Ease the pastry into the flour-dusted tin and gently press it into the sides. Cut off any excess dough. Prick the pastry case all over with a fork, then spread the sour cherry jam on top of the dough, followed by the ricotta mixture.

5 Now take the smaller piece of pastry and roll it out quite thin, to a thickness of about 2mm (1/16in). Use a pastry wheel or sharp knife to cut long strips of different lengths (about 2cm/¾in wide). Place the strips on top of the tart in a lattice pattern and brush with the reserved egg. I usually re-roll any leftover pastry and cut it into fun-shaped biscuits or fingers (then bake them separately on a baking tray until golden).

6 Bake in the oven for about 45 minutes until the lattice is golden and the filling is set, then remove the tart from the oven and leave to cool on a cooling rack for at least 30 minutes before removing it from the tin.

7 Serve the tart warm, at room temperature or straight from the fridge. Its flavour and consistency change as the ricotta thickens as it cools, so test until you find the version you prefer. It keeps well, covered, for a day at room temperature, or in the fridge for up to 4 days.

Pizza Ebraica

NUT AND CANDIED FRUIT CAKES

Preparation:
20 minutes, plus ideally a few hours soaking time (optional)
Baking:
15–22 minutes, plus 30 minutes cooling time

MAKES 15–18 LARGE OR 25–28 FINGER-SIZED CAKES

Ingredients
100g (3½oz/⅔ cup) raisins or sultanas
100g (3½oz/⅔ cup) whole almonds
50g (1¾oz/scant ½ cup) pine nuts
200g (7oz) mixed candied fruit or glacé cherries (or a mix)
100ml (3½fl oz/scant ½ cup) dry white wine
1 teaspoon vanilla extract
230ml (7½fl oz/scant 1 cup) sunflower oil
500g (1lb 2oz/4 cups) plain white flour (ideally 'oo' type), **or** 350g (12oz/2¼ cups) plain white flour and 150g (5½oz/1½ cups) ground almonds (for a more almondy flavour)
170g (5¾oz/¾ cup) caster or granulated sugar
pinch of sea salt

You will also need a large baking tray lined with baking parchment.

Pizza ebraica – *also called* pizza di piazza, Romana *or* di Beridde – *is a traditional biscuit-cum-cake that Roman Jews eat for family celebrations. It was originally made to celebrate the birth of a boy, on the occasion of his circumcision* (Brit Milah *in Hebrew, hence the name 'Beridde' which is Roman Jewish dialect for Brit). Today, it is made for any Jewish celebration, including weddings and bar or bat mitzvahs. It is a unique delicacy and one of the oldest recipes from the Roman Jewish tradition, as its name suggests. In fact, until the 19th century, the word* pizza *was used mostly for cakes, sweets and focaccias; the more commonly known term of* pizza *as a savoury dish is relatively recent.*

These delicious cakes are usually given to guests wrapped in a sachet, together with cinnamon and almond biscotti, at the mishmarah, *a traditional Roman Jewish evening of prayers, study and singing (and food, of course!) held usually on the eve before or on the day of an important family celebration such as a birth, wedding or bar/bat mitzvah.*

Most people would buy the pizza from Boccione, a little bakery in the main square (piazza) of the Jewish quarter in Rome, hence its other nickname pizza di piazza. *They sell – and sell out of – their unique and utterly delicious pizza every day.*

In my family, when it comes to large celebrations, we enjoy baking our own pizza and our recipe is slightly different to Boccione's. I propose here my family recipe. It is a women-only affair and I make it with my mother, sister, aunts and a few of my mother's friends, as well as – lately – my daughters. The photos for this recipe, in fact, show us making Pizza ebraica for 60 people to celebrate my parents' 60th wedding anniversary at our house by the seaside.

In Rome, wonderful candied cedro lemon (etrog) and other candied fruit is used for this recipe – I like to get mine in Campo de' Fiori's market – but in London it is harder to find, so good-quality glacé cherries are a good alternative as they have a vibrant colour and great flavour. The traditional pizza from Boccione usually comes in quite large, brick-like pieces, but you can also make smaller, fat, finger-sized portions; I often do that.

1 Place the raisins or sultanas, almonds, pine nuts and candied fruit or glacé cherries in a bowl. Add the wine and the vanilla extract and leave to soak while you prepare the rest of the ingredients.

2 Preheat the oven to 230°C (210°C fan/450°F/gas mark 8).

> **TIP:** *For a richer taste, and if you have the time, leave the fruit and nuts to soak at room temperature for a few hours or overnight.*

3 Heat the oil in a small saucepan on the hob or in a microwavable container in the microwave until warm, but not hot. Put the flour (or flour and ground almonds) in a large bowl, add the warm oil and mix well with a large spoon. Add the sugar and salt and mix again, this time with with clean hands.

4 Add the soaked nuts, fruit and wine mixture to the flour and oil mixture and mix until everything is evenly distributed. Don't worry if it appears a little crumbly – that's quite normal.

5 On a clean surface, divide the mixture into thirds or quarters. Mould each piece into long, chunky rectangular blocks. Use a sharp knife to cut each block into 5 or 6 brick-type blocks, roughly 10–12cm (4–4½in) in length, 5–6cm (2–2½in) wide and 2cm (¾in) in height. Alternatively, for finger-sized cakes, cut each block into smaller sticks.

6 Place the fruit cakes on the lined baking tray, score a few long lines on the top of each cake, then bake in the oven for 20–22 minutes until golden and slightly burnt – that's one of the trademarks of this pizza, a little burnt on the outside but still moist inside! If you are making the smaller cakes, then 16–18 minutes baking time should be enough. Remove from the oven, transfer to a cooling rack and leave to cool for at least 20 minutes before serving. The cakes will keep well in an airtight container for several days, or you can put a few into clear sachets to wrap and give as little presents...

Pangiallo di Teresa

TERESA'S NUT AND CHOCOLATE CHRISTMAS DESSERT

Preparation:
20 minutes, plus
minimum overnight
soaking time
Baking:
1 hour

 **MAKES 2 LOAVES**

Ingredients
200g (7oz/1⅔ cups) whole hazelnuts (skin-on)
200g (7oz/1⅓ cups) whole almonds
100g (3 1/2oz/generous ¾ cup) walnuts
50g (1¾oz/scant ½ cup) pine nuts
200g (7oz/1 cup) caster or granulated sugar
100g (3 1/2oz/⅔ cup) raisins or sultanas soaked in warm water for 5 minutes
50ml (1¾fl oz/3½ tablespoons) rum, Mistrà (Italian version of ouzo) **or alcohol of your choice** (or a mix!)
½ teaspoon vanilla extract
grated zest of ½ unwaxed orange and ½ unwaxed lemon
1 medium egg
1 tablespoon sunflower oil for the mixture, plus enough to grease your hands
2 tablespoons cocoa powder
80g (2¾oz) dark chocolate, broken into pieces
2½ tablespoons brewed espresso or strong black coffee
about 60g (2¼oz/½ cup) plain white flour (ideally '00' type)

You will need a baking tray lined with baking parchment.

*T*eresa is the amazing lady who, along with her husband Pietro, hid and saved my mum and her family during World War II (see page 31). Our families are still in touch and one of the traditions I love is to receive a piece of pangiallo from them every year after Christmas. Their family is Catholic and pangiallo is a traditional Christmas dessert from the Rome area. So, although this is not an Italian Jewish recipe, it is close to our family's heart, and encompasses what food and traditions represent for me – sharing wonderful flavours with your loved ones and bringing memories back to life.

Teresa's original recipe (pictured here), which her daughters Laura and Felice still use, makes over 20 pangialli using 5kg (11lb) of nuts! That's because pangiallo is one of those wonderful bakes that you make to share. It is made into small loaves, then baked and wrapped to give to family and friends. We are lucky to have been one of the recipients of Teresa's family's pangiallo for over 70 years. Here, I give quantities for two loaves, one for you and one to give (or freeze!), but of course you can halve the recipe, or scale it up if you want to make more for gifting.

Teresa suggests mixing the nuts with the sugar, rum and Mistrà (an Italian version of ouzo), then leaving it to soak for 3–5 days, covered, in a cool room, stirring occasionally. I love doing that because it's like a build-up to the making of pangiallo and the nuts get very tasty. You can do that, too, if you plan well ahead of time. Here, I've cut it to one day, and if you are in a rush, you can cut out this stage altogether, and mix all the ingredients at once – the flavours will just be less rich and the texture less moist, but still delicious!

1 Preheat the oven to 220°C (200°C fan/425°F/gas mark 7).

2 Mix the three different types of nuts, then lay them out on a baking tray and toast them in the hot oven for 5 minutes, shaking the tray halfway through so the nuts toast evenly.

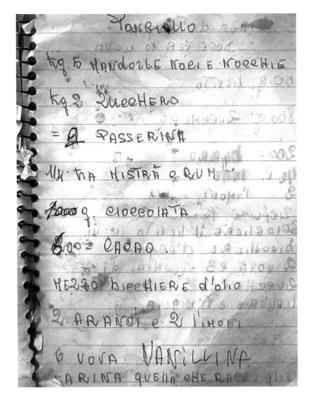

3 In a large bowl, mix the warm toasted nuts with the sugar, soaked and drained raisins or sultanas, alcohol, vanilla extract and the orange and lemon zests. The mixture is quite dry, but you should be able to smell all the wonderful aromas. Mix well, cover and leave to soak ideally in a cool room or at room temperature overnight or for a day (and up to 5 days if you have the time!), stirring once or twice.

4 When you're ready to bake, preheat the oven to 180°C (160°C fan/350°F/gas mark 4). Gently beat the egg in a large bowl, then add the oil and cocoa powder and beat to combine. Place the chocolate and coffee in a small saucepan and melt over a low heat. As soon as the chocolate has melted, add it to the egg mixture and stir. Add the soaked nut mixture and mix well. Finally, add the flour.

5 Grease your hands with sunflower oil and use them to mix all the ingredients, just enough so that they hold together. The mixture should hold its shape, but if it's too wet, you can add a little more flour. Shape the mixture into two oval loaves, about 20 x 10cm (8 x 4in) each, and place them on the lined baking tray.

6 Bake the *pangiallo* in the oven for about 1 hour, until the outer crust is dry. Remove from the oven and leave the loaves to cool down completely before slicing whatever amount you plan to eat there and then. *Pangiallo* keeps well in an airtight container (or wrapped in foil) for a few weeks, or can be frozen. The outer crust may dry a little with time, but it remains delicious and quite moist inside. It is great as an afternoon or midnight snack. Share it with family and friends.

Salame di Cioccolata

CHOCOLATE AND BISCUIT 'SALAMI'

A fun memory of growing up in Rome is of Sunday mornings when my parents cleverly found a way to sleep in by asking us children to surprise them with a dessert or something easy to make in the kitchen. We mostly used the Manuale di Nonna Papera, a cookbook of easy recipes by Walt Disney for children. The salame vichingo – which we called salame di cioccolata – was one of our favourites. It is the first dish I ever made alongside my older siblings, Stefano and Simona. Being the youngest of the three, my role was quite peripheral and mostly involved cleaning up, which I did not mind much as it meant I could lick the bowl at the end!

I like it with just a few simple ingredients, but you can be creative and add nuts, raisins or alcohol, or mix cocoa powder with proper chocolate. The best biscuits to us are the Italian Oro Saiwa (the closest alternative are dry biscuits, such as rich tea).

Note that this recipe contains raw eggs.

Preparation:
20 minutes, plus minimum 4 hours freezing time

 **SERVES 6–8**

Ingredients
150g (5½oz) unsalted butter
2 large egg yolks
2 heaped tablespoons caster or granulated sugar
2 heaped tablespoons cocoa powder
pinch of sea salt
200g (7oz) plain, dry biscuits, such as Oro Saiwa or rich tea
icing sugar to dust the salami

You will also need a string to wrap the chocolate salami (optional).

1 Melt the butter in the microwave or a bain-marie (place the butter in a small heatproof bowl and sit it over a saucepan of just-simmering water), or in a saucepan over a low heat.

2 Beat the egg yolks with the sugar for a couple of minutes in a large bowl until pale and creamy, either by hand or with an electric hand mixer. Once the butter has melted, add it to the egg yolks and sugar, stir well, then add the cocoa powder and salt and mix thoroughly. Roughly break the biscuits into small pieces – about 1cm (½in) chunks – and add them to the chocolate mixture.

TIP: As kids, to break up the biscuits, we used to wrap them in a clean tea towel and bang it on a tabletop, punching any larger lumps; we had a lot of fun! I do the same with my girls today, sometimes using a sealable food bag and a rolling pin.

3 Work the mixture with your hands – you can try using a spoon, but hands work much better here as the mixture is a little crumbly. Tip it out onto some baking parchment and roughly mould it into a log shape about 30 x 5cm (12 x 2in). With clean hands, wrap it in the baking parchment and then again in foil and press it with your hands to help compress it and hold its shape. Freeze the chocolate 'salami' for at least 4 hours, ideally overnight. Take the chocolate 'salami' out of the freezer 10 minutes before serving, remove the foil and baking parchment, then gently roll it over a plate or board dusted with icing sugar. If you want to get creative, tie food string around it to give it a 'salami' look.

4 Slice and serve cold. The chocolate 'salami' will keep in the freezer for several weeks, so you can just cut yourself a slice whenever you feel like having a little sweet treat.

Conversion Tables

WEIGHTS

5g, 4g	1/8oz		275g	9¾oz
10g, 8g, 7g	¼oz		280g	10oz
12g	2/5oz		300g	10½oz
15g	½oz		315g	11oz
20g	¾oz		320g	11¼oz
25g, 30g	1oz		325g	11½oz
35g	1¼oz		340g	11¾oz
40g, 45g	1½oz		350g	12oz
50g	1¾oz		360g	12½oz
55g	2oz		375g	13oz
60g, 65g	2¼oz		400g	14oz
70g	2½oz		425g	15oz
75g, 80g	2¾oz		450g	1lb
85g	3oz		500g	1lb 2oz
90g, 95g	3¼oz		550g, 570g	1lb 4oz
95g	3¼oz		600g	1lb 5oz
100g	3½oz		650g	1lb 7oz
110g, 105g	3¾oz		700g	1lb 9oz
115g	4oz		750g	1lb 10oz
120g, 125g	4¼oz		800g	1lb 12oz
140g	5oz		850g	1lb 14oz
150g, 160g	5½oz		900g	2lb
170g	5¾oz		950g	2lb 2oz
175g, 180g	6oz		1kg	2lb 4oz
190g	6¾oz			
200g	7oz			
210g	7¼oz			
220g	7¾oz			
225g, 230g	8oz			
240g	8½oz			
250g	9oz			

FLUID VOLUME

1.5ml		¼ teaspoon
2.5ml		½ teaspoon
5ml		1 teaspoon
7.5ml		1½ teaspoons
10ml		2 teaspoons
15ml	½fl oz	3 teaspoons/1 tablespoon
20ml	¾fl oz	1½ tablespoons
30ml	1fl oz	2 tablespoons
40ml	1¼fl oz	2½ tablespoons
45ml	1½fl oz	3 tablespoons
50ml	1¾fl oz	3½ tablespoons
60ml	2fl oz	4 tablespoons/¼ cup
75ml	2½fl oz	5 tablespoons/1/3 cup
80ml	2¾fl oz	1/3 cup
90ml	3fl oz	6 tablespoons
100ml	3½fl oz	scant ½ cup
120ml	4fl oz	½ cup
125ml	4¼fl oz	generous ½ cup
130ml	4½fl oz	generous ½ cup
135ml	4¾fl oz	generous ½ cup
150ml	5fl oz	2/3 cup
160ml	5½fl oz	2/3 cup
175ml, 180ml	6fl oz	¾ cup
190ml, 200ml	7fl oz	scant 1 cup
200ml	7fl oz	scant 1 cup
225ml, 230ml	7½fl oz	scant 1 cup
240ml	8fl oz	1 cup
250ml	8fl oz	1 cup [2 cups = 475ml]
260ml	8¾fl oz	generous 1 cup
270ml	9fl oz	11/3 cups
280ml	9½fl oz	scant 1¼ cups

300ml	10fl oz	1¼ cups
330ml	11¼fl oz	13/8 cups
350ml	12fl oz	1½ cups
375ml	13fl oz	12/3 cups
400/410ml	14fl oz	12/3 cups
450ml	15fl oz	scant 2 cups
475ml	16fl oz	2 cups
500ml	17fl oz	generous 2 cups
550ml	18fl oz	2½ cups
570ml	19fl oz	2½ cups
600ml	20fl oz	2½ cups
700ml	24fl oz	scant 3 cups
750ml	25fl oz	3 cups
800ml	27fl oz	3½ cups
900ml	30fl oz	3¾ cups
1 litre	34fl oz	4¼ cups
1.2 litres	40fl oz	5 cups
1.25 litres	42fl oz	5¼ cups
1.4 litres	47fl oz	6 cups
1.5 litres	50fl oz	6¼ cups
1.75 litres	60fl oz	7½ cups
2 litres	68fl oz	8½ cups
2.3 litres	80fl oz	10 cups
2.4 litres	82fl oz	10¼ cups
2.5 litres	85fl oz	10½ cups
2.8 litres	99fl oz	12 cups
3 litres	102fl oz	12¾ cups
3.5 litres	119fl oz	14¾ cups
3.75 litres	127fl oz	16 cups
4 litres	135fl oz	17 cups
4.5 litres	152fl oz	19 cups
5 litres	175fl oz	21½ cups

LENGTH

2mm	1/16in		22cm	8½in
3mm	1/8in		23cm	9in
5mm	¼in		24cm	9½in
8mm	3/8in		25cm	10in
1cm	½in		26cm	10½in
1.5cm	5/8in		27cm	10¾in
2cm	¾in		28cm	11in
2.5cm	1in		29cm	11½in
3cm	1¼in		30cm	12in
4cm	1½in		31cm	12½in
4.5cm	1¾in		33cm	13in
5cm	2in		34cm	13½in
5.5cm	2¼in		35cm	14in
6cm	2½in		37cm	14½in
7cm	2¾in		38cm	15in
7.5cm	3in		39cm	15½in
8cm	3¼in		40cm	16in
9cm	3½in		42cm	16½in
9.5cm	3¾in		43cm	17in
10cm	4in		44cm	17½in
11cm	4¼in		46cm	18in
12cm	4½in		48cm	19in
12.5cm	4¾in		50cm	20in
13cm	5in			
14cm	5½in			
15cm	6in			
16cm	6¼in			
17cm	6½in			
18cm	7in			
19cm	7½in			
20cm	8in			

La Sparsciandata

This gem of a poem was written in Giudaico Romanesco (Roman Jewish dialect) by an anonymous author, most probably at the end of the 19th century, and is taken from Ariel Toaff's *Mangiare alla Giudia* (pp171–173). It is about a Roman Jewish cook, that when asked what she knows to cook, she shares an impressive list of dishes, portraying what Italian Jews cooked at the time, mostly in Rome but across Italy as well, as she also mentions dishes from the centre-north of Italy. The poem is available only in Italian as a translation in English would be challenging and would deserve a publication with plenty of footnotes of its own!

Ad una cuoca ebraica, che intesi decantare,
io volli domandare cosa sapesse fare.
«So fare roba buona, pe vita vostra e mia,
– disse – cucino bene e con economia;
so fare buoni pranzi, so fare buone cene,
cucino all'israelitica, molto pulito e bene,
son cuoca sperimentata, e sempre ho conservato
il vero *cascerudde* e non ho mai *tarfato*.
Grazie al cielo il *hazzirre* non so che cosa sia,
lo posso giurare pe' vita vostra e mia.
E a me non può succedere come alla cuoca Fiano,
che la cacciò di casa *Ribì* Scinguel Toscano,
perché una coratella comprò dall'abbacchiaro,
invece di comprarla da Abram il macellaro,
Ho cucinato spesso per molti *memunnimme*
e sono ricercata da li *ngironimme*.
E adesso voglio dirvi tutta la sparsciandata
della cucina ebraica, di quella ch'ho imparata:
so fare il coscusù, gnocchi, caricioncini,
maccaroni col cacio, sfoglietti e tagliolini,
ceci co li spinaci, ceci coi pennerelli,
facioli, riso e scafe, riso co li piselli,
riso con cucuzzole, lenticchie e faricello,
sfoglietti co la crosta, riso con finocchiello,
minestra di cipolle, luperi, semmolella,
cannolicchi, fettuccie, pennette e farinella,
minestra co li selleri, con burro e bruscatelli,
strozzapreti rizzetti, pastine e tagliatelli,
lagane, *mazzà* pista, riso coll'animelli,
ceci infranti, pulenta, pancotto e frascarelli.
E so fà li salami di tutte qualità,
de carne bene pista di manzo e *cascerà*,
salami d'oca, *vesceli*, *luganeghe*, coscette,
lingua salata, colli, carne secca e coppiette;
so fa la carne in tiano, il fegato in padella,
trippa, boccette in brodo e carne in pignatella,
stentinelli d'abbacchio, milzetti, zaravagli,
ventricelli, ragù, fegatini e regagli,
Ngazzammoddi di pollo, cosciotti di capretto,
pizzette co li selleri, polpette col sughetto,
carne pista in pizzette, polmone scinicato,
pera di carne all'olio e capretto infornato,
coratella d'abbacchio, bianchetta di vitello,
gallinaccio coi selleri, costicelle d'agnello,
milzarelle in aceto, pagliara, cacciunelli,

marghe e treccie in graticola, rognoni ed animelli.
Ndivia soffritta, broccoli allessi e strascinati,
cavoli fiori, sparagi allessi e butirati,
il verde di finocchio, li cavoli stufati,
li torzelli d'indivia soffritti e rosolati,
cocuzzole ripiene, torzuti, broccoletti,
cocuzza marinata, cocuzzole a filetti,
taratufeli arosti, coll'erbetta, stufati,
carciofi alla giudia, stufati e impasticciati,
malignane soffritte, in concia e scinicate,
pastinache in tegame e cipolle infornate,
ndivia coll'aliciotti, rape, gobbi, cardini,
carote, zucca gialla, patate e faciolini,
pomidori ripieni con riso e pan grattato,
baccalà con cipolle e pesce marinato,
pesce allesso e in ferzora, triglie alla livornese,
linguattole, dentale con salsa majonese,
tinche, merluzzi, spigole, in umido e allessate,
verghe d'Aronne, cefoli, triglie fritte dorate,
fritto di baccalà, di pollo, di cervello,
di pastinache, broccoli e testa di vitello,
ova colla *mazzà*, col sugo, frittellate,
e l'ova co li gricioli, barzotte e strapazzate.
E i dolci, che so fare, sono squisiti e fini,
dolci di *Sciavungodde*, *Purim* e *pesahini*,
ciambelle di conforza, roschetti, ciambelletti,
dighimobisi, bolli, pan *cascer* e ginetti,
ciambelle de *beridde*, biscotti, mostaccioli,
e pizza uso Morone con mandorle e pignoli,
pizza e ricotta calda con zucchero e cannella,
zuppa inglese, gattò, bodino e sfogliatella,
gnocchi colla cannella, caciata, cariscioni,
castagne co le mele, tortolicchi e cialdoni,
pastarelle co mandorle, panforti e panpepati,
pizza collo zebibbo, meloni incandidati,
bigné, boccadidama, turchetti, marmellate,
maritozzi, amaretti, pangialli e pignoccate,
Monte Sinai, fotté, croccanti, maritelli,
bianchi mangià, pasticci, tortiglioni e frittelli,
recchie d'*Amanne*, strufoli, mandorle inzuccherate,
scudelluccie, *harosed*, nocchiata e ova filate,
pizzarelle col miele, sfogliate, ammandorlata,
visciolata, canditi, conserve e cotognata,
conserve di briccocole, di mele, di guainelle,
e di tutti li frutti de *Erez Israelle*».

Acknowledgements

This book has been a labour of love, with all the sweet pain that comes with it. Parked and re-ignited a few times along the way, there were moments when I thought it might never see the light of day. I am beyond delighted that it (and I!) made it through, and this has been made possible thanks to the invaluable help and support of quite a few outstanding individuals.

My gratitude goes first and foremost to my dear friend and publisher 'extraordinaire' Michael Leventhal, from Green Bean Books. Thank you, Michael, on so many levels! For supporting my project from the embryo stage, for putting me in touch with countless brilliant people (you are the best and most natural networker I know), for tasting and appreciating my food, and for your friendship and professionalism. It has been a pleasure and privilege working with you. Thank you for taking a gamble on me and believing in my project. I honestly could not have hoped for a better and better-suited publisher and team for my book. You've earned a lifetime's supply of my tiramisù!

Big – humongous – thanks go to my amazing editors, Clare Morris and Laura Nickoll. To Clare, who determinedly and professionally worked on the book with me over the past few years, when I considered self-publishing it, and encouraged me throughout. Your help in structuring and editing, and your invaluable contributions, were precious until the very end, and your perseverance and continuous support, priceless. I am enormously grateful. To Laura Nickoll, outstanding food copy editor, who took the reins with both hands for the last sprint with competence, and swiftly worked through every page. Thank you, Laura, for taking on the project, your astute input and clarity of work made the copy editing sail through. Thank you, too, to Sue Morony and Anne Sheasby for proofreading: your thorough and pertinent queries helped clarify so many details – such an important task! I would also like to thank Hester Abrams for her work, research and valuable initial editorial contribution a few years back.

Huge thanks go to the brilliant team at Green Bean Books, working tirelessly and (literally) out of hours to make this project happen on time. In particular, Kate Baker, for project managing and proofreading meticulously and always being available, attentive and patient – you are a star, and it has been a real pleasure working with you. Many thanks go also to Peter Wilkinson for designing the maps of Italy with care and detail, and to Hugh Allan for the production of the book, not an easy job! Thank you as well to Vanessa Bird for indexing.

There is then the photography, which is an eclectic collection on purpose as somehow it reflects who I am – a lover of different styles. Talking of beauty and style, I am truly grateful to the talented Barbara Toselli for the most stunning photography I could wish for, shooting many of the dishes and snapshots of Rome. I have been lucky to know Barbara for years, well before she became the famous food blogger she is today @pane_burro. We collaborated in Umbria when she came to teach my cookery courses there. Her sophisticated eye and style have elevated the book and given it a modern touch. Thank you, Barbara!

I am also very grateful for the beautiful photography by Inbal Bar Oz, with whom I work regularly for *The Jewish Chronicle* shoots, and her husband, chef and stylist Amir Batito. It is always a pleasure working with you both! Thank you to Jennifer Balcombe for her creative photographic contributions, as well as Charles Taylor for beautifully shooting my Nonna Bianca's lemon sponge. Sincere thanks go as well to David Brandt for his stunning photography during Gefiltefest Dresden 2015 and for generously granting permission to use some in here. Thank you to Armando Moreschi for donating the priceless picture of backstage at the Antico Forno Boccione making *pizza ebraica* on page 24 (top right). Victoria Prever, my brilliant editor at *The Jewish Chronicle*: thank you for your collaboration through the years, for encouraging me to always get better and for granting permission to let us use Inbal Bar Oz's photographs for recipes previously published in *The Jewish Chronicle*.

There are then my friends and family, the rocks of my life, who for years heard (and rightfully asked) about my book. I made it! To my parents, to whom I dedicate this book as they are the pillars who raised me and fed me the most delicious food. You opened my eyes to the world and let me go free with apparent ease, yet have always been there – thank you. To the two Simonas in my life. First, my sister Simona with whom I shared and still share so much. Thank you for being there throughout and unconditionally, for your support, your patience, your valuable feedback and your talented designer eye. Second, my dearest friend Simona Di Nepi, thank you for your advice, time and precious friendship throughout the years, and for always believing in me and my project. Thank you also to my brother Stefano, to Loredana, to Morris, to my wonderful nephews, cousins, aunts and uncles, and to my sister-in-law Anne and my parents-in-law, Nadine and Jean Iarchy. Your support is invaluable. Thank you, dear Anthony for your 'shutafut' and laughs, your camaraderie, creative styling eye and your gorgeous photograph of the no-bake cheesecake. Thank you, too, Nora, for your time and friendship – you are SO talented!

Thank you, Danny, for your friendship throughout the years; I probably would not have started my cookery journey if it were not for you. Thank you, Jodi, for our long walks and talks about the book and life, and our cherished friendship. To ma 'chou' Olivia, for helping me find the 'book of my life'. Thank you, Einav, my only ever 'cooking partner' and an amazing friend. We could literally spend days in the kitchen together, cooking and talking about life – we have such a precious friendship. Mimi, my dear, with you it may not be about the food, but you are so much there, thank you! And thank you to Luca, Marta and all my other friends who fuel my life.

Heartfelt thanks go to Tarryn Klotnick and Stephen Marcus for being my 'official' recipe tasters. Thank you for cooking through the book and liking my food: you have been THE best support! Tarryn, I love our friendship and how it grew, from Gefiltefest to today, from frying pans to nappies, you are the best! Thank you, Linda Dangoor, for your input on the book in its initial self-publishing stage: you made it look so easy, you are truly talented, and I so enjoy our shared passion for food (and books!). Thank you to my lovely book club and for all your support, it means a lot to me.

Thank you to Yotam Ottolenghi for graciously sparing his time to brainstorm about my book ten years ago, letting me in his kitchen at NOPI for a fascinating internship and for contributing his Nonna's *polpettone* recipe.

To my very dear friends Deborah Romano, Sharon Tammam, Claudia Finzi Orvieto and Patty Jaffé and their families for sharing their delicious recipes – thank you. Thanks, too, to Micaela Pavoncello and Hamos Guetta for contributing the recipes for *ngozzamoddi* (photography by Micol Piazza) and fish *haraimi* and for the important work that you both do in the Roman Jewish community: Micaela through the brilliant Jewish Roma Walking Tours and Hamos through the wonderful You-Tube channel, preserving both Libyan and Roman Jewish cuisine. Bravissimi!

Thank you to all my students, clients and readers through the years, for coming to my events, eating and appreciating my food. You are the reason I still do what I do, and it truly brings me joy to cook and teach you all. Thank you for being so loyal!

Finally, my warmest and special thanks go to my husband Marc and my daughters Bianca and Thea, who I love beyond words. Marc, you are my rock. Your patience throughout the writing of this book has been spectacular, especially at the very end, when you could see it was really happening! Thank you for your unceasing support and encouragement and for always believing in me. Bianca and Thea, you are my favourite guinea pigs, giving me honest feedback for all my recipes. Thank you for your patience and support throughout the last year of this project. This book is for you, to keep, to learn about your Italian Jewish roots, and perhaps see your mamma from a different angle. It is for you to hopefully cherish and share with your children one day. I love you.

Thank you to the following for granting me permission to publish their material.

To Edizioni Sonda for granting permission to publish the *cugoli* recipe on page 74, which originally appears in *La Cucina Ebraica in Italia* (Edizioni Sonda, Casale Monferrato 2003).

To Mondadori for the *salame vichingo* recipe in my original 1976 edition of *Manuale di Nonna Papera*, published by Mondadori, which was the inspiration for my *salame di cioccolata* recipe on page 326.

To Random House UK for granting permission to publish Yotam Ottolenghi's meatloaf recipe (see page 142), from *Jerusalem: A Cookbook* by Yotam Ottolenghi and Sami Tamimi, published by Ebury Press. Copyright © Yotam Ottolenghi and Sami Tamimi 2012. Reprinted by permission of The Random House Group Limited. To Random House US for granting permission to publish 'Polpettone di Yotam Ottolenghi' from *Jerusalem: A Cookbook* by Yotam Ottolenghi and Sami Tamimi, copyright © Yotam Ottolenghi and Sami Tamimi 2012. Used by permission of Ten Speed Press, an imprint of Random House, a division of Penguin Random House LLC. All rights reserved.

To Professor Ariel Toaff for his availability and his inspirational work and for granting permission to publish the splendid 'La Sparsciandata' poem from his *Mangiare alla Giudia* (Il Mulino, 2011).

To Professor Sergio Della Pergola for inspiring me to include maps of Italy and allowing me to recreate them on page 19. Sergio Della Pergola, 'The Demography' in R. Weinstein (ed.) Italy. Jerusalem: Ben Zvi Institute, Series Jewish Communities in the East in the Nineteenth and Twentieth Centuries, 2012, 27–38 (in Hebrew).

To the Museo di Roma in Trastevere for granting permission to include and print the watercolour by Ettore Roesler Franz Il Portico d'Ottavia guardando a destra, 1887 © Roma Capitale, Sovrintendenza Capitolina al Beni Culturali, Museo di Roma.

To Guintina for granting permission to include *pollo ezechiele*, *ruota di faraone* and *torta di mandorle e spinaci* from *La Cucina nella Tradizione Ebraica, a cura di Giuliana Ascoli Vitali-Norsa*, ADEI-WIZO, 1987, and for generally being a wonderful inspiration. Also, for the *sefra* and *mielatura* recipes from *La Cucina Ebraica Tripolina* by Rossella Tammam Vaturi, published in 2005 by Giuntina. Special thanks at Giuntina go to Shulim Vogelmann.

To Logart Press for granting permission to include Bruna Tedeschi's recipe 'Baccalà alla Romana' published in *La Mia Cucina Ebraico Romanesca*. Particularly warm regards go to Bruna Tedeschi.

Picture Credits

The publisher would like to thank the following for their kind permission to reproduce their images. All related copyrights and trademarks are the property of their respective owners.

Cover
Front cover photograph by Barbara Toselli; blue motif by Modigliani Italian ceramics

Maps
p19 'Jewish presence in Italy throughout history' by Peter Wilkinson, inspired by a map by Sergio Della Pergola, The Demography. In: R. Weinstein (ed.) Italy. Jerusalem: Ben Zvi Institute, Series *Jewish Communities in the East in the Nineteenth and Twentieth Centuries*, 2012, 27–38 (in Hebrew)

'Cooking for the soul' logo
p344 by Alessandra Spizzichino and Claudia Tagliacozzo

The following photographers generously collaborated in the making of this cookbook. All other photographs not specified below are family photographs © Silvia Nacamulli:

Barbara Toselli front cover, endpapers, and pp8, 15, 22 (bottom), 24 (top left, bottom left and bottom right), 26, 38–39, 68–69, 70–71, 75, 76–77, 78–79, 81, 83, 85, 86, 91, 95, 96, 97, 98, 99, 101, 103, 104–05, 111, 123, 126-27, 129, 131, 132, 144–45, 146, 147, 153, 160–61, 163, 165, 167, 177, 180–81, 186, 190, 191, 193, 194, 195, 197, 200, 207, 215, 218, 221, 226, 229, 233, 234, 243, 244–45, 249, 251, 252–53, 264–65, 293, 295, 315, 327

Jennifer Balcombe pp108, 112–113, 118–119, 135, 136–137, 141, 151, 155, 158, 169, 175, 179, 198–99, 203, 208–09, 211, 213, 231, 239, 246, 255, 267, 269, 274–75, 280, 285 (bottom), 286–87, 291, 300–01, 308-09, 311, 319
Inbal Bar-Oz pp107, 216–17, 237, 279, 283, 285 (top), 297, 299, 303, 317
David Brandt pp63, 64, 67, 335
Anthony Collard p313
Armando Moreschi p24 (top right)
Micaela Pavoncello pp60, 171
Micol Piazza p139
Charles Taylor p263
Steve Hampshire Photography p344

Additional contributors

Museo di Roma
p22 (top) © ROMA CAPITALE – SOVRINTENDENZA CAPITOLINA AI BENI CULTURALI - MUSEO DI ROMA

Shutterstock.com
p17 (top) Mazur Travel; (bottom) photoshooter2o1; p43 Almix p53 (top) ungvar; p54 Sokor Space; p87 (left) MaraZe; p121 (top) Pixel-Shot; p259 Monkey Business Images; p272 Paolo Borella

Wikimedia Commons
p29 Paolo da Reggio (public domain)

Bibliography

Agostini, Maria, *La Cucina Popolare Veneto-Ebraica* (Filippi Editore, 2001)

Arcuri, Italo, *Memme Bevilatte Salvata da Teresa* (Suraci Editore, 2014)

Artusi, Pellegrino, *La Scienza in Cucina e l'Arte di Mangiar Bene* (Einaudi, 1995)

Ascoli Vitali-Norsa, Giuliana, *La Cucina nella Tradizione Ebraica* (Giuntina, 1998)

Rav Bahbout, Shalom, *Seder di Tu biShvat* (Totah.it, 1986)

Bassani Liscia, Jenny, *La Storia Passa dalla Cucina* (Edizioni ETS, 2000)

Belgrado Passigli, Milka, *Nuove Ricette di Casa Mia* (Giuntina, 2005)

Calabi, Donatella, *Venezia e il Ghetto. Cinquecento Anni nel "Recinto degli Ebrei"* (Bollati Boringhieri, 2016)

Capatti, Alberto & Montanari Massimo, *Italian Cuisine - A Cultural History* (Columbia University Press, 2003)

De Benedetti, Ines, *Poesia Nascosta* (Edizioni La Zisa, 2013)

Di Segni, Rav R., 'Guida alle Regole Alimentari Ebraiche', in *Buon Appetito Beteavon Incontro di Culture: Ricette della Cucina Ebraico-Romana*, Roma: GP Edizioni, 2015, pp.5–8

Goldstein, Joyce, *Cucina Ebraica* (Chronicle Books, 1998)

Guetta Hassan, Linda, *La Cucina Ebraica Tripolina* (Gallucci, 2010)

Hazan, Marcella, *The Essentials of Classic Italian Cooking* (Alfred A. Knopf, 1998)

Maffioli, Giuseppe, *La Cucina Veneziana* (Franco Mumio Editore, 1995)

Malizia, Giuliano, *La Cucina Romana e Ebraico Romanesca* (Newton & Compton Editori, 2005)

Milano, Attilio, *Storia degli Ebrei in Italia* (Einaudi, 2017)

Ottolenghi, Yotam & Tamimi Sami, *Jerusalem*, (Ebury Press, 2012)

Rashidy, R., 'La Cucina Ebraica a Venezia: Ieri e Oggi Fra Tradizioni e Usi Locali' in *Mi Racconto...Ti Racconto. Storie e Ricette del Nostro Mondo*, Bologna: Coop Ed. Consumatori, 2007, pp.290–298

Roden, Claudia, *The Book of Jewish Food* (Penguin, 1999)

Rundo, Joan, *La Cucina Ebraica in Italia* (Sonda, 2003)

Sacerdoti, Annie, *Guida all'Italia Ebraica: Fotografie di Alberto Jona Falco* (Marsilio Editori, 2003)

Sacerdoti, Mira, *Cucina Ebraica in Italia* (Piemme, 1994)

Servi Machlin, Edda, *The Classic Cuisine of the Italian Jews I* (Giro Press, 1981)

Servi Machlin, Edda, *The Classic Cuisine of the Italian Jews II* (Giro Press, 1992)

Tagliacozzo, Giordana, *Il Ritorno di Tosca* (Silvio Zamorani Editore, 2021)

Tammam Vaturi, Rossella, *La Cucina Ebraica Tripolina* (Giuntina, 2005)

Tas, Luciano, *Storia degli Ebrei Italiani* (Newton Compton Editori, 1987)

Tedeschi, Bruna, *La Mia Cucina Ebraico Romanesca* (Logart Press, 2008)

Toaff, Ariel, *Mangiare alla Giudia* (Il Mulino, 2000 & 2011)

Index

Author Biography

Silvia Nacamulli is a master in the art of traditional Italian Jewish home-cuisine. London-based, born and bred in Rome, Silvia had the privilege of observing three generations of fine Italian Jewish cooks, surrounded by Italy's culture and love of food.

Silvia runs her business, Cooking for the Soul and has established herself as a much-loved professional cook, lecturer and food writer. She is a well-recognised name on the international food circuit, having written more than 200 recipes for *The Jewish Chronicle*, contributed to numerous recipe books and given hundreds of demonstrations and lectures at cookery schools, universities, charities, synagogues, fairs and festivals worldwide.

She lives in North West London with her husband and twin daughters.